Quine's Epistemic Norms in Practice

Also available from Bloomsbury

John McDowell on Worldly Subjectivity, by Tony Cheng
Philosophy, Literature and Understanding, by Jukka Mikkonen
Quine: A Guide for the Perplexed, by Gary Kemp
The Moral Epistemology of Intuitionism, by Hossein Dabbagh

Quine's Epistemic Norms in Practice

Undogmatic Empiricism

Michael Shepanski

BLOOMSBURY ACADEMIC
LONDON • NEW YORK • OXFORD • NEW DELHI • SYDNEY

BLOOMSBURY ACADEMIC
Bloomsbury Publishing Plc
50 Bedford Square, London, WC1B 3DP, UK
1385 Broadway, New York, NY 10018, USA
29 Earlsfort Terrace, Dublin 2, Ireland

BLOOMSBURY, BLOOMSBURY ACADEMIC and the Diana logo are trademarks of
Bloomsbury Publishing Plc

First published in Great Britain 2023
This paperback edition printed in 2025

Copyright © Michael Shepanski, 2023

Michael Shepanski has asserted his right under the Copyright, Designs and Patents Act, 1988, to be identified as Author of this work.

For legal purposes the Acknowledgements on p. xi constitute an extension of this copyright page.

Cover image: Sergey Ryumin / Getty Images

All rights reserved. No part of this publication may be reproduced or transmitted in any form or by any means, electronic or mechanical, including photocopying, recording, or any information storage or retrieval system, without prior permission in writing from the publishers.

Bloomsbury Publishing Plc does not have any control over, or responsibility for, any third-party websites referred to or in this book. All internet addresses given in this book were correct at the time of going to press. The author and publisher regret any inconvenience caused if addresses have changed or sites have ceased to exist, but can accept no responsibility for any such changes.

A catalogue record for this book is available from the British Library.

A catalog record for this book is available from the Library of Congress.

ISBN: HB: 978-1-3503-0426-0
PB: 978-1-3503-0430-7
ePDF: 978-1-3503-0427-7
eBook: 978-1-3503-0428-4

Typeset by Newgen KnowledgeWorks Pvt. Ltd., Chennai, India

To find out more about our authors and books visit www.bloomsbury.com and sign up for our newsletters.

To Michael McDermott and the memory of W. V. Quine:
influences in equal measure

Contents

Preface   viii
Acknowledgements   xi

Part 1 Undogmatic empiricism

1   Wanted: A normative epistemology in working order   3
2   Epistemological dissociative disorder   7
3   Empiricism without (even mentioning) the dogmas   15
4   Conservatism is not a third norm   25
5   Sufficient logical explicitness is norm zero   33

Part 2 Application to philosophy

6   Touching base   43
7   The armchair   45
8   Adapting to predicate logic   57

Part 3 Case study: Propositional attitude ascriptions

9   Destination and horizon   69
10   Sententialism   77
11   From sententialism to Russellianism   85
12   Sententialism with non-designating names   93

Part 4 Paths not taken

13   The 'Two Dogmas' argument   105
14   Naturalized epistemology   113
15   Attitudes to sets of *possibilia*   123
16   The mythical given   133
17   Epistemology as the theory of knowledge   147

Notes   155
Bibliography   179
Index   185

Preface

This is a book of *normative epistemology*. Normative epistemology is the choosing of *epistemic norms*; epistemic norms, in the sense that I shall use that term, are general principles about how to *theorize*; and to theorize, in the sense that I shall use that term, is to decide which theories to accept. So the natural audience for normative epistemology is everyone who wants or needs to decide which theories to accept.

However, and to my dismay, when I tell philosophers that I am writing a book of normative epistemology, some assume that I am writing a book for fellow normative epistemologists. Then, when I tell them that I want to reach an audience outside that cloister, they assume that I am writing for students who are trying to find a way into it. Now of course I welcome the normative epistemologists and the soon-to-be normative epistemologists, and I hope that they will find something here that engages them; but the idea of directing normative epistemology exclusively to them, or even primarily to them, strikes me as slightly absurd, in the same way that it would be slightly absurd for a moral preacher to preach primarily at preachers' conventions and preaching schools. In epistemology, as in ethics, the natural direction for transmitting norms is outward.

How far outward? For the record, I hold that most people would benefit from receiving some normative epistemology. But this volume is directed to a subset that is easier to reach, viz. those people who have already felt, or can readily be made to feel, a need for epistemic norms. This group includes philosophers who theorize about their special domains – ontology, modality, mental states and others – and scientists who, in the more speculative reaches of their disciplines, have found that what they call scientific method can be unsettlingly indecisive.

For circumstantial reasons, mainly to do with my own background, this book speaks more to the philosophers than to the scientists. This favouritism is prominent in Parts Two and Three, which apply the chosen epistemic norms to philosophical topics, and in Part Four and many of the notes, which debate the views of various philosophers. But Part One is where I choose the norms, and there I do strive to keep the scientists in the conversation. I do so for the sake of any actual scientists who are reading, but also as a means of ensuring that the norms I choose are fit for purpose. For the purpose of epistemic norms is to guide theorizing, which includes theorizing by scientists; and that purpose *excludes* norms that depend on any arcane, improbable or unconvincing philosophy. The scientist in the room, even if she is only a literary device, is a way to keep the arcane, the improbable and the unconvincing in check.

So it might seem incongruous that the norms I choose are from W. V. Quine, who is, according to my students, terribly difficult to read. Nevertheless, the reasoning in Part One leads to those norms, so those are the norms I hold, and I view their difficulty as a problem urgently in need of a solution.

The issue is not one of clarity, since Quine was a master of clear, if terse, expression. What makes Quine difficult is that he had so many doctrines – doctrines about logic, ontology, translation, infant language learning and more – with so many apparent interdependencies among them that it can be hard to know where to start; and if one starts in the wrong place then the road to the epistemic norms can take in some tough and contested terrain. I recall how, as a student, I worked my way through 'Two Dogmas of Empiricism': at first stunned, then perplexed and, eventually, after a steep and arduous climb, persuaded by Quine's contentious claims about meaning, only then to set foot on the sunlit uplands of his epistemology in the final section. When at long last I breathed that rarefied air, it felt as though I had earned an epistemic perspective that only the few could ever attain. Which, of course, was piffle and horsefeathers, because if Quine's epistemology were only available to those who accepted his theses about meaning, then it would not be fit for purpose.

There has to be another way. It must be possible to isolate Quine's epistemic norms from the rest of his philosophy, and to demonstrate that their application does not depend on the rest. That is what this book attempts to do.

Sometimes, in elevator-like environments, I tell philosophers that my book is mainly about Quine, and then they assume that it is either for Quine scholars or for students who want to become Quine scholars. On the contrary, it mines Quine's material for norms that theorists can apply, whether they are interested in Quine or not. Nevertheless, I especially welcome readers who are interested in Quine, and I would like now to say a few words to them.

First to the students: I cannot offer you a broad introduction to Quine's ideas, but I offer something else: a narrow introduction to Quine's ideas. Part One argues for three epistemic norms, and only for them. Let those norms be your portal, your way in. I hope that they will ease your study of Quine by breaching the wall of apparent interdependencies that I mentioned a moment ago. Part

Two travels a little further in, by tracing a route from the portal to a selection of Quine's other theses. It is only a small selection, but it includes some theses that are very distinctively Quinean, so you will see that the norms from Part One lead, not just to theorizing well, but to theorizing like Quine.

Now to the scholars: I should first clarify that the normative epistemology I recommend is the one that Quine partially formulated in the last section of 'Two Dogmas of Empiricism' and clarified through application for most of his life. It is not to be confused with the so-called normative naturalized epistemology that began to emerge a quarter-century later. (The latter doctrine is considered and rejected in Chapter 14. If you are one of the growing company of scholars who see naturalized epistemology as the core of Quine's thought, then you might like to read that chapter first.) You should also know that I extract Quine's epistemic norms by a combination of two methods: I examine his remarks directly on the topic, and I reason by inference to the best explanation from his behaviour as a theorist. Neither method is foolproof: Quine's direct normative assertions were sporadic, incomplete and at times diffident; and inference to the best explanation is always contestable. So you may reasonably dispute some of my attributions. In the end, if you do not agree that the norms I recommend are Quine's, then I would ask you to consider them on their merits anyway. Perhaps I can still convince you that the norms are correct, in which case the conclusion for you – but not for me – might be that Quine didn't follow the norms he ought to have followed. On the other hand, if you agree that the norms are Quine's, then you will see that his normative epistemology is extricable from the rest of his philosophy, a fact that may be of interest insofar as it shows something about the logical ordering of his doctrines.

Acknowledgements

This book would not have been possible without two towering figures: W. V. Quine and Michael McDermott.

I am indebted to Quine for remaking philosophy in such a way that, when I discovered it in the early 1980s, I knew that I wanted to stay and participate. In this sense, as well as in a more obvious sense, he has provided me with a subject.

As an undergraduate, I was willing to believe every word Quine had written, and I imagined that the only thing philosophy still needed was for the non-Quineans to be talked around. I am indebted to McDermott for showing me a broader prospect. A learned Quine scholar and a creative, original thinker, he was proof that one could stand securely on Quine's shoulders and see still further. McDermott was my teacher and doctoral thesis supervisor from 1986 to 1992.

In the northern spring of 1993, I was indebted to Quine all over again. He was so generous as to meet with me each week, in his Harvard office, where we discussed questions arising from my work and questions arising from his. Quine at eight-five, fully engaged in dialogue, was something to behold, as neither age nor eminence had braked his quick wits and open, curious mind.

Over the last thirty years, McDermott's opinions and mine have continued to develop, and more often than not to diverge, yet there is no one today whose opinions I value more highly.

Part One

Undogmatic empiricism

Epistemology without contact with science becomes an empty scheme. Science without epistemology is – insofar as it is thinkable at all – primitive and muddled.

Albert Einstein[1]

1

Wanted: A normative epistemology in working order

In normative epistemology, how you go depends on how you begin.

In times past, cautious epistemologists began by announcing limits to justification. They would pick some category of foundational beliefs, which were typically beliefs about something private, such as sense impressions or 'clear and distinct ideas'; they would endorse some repertoire of forms of inference, which were typically deductive; and together those determined the limits: whatever could be reached from the foundational beliefs, via the endorsed inferences, counted as justified, and everything else was out of bounds.

If that is how you begin, then, unless you either cheat or pull off something supremely clever, you are going to find that none of science is justified, and nor is even the most ordinary talk, as of medium-sized solid objects in physical space. And, once you have arrived at that dismal conclusion, there are only two ways forward. One is to stick to your principles, and withhold your credence from science and everyday things. Take that path and I have no rational objection; all I'll say is that you are unlikely to have navigated the world far enough to be reading these words, and so, with all due respect, you are not my target audience. Now the other way: you accept at least a modest helping of science and common sense, in spite of your professed opinion that none of it is justified. Then I would point out that your high epistemic standards, as noble, venerable and a priori reasonable as they might be, are also inoperative; i.e. they are not functioning to control your accept/reject decisions. Your position is like that of a normative ethicist who renounces the consumption of water: she might have a point, but it's not the type of point that controls her behaviour.

In epistemology, as in ethics, if we want norms that we can use, then we have to set our sights lower. And I do, so I will. Here in Part One, I set out to find epistemic norms that we can put to work, to control our decisions about which theories to accept and which to reject. Unlike a Hume or a Descartes, who *began* with epistemic norms, I shall be *searching* for them. No 'first philosophy' here.

A better role model would be Karl Popper. Long before he crafted his famous falsifiability criterion, Popper set himself the task:

> It was during the summer of 1919 that I began to feel more and more dissatisfied with these three theories – the Marxist theory of history, psycho-analysis, and [Alfred Adler's so-called individual psychology]; and I began to feel dubious about their claim to scientific status. My problem perhaps first took the simple form, 'What is wrong with Marxism, psycho-analysis, and individual psychology? Why are they so different from physical theories, from Newton's theory, and especially from the theory of relativity?'[1]

Observe the sequence: Popper began with a feeling that certain theories should be ruled in and others ruled out, and he asked, *what is the difference?*[2] Later he produced an answer – the falsifiability criterion – and it would come to be the basis for his in- and out-rulings.

Personally, I have been less exposed than Popper to the particular theories of Marx, Freud and Adler, so I am not as ready to pass judgement on those three, but that is a small detail. I am with Popper in favouring the sort of theories that are usually described as 'hard science', and in deploring anything supernatural, mystical or incomprehensible; and with Popper I ask 'What is the difference?' But, as we shall see, my answer will not be the same as his.

Thus I deviate from Popper in specifics, but my strategy is identical: I begin with certain preconceptions about what to rule in and out; I ask 'What is the difference?'; and later, when I find my answer to that question, it will become the basis of my in- and out-rulings. And you are about to tell me that this strategy is circular.

Very well, it is circular; but not all circles are wrong. Democracy is a kind of circle – the government rules the people and the people rule the government – yet somehow the whole thing keeps turning. Why can't the relation between epistemic norms and the theories they rule over be something like that?

Perhaps the circularity objection comes down to this: there is no way to persuade someone who is off my circle to get on. Someone who has a different selection of theories might find a different set of norms to fit it, and there will be nothing I can say against that whole package. She will say that her norms work fine because they support her selection of theories, which is precisely parallel to what I'll say about my norms (after I find them).

And this is true, at least in principle. Indeed we have mentioned just such a theorist already, viz. the hypothetical character who rejected objects in physical space. When combined with an old-school foundationalist–deductivist epistemology, that was a position to which I had no effective retort. Let us face it: there are some (hypothetical) people we will never convince.

In practice, however, I remain optimistic. In debates with real people, even those who disagree with us about epistemology and theory at the same time, some headway is often possible, for a combination of three reasons.

Firstly, any real-life disagreement takes place against a vast background of agreement. Our interlocutor almost certainly accepts most of the day-to-day realities of common sense and well-known science, and rejects a lot of stuff that she describes as airy-fairy, hippy-trippy or cloud-cuckoo. Perhaps she believes in angels – hence the disagreement – but she doesn't believe in fairies; or if she does then she doesn't believe in pixies. So we can open a debate about angels by plying Popper's question, 'What is the difference?'

Secondly, finding a set of norms to fit *any* remotely plausible sorting of theories is extremely hard. This fact was not always known, but, now that we have got the twentieth century in our hindsight, we can see how many epistemologists and philosophers of science did their best to draw a line between science and metaphysics, only to find either that the line was unclear, or that it didn't land where they wanted it to, i.e. it inadvertently ruled in some of what they wanted to rule out or vice versa. So they would erase that line and draw another, followed by another, and another. (See, e.g., the preface to the second edition of Ayer, *Language, Truth and Logic*.) How much harder will it be, then, for our friend to draw a line that rules angels in while keeping everything else on whichever side she wants it?

Thirdly, if we do run into someone whom we cannot convince, progress might still be possible in another direction: that person might convince us, because we might be wrong. To see how it could happen, we need only to imagine being Rudolf Carnap. Carnap was dead set against *ontological* statements. (We can characterize these roughly as statements about which categories of objects there are – numbers? sets? properties? – but it is better done in logical notation; see Chapters 7–8.) It is fair to say that Carnap's prejudice against ontology was at least as firm as my prejudice against angels. Then Carnap encountered W. V. Quine. Quine brought his own set of epistemic norms, and on that basis ruled some ontological statements in. It sounds like a tale of irreconcilable differences, but it isn't. Quine was able to show that Carnap's norms depended on notions that were, by Carnap's own standards, inadequately defined; so in the end Carnap's package of views was untenable.

In a nutshell: my working hypothesis is that, when rival epistemologies collide, at least one of them has either not been fully thought through, or not been fully put into practice, or both.

2

Epistemological dissociative disorder

We all need epistemic norms. We need them to decide which claims to accept and which to reject, or, at the very least, to explain the accept/reject decisions we were going to make anyway. Yet it is hard to find norms that actually perform that function. That leaves many of us in a tight spot, and humans can behave erratically when cornered.

Take a typical person on the street. You ask his opinion of chakras, auras and homeopathic water memory, and he tells you they are all rubbish. So far so good. But if you ask him to explain that assessment, he becomes agitated and snaps 'I only believe in what I can see with my own eyes!' His tone is emphatic, yet what he says is not true, and if he were to allow himself a moment's reflection he would realize that it is not true, because he, like most of us, believes in atoms, Julius Caesar and the inside of Fort Knox. Of the myriad purported entities that our sample citizen cannot see with his own eyes, he believes in some, he barks his rhetorical line at others, and, for all his braggadocio, he has no clear idea how to decide which is which.

Of course present company is more sophisticated than that. You and I would never say 'I only believe in what I can see with my own eyes.' Yet it seems to me that all of us, sophisticates included, are prone to the same underlying blunders, viz.: (i) the use of an epistemic criterion that is easy to push over; (ii) the selective, or rather, *capricious*, application of the criterion, i.e. applying it in some cases and waiving it in others, without any further criterion for deciding which cases are which; and (iii) a reluctance to examine this behaviour.

♦

Take a typical scientist in a laboratory. She, like the person on the street, agrees with us that chakras, auras and homeopathic water memory are rubbish, but she arrives at that verdict by a different route. Her procedure for evaluating any claim p begins by asking the claimant a question: 'What possible observation would, if it occurred, lead you to deny p (i.e. assert p's negation)?' If she receives a clear, definite answer, then she knows that *p* takes some empirical risk – it is *falsifiable* – and she counts that as a point in its favour. But if no answer is forthcoming, then she rates *p* as empirically empty – *unfalsifiable* – which, for her, is sufficient grounds to rule *p* out.

Readers will recognize this as a version of Popper's famous falsifiability criterion. It is stricter than some versions, however, since our scientist does not allow the excuse that *p* belongs to some conjunction of claims that is falsifiable as a whole. She does not allow it because, if she did, she would be at a loss to prevent such a farcical exchange as the following:

'This chakra has a knot in it.'
'How is that falsifiable?'
'It is part of a larger claim, viz. "This chakra has a knot in it *and* snow is white", and the larger claim is perfectly falsifiable: I would deny it in a heartbeat if I observed black snow.'

The demand for falsification conditions *of each sentence* blocks this stunt, and it is the only principle our scientist can think of that does, so that is the principle she adopts. And it serves her well for much of the time; e.g. it allows her to prohibit most, if not all, claims about chakras, auras and homeopathic water memory. But of course, our sample person on the street got that far too, before coming a cropper over atoms, Julius Caesar and the inside of Fort Knox. So let us see how the Popperian scientist handles those cases.

Starting with Caesar: I claim Julius Caesar once lived, so she asks me 'What possible observation would, if it occurred, lead you to assert "Julius Caesar never lived"?' I cannot think of any isolated observation that would do it, but I suppose that some prolonged sequence of observations would. I think I can imagine a novella-length story, in which an intrepid classicist makes one stunning observation after another, eventually leading to[1] a radical, Caesar-excluding revision of history. So okay: 'Julius Caesar once lived' passes the test. Also, and for similar reasons, 'The inside of Fort Knox exists' passes. So far, then, the strict falsifiability criterion is holding up in places where the earlier, crude criterion did not.

What about atoms? I claim that there are some atoms in the universe, so what possible observation (or sequence of observations) would lead me to assert 'There are no atoms in the universe'? Here I draw a blank. If you insist on asking me this question I will stall and prevaricate for so long that you won't be able to tell the difference between me and a quack who has been asked what observations would disprove 'Water has homeopathic memory'. Of course this may be a reflection on my lack of imagination, or my lack of some key scientific knowledge, so maybe you should ask a more competent scientist; but if you do, I suspect that she will let you know you are making an unreasonable demand: 'There are some atoms in the universe' is blue-chip science, regardless of whether she can dream up some answer to your far-fetched question.

It is not just that the question 'What observations would, if they occurred, lead you to assert "There are no atoms in the universe"?' is far-fetched. It's that it is more far-fetched than it needs to be. To see this, try flipping the question around, like so: 'If you decided that there are no atoms in the universe, what observational consequences would you lose?' Now *that* question is easy to answer: we would lose almost all of chemistry (and more), so we would lose most of the observational consequences that depend on chemistry (and more). I am suggesting that the flipped-around question makes a better test than the original question does. But I am also getting ahead of myself. My preferred set of epistemic norms is a topic for Chapters 3–5.

Returning, then, to our hard-line Popperian scientist, I would next like to inquire what she makes of mathematics. I don't mean the mathematical equations that express physical laws, relating temperature to pressure and so forth; I mean straight mathematical laws, such as the binomial theorem and Euler's identity. Are there possible observations that would discredit those? Perhaps there are: perhaps future observations of the universe will turn out so strange that they call for a revision of mathematics itself. That, however, is hard to imagine right now. Right now, we have no answer to questions like 'What observation would lead us to deny the binomial theorem?', and so – speaking in the present tense – mathematics fails the falsifiability test.

In response, our scientist might try to adjust her position by allowing some alternative sort of justification, specifically for mathematics. Perhaps she will say that mathematics is all proven from intrinsically obvious beginnings by intrinsically obvious steps. Unfortunately, that old saw doesn't survive a fact check. Mathematics is usually grounded in set theory, and the basic postulates of any modern set theory are nowhere close to obvious.

I have just one more kind of example to make trouble for our professed Popperian. Suppose that some bundle of statements, taken together, has observational consequences, but none of the individual statements in the bundle does. In that case, the bundle as a whole (or if you prefer, the *conjunction*) is falsifiable, but each statement in it is not. So the strict falsifiability criterion will allow the bundle, while disallowing every statement in it. Clearly we can't have the former without the latter; so what will we do if the former turns out to be excellent science?

This type of case has been much discussed in philosophical circles, with Quine in particular seeing it as almost ubiquitous. That is as may be. For present purposes, we only need one example, as long as it is credible to our scientist. So I'll quote Albert Einstein:

> We have seen how experience led to the introd. of the concept of the quantity of electricity. it was defined by means of the forces that small electrified bodies exert on each other. But now we extend the application of the concept to cases in which this definition cannot be applied directly as soon as we conceive the el. forces as forces exerted *on electricity* rather than on material particles. We set up a conceptual system the individual parts of which do not correspond directly to empirical facts. Only a certain totality of theoretical material corresponds again to a certain totality of experimental facts.
>
> We find that such an el. continuum is always applicable only for the representation of el. states of affairs in the interior of ponderable bodies. Here too we define the vector of el. field strength as the vector of the mech. force exerted on the unit of pos. electr. quantity inside a body. But the force so defined is no longer directly accessible to exp. It is one part of a theoretical construction that can be correct or false, i.e., consistent or not consistent with experience, only *as a whole*.[2]

Einstein broke from sentence-by-sentence falsificationism by asserting statements about forces exerted on electricity – statements that are 'no longer directly accessible to experience'. If our typical scientist agrees with Einstein (and trust me, she does), then we can add these to the list of claims for which she needs to flout her professed epistemic norm.

The inconvenient cases are starting to rack up. So why does the typical scientist cling to her version of Popper's criterion? I suspect it's because it's the best weapon she currently has against quacks and mystics. So she soldiers on, wielding her weapon against foes but not friends, which leaves us to wonder: How does she decide which is which? How does she prefilter claims, to work out which ones are subject to her falsifiability criterion and which ones get a waiver?

All I can think is that her prefilter is sociological: she assesses claims by their authors' reputation, place of employment, peer review and so forth. That could work – in fact I'm sure it works for a lot of scientists a lot of the time – but, like all buck-passing, it cannot work forever. Eventually the oracles who dispense peer reviews etc. will have to distinguish science from non-science in some other way.

And then there are the times when sociological prefiltering doesn't work at all. Once in a while, scientists of great – and equally great – eminence are split between those who applaud some new theory as a profound innovation and those who deplore it as metaphysics. String theory is perhaps a current example. I don't have a position for or against string theory but, philosopher to scientist, I'll offer one piece of advice: don't try to solve new problems by applying a norm that you already know you don't trust.

◆

Oh, and one more piece of advice: beware of advice from philosophers. Contemporary philosophy has its own set of problems, to which I now turn.

Huw Price tells it like it is:

> Back in the late 1940s, ... metaphysics, like poverty, was supposed to be on its last legs. Yet everywhere that [one] turns these days, there is a philosopher espousing a metaphysical position – someone claiming to be a 'realist' about this, an 'irrealist' about that, a 'fictionalist' about something else. Out in the college towns of New Jersey and New England, ... there are more ontological options than kinds of coffee, more metaphysicians than homeless people. And it isn't simply an affliction of the aged, infirm and mentally ill. ... [C]ontemporary metaphysics seems to have claimed the best and brightest of a generation.[3]

Clearly, Price is tarring with a broad brush. Some of what he calls 'metaphysics' I would endorse, though there is also much that I would not. I'll come to specifics in Chapter 7, after I have shown how I draw the line.

My present concern is with philosophers who draw no line. These are philosophers who are well aware of the points I raised a moment ago against strict falsificationism; they understand that those points or others can be made against all of the early twentieth-century attempts to demarcate science from metaphysics; and now they have surrendered: they set no limit to metaphysics' advance.

How far will these philosophers' tolerance extend? Will they, for instance, endure the metaphysics of F. H. Bradley ('The Absolute enters into, but is itself incapable of, evolution and progress') and Martin Heidegger ('The nothing simply nothings')? How far is too far? Of course, to ask them that question is to ask them to draw a line, which is the very thing they will not do.

Yet contemporary philosophers do not, on the whole, brook the full spectrum of metaphysics. Each one has a threshold; she just can't say what it is. That is an odd position for a philosopher to be in, and you only need to scratch the surface a little to see the incoherence of it.

Ask a contemporary philosopher what is wrong with, say, Bradley's theory of the Absolute, and you might get a lecture on the arc of philosophical progress: 'Bradley was writing in 1893, you see, and since then philosophy has taken two great strides. First the logical positivism of the inter-war years debunked Bradley, and then subsequent developments debunked logical positivism. Onwards and upwards!' (For added *gravitas*, Wittgenstein's remark about kicking away a ladder after climbing it might get an airing.) It is a story that sounds reasonable until you condense it, and then what you have is 'I reject Bradley's theory on the basis of norms that I reject' – which is as egregious a case of epistemological dissociative disorder as any we have seen.

Sometimes you find a glimmer of self-awareness. When a seminar paper crosses some philosopher's ineffable threshold, you occasionally hear a response such as this: 'I have a bit of a verificationist worry here. Mind you, I'm not technically a verificationist, but, that being said, I can't quite let this worry go.' On other occasions, however, there is no glimmer of anything. As David Lewis once complained, his theory of modal realism 'met with many incredulous stares, but few argued objections'.[4]

I sense that empiricism – the project of demarcating responsible theory from irresponsible metaphysics – has also become unfashionable for another reason, apart from the difficulty of achieving it. I sense that it is seen in some quarters as oppressive; as something that jerks use to shut down voices other than their own. So let me point out, very gently, that when one party accuses another of metaphysics, it is often in the accused party's interest to obtain a clear statement of the alleged norm that was allegedly violated. Then she can either dispute the violation, or (as I did in the case of strict falsificationism) dispute the norm. That has got to be better than trying to mount a defence against an incredulous stare.

◆

Let's recap. In the course of this chapter we have found that sentence-by-sentence falsificationism is too strict, forcing its exponents to issue unexplained waivers for claims that they dare not rule out; and then we found that contemporary non-empiricism is too lax, forcing its exponents to trump up incoherent charges against claims that they dare not rule in. Like Goldilocks, we have found one bed too hard and another too soft. Can we now find one that is just right? Has any epistemologist ever made a bed that he can lie in?

I believe that one has. Right in the centre of the twentieth century, Quine sketched the main elements of a normative epistemology that he was able to follow, without the need to overrule it in one direction or the other. And we can follow it too. Sneak preview: this epistemology rules chakras, auras and homeopathic water memory out; it rules atoms, Julius Caesar and the inside of Fort Knox in; mathematics and statements about forces exerted on electricity are also in; and the line cuts through the middle of philosophical theorizing, inviting reasoned discussion about which philosophical theories fall on either side.

But there's a catch. Quine never did write an essay titled 'My Epistemic Norms' that lays the whole system bare. Instead he wove his epistemic norms into discussions of other theses for which he is better known, particularly his negative theses about semantic concepts. What is worse, there is a part of Quine's normative epistemology that, to my knowledge, he hardly stated at all (see Chapter 5), though we can see it at work in his practice (Chapters 7–8). And of course Quine's opinions on normative epistemology went through changes, as opinions will in the span of a long career. (There were even times when he hid his light completely under a bushel, renouncing normative epistemology altogether; see Chapter 14.)

Quine once wrote:

> Not all of what is philosophically important need be of lay interest even when clearly expounded and fitted into place. I think of organic chemistry; I recognize its importance, but I am not curious about it, nor do I see why the layman should care about much of what concerns me in philosophy.[5]

I agree: the layman may well not care about many of Quine's themes. Nonetheless, if my reflections so far are correct, every conscientious thinker has an interest in finding serviceable epistemic norms. So I undertake to extract that filament of Quine's philosophy: to show that it does not depend on the rest; to say the part of it that Quine left unsaid; and to resolve, as best I can, the few internal tensions that I find within it.

3

Empiricism without (even mentioning) the dogmas

'Empiricism without the Dogmas' is the title of §6 of Quine's famous essay, 'Two Dogmas of Empiricism'. The last of six sections, tucked behind a deep critique of the analytic–synthetic distinction and phenomenalistic reductionism, this is the site where Quine announced to the world the main features of his normative epistemology.

From my perspective he was burying the lead, but he had his reasons. Quine wanted not only to announce his epistemology but also to argue for it, and his argument was roughly this: 'You, the reader, currently accept some version of modern (for 1950) empiricism; but it rests on two mistakes; and when you correct those, here's what you get.'

It is an intriguing argument, and I dip into it in Chapter 13, but nothing in this book depends on it. For now I am more interested in getting Quine's epistemology onto the table, and then arguing *from* it, to show in a range of cases that it leads to rule-in/rule-out decisions that we can live with. If I can do that, then my argument *for* it will be as simple as this: 'We need an epistemology that we can put to work; we couldn't find one before; and now we have.'

Here are some key passages:

> The totality of our so-called knowledge or beliefs, from the most casual matters of geography and history to the profoundest laws of atomic physics or even of pure mathematics and logic, is a man-made fabric which impinges on experience only along the edges. ... A conflict with experience at the periphery occasions readjustments in the interior ... Reëvaluation of some statements entails reëvaluation of others, because of their logical interconnections – the logical laws being in turn simply further statements of the system, certain further elements of the field. ... But the total field is so underdetermined by its boundary conditions, experience, that there is much latitude of choice as to what statements to reëvaluate in the light of any single contrary experience. ...[1]

> Physical objects are conceptually imported into the situation as convenient intermediaries – not by definition in terms of experience, but simply as irreducible posits comparable, epistemologically, to the gods of Homer. For my part I do, qua lay physicist, believe in physical objects and not in Homer's gods; and I consider it a scientific error to believe otherwise. But in point of epistemological footing the physical objects differ only in degree and not in kind.[2]
>
> Physical objects, small and large, are not the only posits. Forces are another example …. Moreover, the abstract entities which are the substance of mathematics – ultimately classes and classes of classes and so on up – are another posit in the same spirit. Epistemologically these are myths on the same footing with physical objects and gods, neither better nor worse except for differences in the degree to which they expedite our dealings with sense experiences. …
> … The edge of the system must be kept squared with experience; the rest … has as its objective the simplicity of laws.[3]

Now let me spell out, in less poetic language, what I take from this.

The first thing I notice is that the object of epistemic appraisal is a *total theory*; that is to say, the totality of sentences that some person or community accepts, together with all of their consequences under the logical laws that that person or community accepts.[4] So if we are asked whether some individual sentence *s* is warranted, we cannot quite take the question at face value. Usually the question to be decided is whether some envisaged total theory that includes *s* is better or worse than some envisaged alternative total theory that does not.

Focusing, then, on the assessment of theories, one norm is paramount, which I'll call *empirical correctness*. In Quine's words, 'The edge of the system must be kept squared with experience'. This norm guides scientists, and indeed all of us, every day:[5] when our theory leads us to expect experience to go a certain way, and actual experience does not comply, we understand that, somewhere along the line, the theory is at fault. There may be debate about precisely where to pin the blame, but we know that the *total* theory must not be allowed to survive as is.

The experiences that count here are experiences (ours or others') that we already know about, not experiences that we are yet to discover. Naturally we have an interest in predicting the future, but, in each moment, as we contemplate our choices, we must go on what we have.

The norm of empirical correctness narrows the range of acceptable total theories, and the more experience we acquire, the narrower the range becomes. We can accelerate the process by conducting experiments, i.e. deliberately putting ourselves in the way of experiences that stand a good chance of knocking out one contender or another, but this will never cut the range down to one. As Quine put it, 'the total field is … underdetermined by its boundary conditions, experience'.

This is where the second norm, *simplicity*, enters the picture: simplicity is the tie-breaker. When faced with a choice among empirically correct theories, take the simplest.

◆

There is a puzzle here. The norm of empirical correctness, as I have defined it, is purely negative: it is a matter of getting no observations wrong rather than getting many observations right. Thus it favours the meek, not the brave: the less you say, the less risk you run of tripping over something in past or present experience. At an extreme, the null theory, i.e. the theory consisting of no sentences at all, always counts as empirically correct. And what does the norm of simplicity have to say about this? Surely it gives the null theory full marks, for what could be simpler than silence? It would seem, then, that both of our norms are contractionary. The puzzle is to find a countervailing expansionary force, to save our total theory from implosion.

Let me break this into two parts. First there is a bootstrapping part: Why do we accept something rather than nothing? I say it's because we have no choice. Any time we are awake, with our eyes open, we learn something from our senses, whether we choose to or not. We have some control over how we frame what we learn; but, even if we're being exceptionally cagey, and limiting ourselves (as best we can) to bare reporting of sense data, that is still something rather than nothing. At this level, epistemic norms are beside the point: norms are for guiding decisions, not compulsions.

Now the other part: Why do we accept a theory of physical objects rather than a theory of sense data? That is indeed a question for normative epistemology, and it has a Quinean answer: we prefer the physical object theory because it is simpler. Once we have got past the null theory, the norm of simplicity takes on an expansionary role.

This might be counterintuitive. If you are visualizing a theory as a flat list of sentences, then you might suppose that adding any sentence to it would make it more complex. But a theory is not a flat list; it has structure, thanks to the presence within it of logical laws. A theory, which typically contains an infinite number of sentences, can be presented in compact form by listing a subset of its sentences, plus a suite of logical laws that lets the unlisted sentences be deduced from the listed ones. When I speak of simplicity of a theory, I am concerned primarily, or perhaps even exclusively, with simplicity of the compact presentation.

On this reckoning, the addition of new sentences can leave a theory simpler than it was before, if the addition pays for itself by enabling tighter compaction. Let me illustrate this with a couple of examples, before I return to the pending question about physical objects versus sense data.

Consider, first, a theory consisting of standard logical laws plus the sentences 'A is a swan', 'A is white', 'B is a swan', 'B is white' and so on through two thousand sentences describing a thousand white swans. Each of those two thousand sentences is logically independent of the rest, so we cannot compact this theory as it stands. But if we add 'All swans are white', then we can de-list the thousand sentences 'A is white', 'B is white', etc. They will still be in the theory, but they will be deducible. In logicians' jargon, they will be theorems rather than axioms. On my reckoning, then, the theory with 'All swans are white' is simpler than the theory without it. Therefore we should prefer the theory with 'All swans are white' – until the day when it becomes empirically incorrect.

It is a bit of a leap, going from a thousand swans being white to all swans being white, but the pursuit of simplicity has notched up bigger leaps than that. Take astronomy. The ancients once held that planets were mere spots on a dome, or firmament, above our heads. When they looked at, say, Venus, and saw it wandering to and fro, they took that as reality: Venus was wandering to and fro on the dome. There was no obvious pattern, so if those ancients took notes, in the form of azimuth–elevation pairs for various times and dates, then that stack of notes was their theory of Venus, and they were hard-pressed to simplify it. Maybe they could devise equations from which the azimuths and elevations could be calculated, but the equations would have had to be awfully complex. Add to that a similar amount of complexity for Mars, and again for Mercury, and for Jupiter. Fortunately, Copernicus and Kepler had another idea: accept that there is a gigantic solar system, with the sun at its centre, and then the observed planetary motions fall out of a few general laws. In net terms, it was a great simplification. The expansion of theory (not to mention the cosmos) was more than offset by the saving in basic principles.

The choice between sense data and physical objects is, in its small way, analogous to the choice between dots on a dome and the gigantic solar system. Our private parades of sense data are what William James called 'a blooming, buzzing confusion': sights and sounds darting about with less rhyme or reason than the apparent retrograde motion of Mars. By contrast, the alternative theory, the theory of physical objects, is a paragon of orderliness. Physical objects obey physical laws – conservation of momentum and the rest – as well as more obvious regularities of the type that David Hume documented:

I never have observed, that this noise coued proceed from any thing but the motion of a door; and therefore conclude, that the present phaenomenon is a contradiction to all past experience, unless the door, which I remember on the other side the chamber, be still in being. Again, I have always found, that a human body was possest of a quality, which I call gravity, and which hinders it from mounting in the air, as this porter must have done to arrive at my chamber, unless the stairs I remember be not annihilated by my absence.[6]

So the norm of simplicity is what justifies the common-sense doctrine of physical objects, in much the same way as it justifies heliocentrism, and in somewhat the same way as it justifies (until it doesn't) 'All swans are white'. I rate all three as examples of excellent theorizing. Faced with a slab of raw data, we invent the smallest possible doctrine that will convert the greatest possible part of the slab into deducible consequences.[7] Ernest Rutherford over-egged it when he said, 'That which is not physics is stamp collecting', but perhaps we can see what he was getting at.

◆

What I have just given is a very broad characterization of good theorizing, and it would be remiss of you not to point out that I have assimilated things that are different: the move to 'All swans are white' is *inductive reasoning*, whereas the move to physical objects, or to heliocentrism, is *abductive reasoning* (also known as *inference to the best explanation*).

Yes, I have assimilated them, and yes, they are different. They are both similar and different. On one hand, induction and abduction are conspicuously different operations, each with its own rules of thumb, studied in its own part of the literature. On the other hand, what ultimately distinguishes a good induction from a bad one is the same as what ultimately distinguishes a good abduction from a bad one, viz. a net simplification of total theory, that holds the line on empirical correctness.

We do not have to choose between these two ways of looking at the situation: the traditional non-deductive inferences 'versus' the unified pursuit of simplicity. In fact we had better not choose between them, because I don't think we understand either of them terribly well just yet, and we stand to learn something about each one by looking from the other point of view.

Take the pursuit of simplicity. At several points in this chapter, I have judged one theory to be simpler than another. In each case the judgement was pretty obvious, but a judgement nonetheless; Quine did not have any formula for simplicity, and neither do I. And, come to that, I don't have much judgement about it either. Like most humans, I have not often run my eye over a total theory to judge how simple it is; nor have I often placed two total theories side by side to judge which one is simpler. We (or most of us anyway – scientific geniuses might be different) are not used to taking such a direct approach.

What we are good at is performing inductive and abductive reasoning, and thereby letting the invisible hand of simplification do its work under our noses. So one way we can learn about simplicity is by carrying on with our traditional non-deductive inferences, but paying more attention to how theory changes as we go.

To illustrate, let's suppose that we have the two thousand sentences 'A is a swan', 'A is white', 'B is a swan', 'B is white', etc., as before; but this time suppose that we also have several other sentences, from a range of topics, that together imply 'A is white'. (Perhaps that is how we came to accept 'A is white' in the first place – we deduced it from those other sentences.) And we have another lot of sentences, from another range of topics, that together imply 'B is white', and another lot for 'C is white', 'D is white' and so on. In this situation, our intuitive flair for induction still tells us that we are justified in adding 'All swans are white'. But notice: this time, there are no non-deducible sentences in our theory that are becoming deducible, so 'All swans are white' is not simplificatory in the same way as it was in the previous white swans example. This time we gain simplicity of a different sort: we *systematize* the deductions of whiteness. Where the particular attributions of whiteness had been deducible in miscellaneous ways, now they are deducible in a uniform way. That counts, apparently, as a win.

So there you have a case where a traditional non-deductive inference teaches us something about simplicity. I also suspect – though I am less sure – that considerations of simplicity can teach us something about traditional non-deductive inferences.

My example here is Carl Hempel's famous quandary about the non-black non-ravens. If A, B, etc. are a thousand green leaves, then, given that whatever is green is not black, and that no leaf is a raven, it follows deductively that A is non-black, A is a non-raven, B is non-black, B is a non-raven and so on for a thousand non-black non-ravens. Then an induction, in what appears to be the same pattern that worked well in previous examples, leads to 'All non-black things are non-ravens', whence we can deduce 'All ravens are black'. But that is absurd: a thousand green leaves obviously do *not* support 'All ravens are black'. So where did we go wrong?

I think we can safely narrow it down to the inductive step: the inference to 'All non-black things are non-ravens'. We drew that inference entirely because of the so-called premises: 'A is non-black', 'A is a non-raven', 'B is non-black', 'B is a non-raven', etc. Perhaps the core of our mistake was to be so fixated on premises. If we switch perspectives, and look at it from the point of view of simplifying total theory, then we can see more. The sentences 'A is a non-raven', 'B is a non-raven', etc. were already deducible from the sentences 'A is a leaf', 'B is a leaf', etc., respectively (plus 'No leaf is a raven'). So the addition of 'All non-black things are non-ravens' did not make any non-deducible sentence in the theory become deducible. Moreover, 'A is a non-raven', 'B is a non-raven', etc. were already deducible in essentially the same way as each other, so there was no significant gain in uniformity. In short, the addition of 'All non-black things are non-ravens' was not simplificatory, and that is why it was not justified.

I do not know whether this solution of Hempel's paradox is correct, and I do not rest anything on it. My point is merely that, by looking at non-deductive inferences from the point of view of total theory simplification, we can take more factors into account than we could when our sights were restricted to the so-called premises and conclusion.

We have seen how a non-deductive inference could elucidate the pursuit of simplicity, and how the pursuit of simplicity might elucidate a puzzling non-deductive inference. Now there is a third kind of elucidation that I would like to mention. This is where, by pursuing simplicity, we expand theory in ways that are not covered under either of the traditional modes of non-deductive inference.

The *locus classicus* of this point is our acceptance of mathematics. Here I mean modern, systematic mathematics, in which many theorems, useful and otherwise, are derived from a foundation in pure mathematics; typically in set theory. If we accept the foundation then the theorems follow, but the question is, Why do we accept any of it? Our logical laws do not let us deduce it from non-mathematical statements; nor does it follow from non-mathematical statements by induction. How about abduction? Well, how do you understand abduction? If you think of it as inference from effects to causes, then no, abduction does not lead to mathematics, because mathematics per se does not describe causally powerful states or events. And if you think of abduction as Bayesian confirmation, then no again: we cannot meaningfully calculate the probability of an event conditional on mathematics, as distinct from its unconditional probability.

Philosophers might seek other ways to treat our acceptance of mathematics as an abductive inference, but, as I see it, there is no need. If we thought it was an abductive inference, then we would want to know whether it is a good one, and thus we would come to the crucial question, 'Is our total theory, which includes mathematics, simpler than any empirically correct total theory we can envisage that does not include mathematics?'; but we do not need to come to the crucial question that way. We can ask it directly, and the answer is 'yes'. Mathematics is a prerequisite for most of the science of the past 400 years; the science is part of the simplest empirically correct total theory we can envisage; therefore the simplest empirically correct total theory we can envisage includes mathematics.[8]

♦

The example of mathematics shows that we are open to expansions of theory that are neither directly experiential, nor deductive, nor inductive, nor abductive. Little wonder that Quine reached for the poetic language: 'these are myths on the same footing with physical objects and gods'! And, just as this epistemological open-mindedness worked to our advantage in admitting mathematics, perhaps it will help us again, somewhere on the speculative frontiers of science and philosophy. But even this heady liberality has its limits, and friends don't let friends theorize irresponsibly, so you must forgive me for closing this chapter with three sobering thoughts.

First, while I concede that the norm of simplicity is not fully clear in all cases, that is not a licence to make it say whatever we want. Sometimes its dictates are black-and-white. In particular, any change that only adds complexity, without removing some as well, is not simplificatory on any measure. So if your theory is in good shape and you are wondering whether to annex some body of doctrine about undetectable spirits, then just don't. And the same applies to auras and the rest. Our epistemology does not have a special norm to rule out metaphysics, but metaphysics is what the norm of simplicity rules out, when the balance of pros and cons is all one way.

Second, justification by the lights of this epistemology is not the same as truth. It is not even the same as likelihood of truth. Our epistemology calls on us to make a range of expansionary moves, each of which leaves our theory stronger, in the logical sense, than it was before. That usually makes it less probable; never more probable.

Here is how it typically plays out. We expand our theory in some way that brings in new predictions, e.g. that the next swan will be white. This increases the risk that future experience will discredit the theory, leading our future selves to say, not 'The theory just turned false', but rather 'The theory has been false all this while'.[9] From our present point of view, therefore, the expansion increases the risk that the theory is false now.

The moral is not that we should refrain from expansionary moves, but rather that, as a matter of prudence, we should treat the expanded theory with caution. In particular, if it is the sort of expansion that adds new predictions, then, in the interests of not being wrong for long, we should conduct experiments that give it every chance to fail early.

And third: we do not have the whole epistemology yet.

4

Conservatism is not a third norm

I believe in judging any theory, old or young, on its epistemic merits, and at this stage I recognize precisely two: empirical correctness and simplicity, in that order.

That is how I keep score; and on that score I find that our current total theory, which is the product of several centuries' labour, is doing extremely well. Furthermore, though we still throw out parts of it every day, and we add new parts, and we'll never stop doing that, I am quietly confident that most of the statements that earn our assent inter alia today will earn our assent inter alia tomorrow and for the foreseeable future – provided that we continue to judge on merit. If that opinion counts as conservative, then very well: sign me up to conservatism.

There is another strain of conservatism, however, that I oppose. I oppose building chronological factors into the normative epistemology – into the scorekeeping – to bias it towards older claims over younger ones, or towards incumbent claims over fresh candidates. That brand of conservatism crosses the line into age-based discrimination.

Scientists are often accused of conservative bias, and they may sometimes be guilty of it, but on the whole they seem to understand that it's poor form. Scientists take professional pride in their willingness to cut any claim loose, should the facts of experience turn against it or a better theory be proposed. In Carl Sagan's words,

> It often happens that scientists say, 'You know that's a really good argument; my position is mistaken', and then they would actually change their minds and you never hear that old view from them again. They really do it. It doesn't happen as often as it should, because scientists are human and change is sometimes painful. But it happens every day.[1]

If you are such a scientist, then *bravo*: you do not need me to talk you out of conservative bias. Feel free to skip to the next chapter.

Philosophers, on the other hand, or some of them, have openly embraced conservative bias. Not that they'd ever call it 'bias', but all the same they nominate conservatism as a factor in their epistemic scorekeeping. I disagree with those philosophers; and, since this is a matter of basic epistemic norms, I *fundamentally* disagree with those philosophers.

Fundamental disagreements need not be terminal, however. Impasses can be broken, and in our present fix I take heart in the observation that almost all philosophers reject conservative bias *some of the time*. It is an observation that David Christensen makes vividly:

> Insofar as my attachment to one of my own beliefs outstrips my justification for it, I hold the belief in question dogmatically. Perhaps the ultimate expression of the dogmatic attitude is to say 'I happen to believe it – and that's all the justification I need for continuing to believe it!' Philosophers, of course, have traditionally prided themselves on ferreting out such dogmatically held beliefs, and exposing them to the light of rational criticism.[2]

Here, then, is our foothold. Since most philosophers reject conservative bias some of the time, we can ask them 'Why not the rest of the time?' It becomes an instance of Popper's excellent question (from Chapter 1): 'What is the difference?'

◆

Let's start with Quine. I regret to report that he endorsed conservative bias, or at least he wrote things that invited that interpretation. Here are some parts of 'Empiricism without the Dogmas' that I withheld from the earlier discussion:

> We can imagine recalcitrant experiences to which we would surely be inclined to accommodate our system by reëvaluating just the statement that there are brick houses on Elm Street, together with related statements on the same topic. We can imagine other recalcitrant experiences to which we would be inclined to accommodate our system by reëvaluating just the statement that there are no centaurs, along with kindred statements. A recalcitrant experience can, I have urged, be accommodated by any of various alternative reëvaluations in various alternative quarters of the total system; but, in the cases which we are now imagining, our natural tendency to disturb the total system as little as possible would lead us to focus our revisions upon those specific statements concerning houses or centaurs. …
>
> Conservatism figures in such choices, and so does the quest for simplicity.[3]

Quine seems to be advocating conservatism as a third norm, roughly on par with simplicity. I'm not sure that that interpretation is correct, but let us suppose it is. Then I would like to know what this third norm is for; what work it does. I would have expected Quine to show how a triumvirate of empirical correctness, simplicity and conservatism reaches better decisions than a duumvirate of empirical correctness and simplicity; but he does not. He does not even show how it reaches *different* decisions. He gestures towards a couple of examples, about brick houses and centaurs, but there is no attempt to calculate what 'reëvaluations' the duumvirate would recommend, as opposed to the triumvirate, nor to work out which of them is better.

I am unmoved, therefore, from my two-norm position. I remain happy to accept whatever the simplest empirically correct total theory tells me, on the subject of houses or centaurs or anything else. But that leaves me with a practical problem. At any moment, there are many (in fact, infinitely many) empirically correct total theories, and my hominid brain is a poor tool for judging the simplicity of any of them; so how can I find the simplest one?

Clearly I cannot. I can only make approximations, and I need all the help I can get just to do that. Induction and abduction are two handy heuristics, and yes, conservatism is another. As far as we can tell, the simplest empirically correct total theory on day d has been almost the same as the simplest empirically correct total theory on day $d-1$, for almost all values of d. Moreover, certain widely used elements, such as logic and mathematics and physics, have been *exactly* the same, in the simplest empirically correct total theory on day d as in the simplest empirically correct total theory on day $d-1$, for almost all values of d. So, if we managed to approximate yesterday's best theory yesterday, then chances are that conservatism, especially with respect to the most widely used elements, will help us to approximate today's best theory today.

Confined to that heuristic function, conservatism is as unobjectionable as it is indispensable. It conduces to empirical correctness and simplicity, rather than competing with them. It can never outweigh them. In a word, it is not a part of the scorekeeping.

I believe that Quine was wavering, in 'Empiricism without the Dogmas', between conservatism as heuristic and conservatism as bias, and the wavering continued in his later writings.[4] It was part of a broader wavering over whether norms and heuristics are the same thing. I take that up in Chapter 14.

For now, though, let us stay on track. The task of Part One is to find a normative epistemology that we can put to work, to decide which claims to accept and which to reject. The task of this chapter is to decide whether such an epistemology should include a conservative bias, and the task of the moment is to discover Quine's opinion on that question. One way to get at it, without courting confusion with other questions, is by looking for the fingerprints of conservative bias on Quine's actual decisions. Did Quine ever, for the sake of conservatism, knowingly choose the less simple of two empirically correct theories, or an empirically incorrect theory over an empirically correct one?

I have never seen it. On the contrary, Quine was so consistently on the maverick, avant-garde side of theoretical debates, it is hard to conceive that conservatism had any sway on him at all. He was fascinated with antinomies, i.e. arguments that challenge our core beliefs, and with non-naïve set theory, i.e. the branch of mathematics that dwells on antinomies the most. But even that iconoclastic field had an established base, and Quine challenged it too, by offering a simpler alternative, aptly named 'New Foundations'. His most famous essay, 'Two Dogmas of Empiricism', confronted received opinion as defiantly as its title suggests. He was an early adopter of mind–body identity theory, at a time when it was widely considered counterintuitive. His theses of indeterminacy of translation and inscrutability of reference are of interest precisely because they contradict popular conceptions about semantics. And, when Quine did side with an ancient doctrine, viz. the existence of the external world, he was sure to make the case in a way that owed nothing to *argumentum ad antiquitatem*. We saw that in the previous chapter, but, to refresh the point, here is Quine in 'On What There Is':

> A physicalistic conceptual scheme, purporting to talk about external objects, offers great advantages in simplifying our over-all reports. By bringing together scattered sense-events and treating them as perceptions of one object, we reduce the complexity of our stream of experience to a manageable conceptual simplicity.[5]

Have I missed a spot? Is there a passage somewhere in Quine's oeuvre that shows him siding with conservatism against simplicity?[6] Suppose there is. Then I would disagree with the passage, quoting Quine as I do: 'There is room for choice, and one chooses with a view to simplicity in one's overall system of the world.'[7] A philosophy that takes this typically Quinean stance most of the time, but flouts it on some odd occasion, would owe us an answer to Popper's question: *What is the difference?*

♦

Let me turn, now, to another sort of argument for conservative bias: the argument from *lost evidence*. Christensen, who opposes the argument and attributes it to Gilbert Harman, begins his exposition with the following example. He, Christensen, currently holds that India is more populous than the United States. He came to believe this a long time ago, and presumably it was justified then, but the intervening years have erased any memory of the experiences that made it justified. Nevertheless he carries on believing that India is more populous than the United States. Moreover, Christensen judges – and I agree – that he is justified in continuing to believe it.

This sounds like a case of conservative bias, since he is running on nothing except the inertia of the belief. Yet we also know there are cases where inertia counts for nothing, and Christensen gives an example:

> Suppose you flip a coin, and it lands out of my sight. Without going over to look, I decide that it has landed 'tails' up. I do not believe the coin to be biased, nor do I believe myself telepathic, nor am I a victim of the gambler's fallacy who has just seen several 'heads' in a row. I simply believe that the coin has landed 'tails' up. Now, it seems to me that the fact that I now believe that it landed "tails" up does not justify me – in any measure at all – in maintaining my belief that it landed 'tails' up. ... To the degree that I favor 'tails' over 'heads' ..., merely on the basis of the fact that I currently believe it landed 'tails' up, I am being dogmatic.[8]

We approve of the belief about populations but we disapprove of the belief about the coin, so I would reflexively ask 'What is the difference?', except I don't have to: Christensen is right onto it:

> What, then, accounts for the difference between our intuitions in the coin case and our intuitions in the case of my beliefs about the population of India?[9]

Furthermore, he compares both kinds of example with analogous examples involving statements that reside in a friend's theory rather than his own, and he looks for similarities and differences across the matrix of cases.

What Christensen finds is that the crucial factor is his indirect evidence about the origin of the belief, i.e. his evidence that there had once been good evidence, even if he can't put his hand on that original evidence now.

> In the case of my belief about the population of India, I suspect that I originally formed this belief (like most of my geographical beliefs) based on the testimony of my mother, or a teacher, or some other generally reliable source. Furthermore, since India is a common topic of conversation in my family, I would have had a good chance of discovering an erroneous belief on this topic if I had one.[10]

In effect, he is treating his own current beliefs in the same way as he treats a newspaper article: he doesn't know what evidence the reporter had, but he can form a view about it, favourable or unfavourable, on the back of indirect clues, such as the reporter's access to reliable sources and her track record of careful checking. In the end, therefore, Christensen's example about the population of India demonstrates nothing more than an ordinary use of testimony. It only looks like conservatism because the testimony in question is his own.

I agree with Christensen's analysis, and I find it helpful because, by assimilating his own testimony to the testimony of others, it alerts us to the ways that our own testimony can go wrong: they are just the old familiar ways that other people's testimony goes wrong. In the words of Quine and Ullian, people 'misremember, misjudge, and misreason'.[11] And I would add that, even when an informant does none of those things, we still should not take his testimony as gospel. At best it tells us something about his epistemic situation, from which we *might* conclude that the testimony is true, or we might conclude something else.

Thus take the case where the informant is Isaac Newton and his testimony is the laws of classical mechanics. Knowing that Newton was not one to misremember, misjudge or misreason, and knowing that he had access to many observations of planets, cannonballs, billiard balls, pendulums and the odd falling apple, we can reasonably conclude that all of those observations, including any that have been lost, matched the predictions of classical mechanics, as near as Newton could tell. That is all good to know, but what we do with the information is up to us. As it happens, we also have access to more recent observations, involving higher speeds, greater masses and longer distances; and it turns out that the simplest theory that squares with all the observations, both old and new, does *not* include Newton's classical mechanics. It includes relativistic mechanics, and that contradicts classical mechanics; so classical mechanics is out.

Notice that we do not ignore Newton's testimony. We allow it to teach us something, indirectly, about some old empirical data, which in turn informs our search for the simplest empirically correct theory. In that way we give it its due. And in the same way we should give our own testimony its due; but whether we end up agreeing with it or not will vary case by case according to the sum of available evidence. Let us judge each theory on its merits.

◆

The argument from lost evidence, like Quine's remarks on conservatism, was about theorizing in general. I would like to deal now with another strand of conservatism, which specifically counsels *philosophers* to be conservative, in the sense of steering their own theories close to pre-philosophical opinion. Here, for example, is Scott Soames:

> Even theorists whose aim is one of substantial conceptual reform cannot afford to stray too far from our ordinary, pre-philosophical judgements. The further one goes down the reformist path, the more implausible the consequences of one's theory are likely to become, until at some point the implausibility of the consequences comes to outweigh the initial attractiveness of the theory. This is not to say that no philosophical revisions of our ordinary judgements, or of our ordinary pre-philosophical concepts, can ever be justified. In some cases, they can. However it is to say that our ordinary pre-philosophical judgements substantially constrain even the most philosophically well-motivated theories.[12]

Insofar as this passage can be construed as an argument, a key premise is that counterintuitive claims – i.e. claims that contradict 'our ordinary, pre-philosophical judgements' – are implausible. Or I should say, counterintuitive claims *in philosophy* are implausible, since science does not seem to bear this burden. Science strides confidently into areas that boggle the lay mind; and not just confidently but *plausibly*, according to a scientific standard of plausibility that is not tethered to vulgar opinion. So why doesn't philosophy get to do that? What is the difference?

One line of argument, sometimes attributed to G. E. Moore, targets philosophers because philosophers are vulnerable to accusations of getting their epistemology wrong. To take the most famous example, when a sceptical philosopher's epistemic standards demand that she reject the existence of the external world, the Moorean move is to fault the epistemic standards, as they are less certain than the common-sense view that the external world exists.[13]

I agree with this, up to a point. I agree that, in a case of this kind, the epistemic standards are at fault, and I said as much in Chapter 1. Unlike Moore, however, I don't rest anything on the 'common-sense' status of belief in the external world. Arguing from common-sense status only has persuasive force against someone who thinks that that status matters, which our sceptical philosopher presumably does not. So I would set aside the issue of what is or isn't common sense, and focus on my interlocutor's own everyday assertions about the world and its contents. Then I would set aside the fact that she has been making those assertions already, and focus on the fact that she will not quit making them. On *that* basis, I would argue that her strict epistemic standards are hypocritical, or, as I put it in Chapter 1, inoperative.

I might fail. The philosopher in question might escape my accusations by keeping true to her principles and giving up the world. Then the situation is truly desperate, and make no mistake: proclaiming commonsensicality as a fundamental epistemic norm will not save it, unless I can convince this philosopher to do the same, which seems unlikely in her case. Conversely, if I had the rhetorical skill to persuade her of new epistemic norms, then I would not need conservatism; the norms of simplicity and empirical correctness would do just fine.

In contemporary philosophy, the reverence for common sense runs deep, and I sense that I have not yet fathomed it. Let me see what I can find in this passage from David Lewis:

> For it is pointless to build a theory, however nicely systematised it might be, that it would be unreasonable to believe. And a theory cannot earn credence just by its unity and economy. What credence it cannot earn, it must inherit. It is far beyond our power to weave a brand new fabric of adequate theory *ex nihilo*, so we must perforce conserve the one we've got. A worthwhile theory must be credible, and a credible theory must be conservative. It cannot gain, and it cannot deserve, credence if it disagrees with too much of what we thought before.[14]

I agree with this part: 'It is far beyond our power to weave a brand new fabric of adequate theory *ex nihilo*'. That is why I favour conservatism as a heuristic: it helps creatures like us to get by with our meagre intellectual powers. But I think Lewis is getting at something much stronger than that. His four 'must's and four 'cannot's, and particularly the phrase 'cannot deserve', suggest that conservatism has seeped into his epistemic scorekeeping.

This interpretation is both reinforced and explained by the slide Lewis makes, from 'earn … just by its unity and economy' to 'earn' *simpliciter*. Of course those expressions are not interchangeable: earning credence involves not just 'unity and economy' but experience too. By treating them as interchangeable, Lewis reveals that he has forgotten the role of experience. That leaves a gap in his epistemology, and conservatism becomes the plug.

This is not a mistake one would make if one were thinking about science. No one forgets about experience there. But think of a philosopher, and you probably picture an armchair in a library; and once you have that image, the role of experience is easy to overlook. Such an oversight is, I believe, the root of the felt need for conservatism within philosophy. It is an oversight that I try to correct in Chapter 7.

5

Sufficient logical explicitness is norm zero

Quine's 'Empiricism without the Dogmas' included this phrase:

> the logical laws being in turn simply certain further statements of the system, certain further elements of the field[1]

I quoted that in Chapter 3, but I didn't pause to scrutinize it, and neither did Quine. I suspect that, in his world, the notion that one *states* logical laws was barely worth mentioning. The early Quine was a logician through and through. Systems of codified logic were his habitat and, as the saying goes, a fish doesn't know it's in water.

For my part, I try to extricate Quine's normative epistemology from the rest of his philosophy whenever I can. So I would like, as a thought experiment, to do away with codified logic and see how the epistemology functions in its absence – but I regret that that will not be possible. I can set aside Quine's preference for some kinds of logic over others, but the need to have some codified logic rather than none, and to reason by applying its laws explicitly, at least some of the time, is so entangled with Quine's epistemic norms that I cannot pull it and them apart.

In this chapter we shall explore the entanglements, and it will turn out that they force epistemology to include more than just the two norms of simplicity and empirical correctness. But, before we go on, I need to draw a distinction.

I distinguish two sets of sentences, each of which is sometimes called 'our theory'. On the one hand, there is the set of sentences that we have actually spelled out and endorsed, whether on paper or in our heads or somewhere else. Call this *the explicit theory*. On the other hand, there is the set of sentences to which we have committed ourselves by endorsing the explicit theory. Call this *the implicit theory*. It is typically a larger set than the explicit theory, and it includes the explicit theory as a subset.

Whether 'our theory' refers to the explicit theory or to the implicit theory depends on context. When we say 'We must revise our theory', we are referring to the explicit theory, since revising is a process of expressly endorsing sentences that we did not formerly endorse or expressly disendorsing sentences that we formerly endorsed. But when we say 'Our theory conflicts with experience', we are referring to the implicit theory. To see this, suppose that we have expressly endorsed:

(1) Anything with feet like a duck and a bill like a duck that lays eggs like a duck is a duck.

and:

(2) All ducks have feathers.

but we have never expressly endorsed (nor disendorsed):

(3) Anything with feet like a duck and a bill like a duck that lays eggs like a duck has feathers.

And suppose that we now catch a clear view of a platypus laying eggs. Then *our theory conflicts with experience*, but only because our theory – that is to say, our implicit theory – includes (3).[2]

♦

With the concepts of explicit theory, commitments and implicit theory in mind, let us look again at our norms of empirical correctness and simplicity.

First, empirical correctness. This norm would be very straightforward if all of our logic was explicit. Thus imagine (i) that our explicit theory is the union of two sets L and O, where L is the set of all the logical laws that we have spelled out and endorsed and O is the set of all the other sentences that we have spelled out and endorsed; (ii) that the laws in L cover every kind of deduction that we use and (iii) that the sentences in O are all logically transparent.[3] In this tidy scene, if our theory leads us to expect experience to go a certain way, and actual experience does not comply, then we can be sure that the fault lies in the explicit theory – i.e. somewhere in L or somewhere in O – since there is nowhere else for it to lie. But this tidy scene is a logicians' fantasy. How does the norm of empirical correctness apply in real life?

In real life, our explicit theory contains sentences of natural language, and, when we discover our commitments, it is rarely by instantiating stated logical laws. Instead we employ a knack that we call *informal logic* – a knack that, being uncodified, cannot be part of the explicit theory. In this untidy scene, if experience does not go as we expect, then we cannot be sure that our explicit theory is at fault, because an alternative explanation is available: our informal logic might have malfunctioned. Perhaps we allowed some unavowed falsehood to slip in as a suppressed premise, somewhere along the daisy chain of our informal reasoning; or perhaps we read some ambiguous construction the wrong way; or perhaps, without any ambiguity, we were mistaken about which sentences follow from which. (We know that formal logicians sometimes disagree about which sentences follow from which, and express their differences in competing systems of logical laws, so presumably there is room for disagreement – and a fortiori room for error – among informal plodders too.)

The possibility of informal logic failure prevents us from pointing to the explicit theory and saying '*That theory* is empirically incorrect, so *that theory* needs to change'; and if we cannot say it while pointing to the explicit theory, then we cannot say it at all, since we have no other way to identify *that theory*. The most we can say is, 'Something is wrong in the theory-plus-reasoner complex.'

Now consider the norm of simplicity. Simplicity is a matter of judgement rather than formula, but still we would like to be clear about the object of the judgement: what is the thing that is to be kept simple? In the logically ideal case, it is the explicit theory (or its compact presentation – see Chapter 3); but what is it in untidy real life, where we depend on informal logic?

Now we are back in the woods. We cannot judge the simplicity of the theory-plus-reasoner complex, since a reasoner's cognitive mechanisms are hidden from view and poorly understood, even when the reasoner is oneself. The best we can do is to judge the simplicity of what we can see, i.e. the explicit theory, but that restricted measure is not satisfactory either, because it is too easily gamed. It invites theorists to sweeten their simplicity scores by the cynical expedient of theorizing less explicitly, also known as obscurantism. An unscrupulous mathematician could, for instance, 'simplify' the calculus by deleting the intricate definitions of derivatives and integrals and replacing them with hand-waving about actual infinitesimals.

In summary, then, both of our norms can break down when we apply them to theories that rely on informal logic. And, by 'break down', I do not mean that the norms rule such theories out. I mean that the norms can fail to rule on them at all.

◆

Could we remedy the situation by a change of ontology? E.g. if we helped ourselves to *propositions*, and to a relation of *entailment* between propositions, and a relation of *expressing*, between ordinary-language sentences and propositions, then we might say that our ordinary-language theory is empirically incorrect whenever the propositions expressed by the sentences of the explicit theory together entail a proposition that conflicts with experience. Or if we helped ourselves to *beliefs*, considered as something like sentences, but capable of latent, unformulated residence in a reasoner's mind, then we might try to measure a theory's simplicity by taking account of all the beliefs that are involved in holding it.

I do not dismiss any of this. In my opinion, ascriptions of belief (along with ascriptions of desire) can be justified, and in Part Three I shall venture some steps in that direction. And if a theory of belief and desire were developed further, it might enable a theory of linguistic convention (perhaps along the lines of Lewis, *Convention*); and that, in turn, might enable a defensible theory of propositions and their expression. But I speak of future developments. In the present, I have no clearly correct theory of propositions, nor of mental content. Those are matters of dense philosophical debate, in which I cannot find my way without an epistemological compass. Therefore I need to build a working set of epistemic norms *beforehand*, and that means building it without science from the future.

◆

Let's back up. Recall that our two norms, simplicity and empirical correctness, were working fine until we asked them to assess theories that use informal logic. That suggests another approach: we could assert a new norm – call it *total logical explicitness* – that outlaws any theory that uses informal logic at any point. We could make it our policy to apply this norm before the others, so that only theories with 100 per cent rule-based deductions would go on to be assessed for empirical correctness and simplicity. Those two norms would then run smoothly on filtered fuel.

The trouble with this plan is that the new norm would be too demanding. Even Euclid's *Elements* would not pass, since Euclid only wrote down mathematical postulates, not logical ones. Now we can correct that, as it turns out, because nowadays we can formalize geometry quite thoroughly, but the point is this: unless we are ready to forgo every bit of theory that is stuck at Euclid's level of clarity or below, we cannot sincerely claim to have adopted total logical explicitness as a norm.

Here is our dilemma. On the one hand, if we declare a norm that bans all reliance on informal logic, it will ban so much of what we actually say and, frankly, won't quit saying, that it will not be operating as a norm at all. On the other hand, we have seen how our two existing norms can break down when applied to theories that use informal logic; so if we don't have another norm to act as a filter, we can expect a lot of breakdowns.

◆

Here is what I propose. If we analyse the conditions under which our two norms need logical explicitness in order to function, we will see that neither of them needs 100 per cent logical explicitness 100 per cent of the time. Let us find out what they do need, and then frame a nuanced norm of logical explicitness: one that is less of a blanket and more of a tailored fit.

First take empirical correctness. We saw how this norm breaks down when informal logic leads to a conflict with experience, but that is not the fate of every theory that uses informal logic. For one thing, the breakdown only happens when there *is* a conflict with experience, and sometimes there is not. And even when there is a conflict, it might have nothing to do with informal logic: it might be that the explicit theory alone is in conflict with experience; or perhaps the theory is partially formalized, and the set of sentences that can be formally deduced from the explicit theory is in conflict with experience. In either of those cases, the norm of empirical correctness arrives at a verdict – a negative one – so again: no breakdown. Evidently, then, we can operate the norm of empirical correctness without filtering out every theory that uses informal logic; it suffices to filter out *those theories from which conflicts with experience arise via informal logic and not otherwise.*

Now simplicity. Recall how this norm comes into play: rival theories A, B, C ... have passed the empirical correctness test, and we must find the simplest, because that is the one we should accept. So the simplicity judgement we need to make is comparative, not absolute. Consider, now, the case where A, B, C, ... all include a common part Φ. (Perhaps A, B, C ... are rival economic theories and Φ is high school mathematics.) It seems plausible that Φ's complexity contributes an equal amount to the complexity of each rival theory, and therefore, for comparative purposes, it doesn't matter what that amount is: it cancels out. So even if we cannot assess the complexity of Φ – e.g. because Φ relies on informal logic – that does not prevent us from making the comparative simplicity judgement that we need to make. Evidently, then, we can operate the norm of simplicity without filtering out every theory that uses informal logic; it suffices to filter out *those theories that have informal parts that their empirically correct rivals do not have.*

Let us pull together the conclusions of the last two paragraphs. In order to operate the two norms of empirical correctness and simplicity, it suffices to filter out both (i) those theories from which conflicts with experience arise via informal logic and not otherwise, and (ii) those theories that have informal parts that their empirically correct rivals do not have. So let us make this our norm of *sufficient logical explicitness*:

Do not accept any theory from which conflicts with experience arise via informal logic and not otherwise, and do not accept any theory that has informal parts that its empirically correct rivals do not have.

This rule is inelegant, it must be said, and what's worse is that there could be more warts and epicycles to come before it is settled. For, while this version demands conditions that are sufficient for the operation of the other two norms, I have not shown, and I do not know, that those conditions are necessary for the operation of the other two norms. To put it another way, it might transpire that the other two norms can assess theories that meet some weaker set of conditions. If so, then we should be able to amend the norm of sufficient logical explicitness again, in ways that make it even less demanding. But I shall not pursue that here.

For the space of this book, then, the norm of sufficient logical explicitness is finished, and so too is my (tentative, revisable, undogmatic) list of epistemic norms. For the space of this book, then, here is my criterion of epistemic justification:

> If you have a theory that is sufficiently logically explicit, and if it has never led you to a conflict with experience, and if it is the simplest theory you have found that meets those conditions, then that theory is epistemically justified.

◆

Note the present tense: if a theory complies with the three norms, then it *is* epistemically justified. Yet we know, as responsible theorists, that present epistemic justification is not our only concern. It is also our business to consider the future, because, as we saw near the end of Chapter 3, a theory that is justified now might be superseded and denied later; and then we shall say that it had been false along. We would prefer today not to hold until tomorrow a theory that will turn out next year to have been false all along; so what can we do to avoid it?

One thing we should *not* do is to reject the theory that our normative epistemology is telling us to accept. That would be hypocrisy of a type that we have been taking pains to avoid since Chapter 2. Happily, there are other ways to reduce risk.

At the end of Chapter 3 I mentioned experimentation. Experimentation is a tactic for bringing failures of empirical correctness forward, so a theory that is at risk of becoming empirically incorrect in the distant future becomes empirically incorrect in the near future instead. That obliges us – and a fortiori permits us – to revise it soon, thereby cutting short our time spent holding a doomed theory.

Similarly, we would like to bring failures of sufficient logical explicitness forward.

Consider the common situation, where our current theory T is sufficiently logically explicit but not totally logically explicit. In this situation, we run the risk that, at some unknown time in the future, T will become insufficiently logically explicit and we will have to revise it. There are three ways that that could happen: (i) the implicit theory could lead, via informal deductions already made and not otherwise, to conflict with future experience; (ii) the implicit theory could lead, via informal deductions yet to be made and not otherwise, to conflict with past, present or future experience and (iii) some alternative empirically correct theory U could be proposed that beats T on logical explicitness. Fortunately, we can reduce the risks of all three by devising a more explicit alternative theory *now*. If we can propose a theory U that dispenses with some of T's parts that rely on informal logic, and if U does not introduce any new parts that rely on informal logic, and if U is empirically correct, then U's mere presence, as a rival to T, will render T insufficiently logically explicit by the definition above. That will oblige us – and a fortiori permit us – to switch from T to U, thereby cutting short our time spent holding a doomed theory.

(We can also play mixed tactics. E.g. suppose we plan an experiment, hoping to bring failures of empirical correctness forward, but before we conduct the experiment we notice that our theory predicts an outcome only via informal logic. Foreseeing that that will create unwelcome wriggle room, between the theory and oncoming experience, we move to pin down the deductions before the experiment starts.)

To summarize this chapter so far: there are two good reasons why we might revise a theory in the direction of logical explicitness. One is an epistemic duty in the present, and the other is our interest in dispatching theories that have epistemic discredit in their future. The first demands sufficient logical explicitness, and the second beckons us beyond what is currently sufficient.

◆

It is almost time to pivot from the norms of theorizing to theorizing itself, but, before we do, let me close this chapter with an objection and reply.

The objection is that the norm of sufficient logical explicitness is still too demanding. For, while it does not demand perfection, it does demand that we always do our best, in the following sense: we must never accept a theory that is informal in an area where we have a formal alternative. Yet many of us do less than our best for much of the time. We achieve a high degree of logical explicitness in some area, and then we backslide. There are, e.g., entirely formal geometries, couched in the language of first-order predicate logic, but no matter how well we know them, there are still times when we intone, in our schoolteacher's English, 'The square on the hypotenuse is equal to the sum of the squares on the other two sides.' And let us not pretend that we are about to quit talking this way. Sometimes we have no other choice, e.g. when we are the schoolteachers, imparting geometry to students who know nothing of formal logic; and even when the discourse is expert-to-expert, a certain degree of informality is often helpful and we feel no obligation to censor it. Don't these practices expose our norm of sufficient logical explicitness as hypocritical – or, in the terminology of Chapter 1, *inoperative*?

In order to meet this objection, I need to look more closely than I have so far at the role of epistemology.

Epistemic norms tell us what to accept and what to reject, but their role is not, and never has been, to exert direct control over every noise that leaves our mouths. Some of our noises bear no relation to epistemic warrant – 'hello', 'ouch', 'ho hum' – and others bear only an indirect relation to it.

Take metaphor. We say, 'She is skating on thin ice.' If we are challenged, our first response is to signal that the sentence is metaphorical, and if necessary offer some non-metaphorical sentence N in its place. Questions may be asked about the poetic or social aptness of the metaphor, but those are not questions of epistemology. If, however, the challenge turns from the aptness of our remark to its accuracy, then we will need to justify the non-metaphorical sentence N – and that is where epistemology enters.

The same applies to a range of utterances: not only metaphor but also irony, ambiguity, rough sketches and white lies. There are differences among them, of course, but in each case, when we are called to account for what we have said, one part of our apologia is non-epistemological, and another part is to justify some sentence or sentences other than the one we uttered.

Now I submit that statements of colloquial geometry, spoken while in possession of a formal geometry that is epistemically superior, are members of the same extended family. If they are challenged, there may be some discussion about our rhetorical or pedagogical judgement; but, when the argument turns to substance, what counts is the justification, not of the sentence we uttered, but of something else: some sentence or sentences of our best geometry (and what *ultimately* counts is whether that best geometry forms part of an epistemically warranted total theory).

Part Two

Application to philosophy

The same motives that impel scientists to seek ever simpler and clearer theories adequate to the subject matter of their special sciences are motives for simplification and clarification of the broader framework shared by all the sciences. ... The quest of a simplest, clearest overall pattern of canonical notation is not to be distinguished from a quest of ultimate categories, of a limning of the most general traits of reality.

W. V. Quine[1]

6

Touching base

To scientists

The epistemology at which we have arrived might strike you as very new and strange. In practice, however, it mostly asks you to do what you were doing anyway. It calls for induction and abduction to carry on (although both are now seen as special cases of theoretical simplification); it backs your rejection of idle metaphysics (though this too becomes a case of simplification, rather than an issue of Popperian falsificationism); it applauds your drive to express scientific laws in the language of mathematics (because this imports the hard-won logical explicitness of mathematics into science); and, in those sciences that are not ready to be expressed mathematically, it commends your discipline of staying close to observable facts (because this limits the amount of informal reasoning needed to reach those facts). In all of these ways, the counsel of our epistemology is for science to continue its business as usual, including its usual business of improving itself.

Is there any way that our epistemology might change science? Well, it opens doors to some new lines of inquiry, e.g. 'We can simplify theory by induction, abduction and what else?' and 'We can make deductions explicit by employing mathematics and what else?'; and it is conceivable that these might lead scientists onto some new path. But, in the shorter term, it might be leading *philosophy* towards something that counts as science. Here in Part Two, we shall meet a type of philosophy that is heading that way.

To Quine scholars

The epistemology at which we have arrived might strike you as very new and strange. You might be surprised to see theoretical conservatism rejected as an epistemic norm, after Quine appeared to assert it, and surprised again to see sufficient logical explicitness proposed as an epistemic norm, when Quine made no such proposal. Above all, you might be perplexed at the very idea of 'Quine's normative epistemology', considering that Quine appeared to disown normative epistemology on more than one occasion.

But this last point is a sign that we are at cross purposes. By 'normative epistemology', I mean no more than the principles one uses to decide which claims to accept and which to reject. Quine was full of interesting and controversial decisions of that type; I assume that those decisions were guided by principles; and I would like to know what the principles were, even if Quine himself was not always forthcoming on the question. I submit that my three epistemic norms are a good fit, in the sense that they lead to much the same decisions as Quine reached. In this part we shall follow them a little way and see.

To philosophers more generally

I imagine that you find this epistemology not so much new and strange as old and strange, what with its revival of the quaint word 'empiricism' and all the *passé* prudery about metaphysics that comes with it. To you, I am afraid, there can be no assurance that it supports business as usual. It supports some of the things you do, but only some, and our next task is to work out which things they are.

7

The armchair

We know that our epistemology is pro-science and anti-metaphysics, but where does it stand on philosophy? Which of philosophers' ranging activities does it rule in, and which does it rule out? These are daunting questions, but we can make a start on them by confronting three arguments that purport to show that our epistemology rules out philosophy in toto.

To begin, then, let it be argued that our epistemology, being empiricist, is opposed to all a priori claims, and that philosophy is nothing but a priori claims, because philosophers do not make observations. After all, the philosopher's place of business is the armchair, not the laboratory or field or observatory.

And yes, it is true that our epistemology opposes a priori claims. It opposes them in precisely the following sense: for anyone who has no experience, the best theory is the null theory, i.e. no claims at all. But philosophers, even those in armchairs, are not without experience. They might be lacking in novel or interesting experience, or they might not; but in any case they have ordinary experience, and that is enough to disarm anti-philosophy argument #1. Furthermore, philosophers enjoy the benefit of everyday testimony, as we all do, from friends, family, news reporters etc. What any philosopher hears in a day might be novel and interesting or it might not, and it might be true or it might be mistaken, but it often carries clues about the experience of others.

Next, let it be said that science, and specifically physics, has reached a stage where it describes the whole universe with such consummate logical explicitness and simplicity that there is no room left for improvement; or, if there is room, then it belongs to those specialists who understand the open problems at the scientific frontier. On that basis, let it be argued that there is nothing left for philosophy to contribute; or as Stephen Hawking was kind enough to put it, 'Philosophy is dead.'

And yes, I accept that physics describes, or is very close to describing, the whole universe, and I also accept the part about its consummate logical explicitness and simplicity; but this does not add up to physics being all the theory we need. If it did, then we could dispense, not only with philosophy, but with botany, geology and so forth as well – which is absurd.

And why is it absurd? Because, though a plant's flowering or a volcano's erupting might, in principle, be calculated using physics alone, the calculation would require masses of detailed information and computing power that nobody actually has. That is why, when we employ induction and abduction to systematize our observations of plants and volcanoes, we do so in a way that produces sciences other than physics.

Moreover, in the same way that sciences like botany and geology help us to deduce observations that physics alone cannot, some of the less rigorous sciences help us to deduce observations that sciences as rigorous as botany and geology cannot. And even if we were to pool the entire published output of hard science, soft science and worse, there would still be room for more theory. Nothing in the Library of Congress will tell me where I left my car keys, or which dog chewed my rug. Those are things I must work out for myself.

So we each find ourselves holding a total theory that is large, multilayered and of uneven quality. I take the point that physics is not to be improved upon, at least not by the likes of you and me, but that leaves plenty of room for improvement elsewhere.

The task can be divided, very roughly, into two parts. One is to make the less rigorous sciences more rigorous. Practitioners of the less rigorous sciences often undertake that part themselves, though philosophers can always train up and join in. And the other part is to improve the portion of our theory that, though we rely on it every day, we do not usually grace with the name of 'science'. We relegate it, rather, to the category of common sense.

In the jungle of possible theoretical improvements, the improvement of common sense is the low-hanging fruit: 'low-hanging' because it requires no specialized experience, and 'fruit' because it offers the prospect of great advances, especially along the axis of logical explicitness. Here, then, is an opening for philosophers to do epistemically valuable work. As to the nature of this work, Quine offered this list of examples:

> One example ... is Frege's 'definition' of number. Another is the avoidance, by means of quantification theory, of the misleading substantive 'nothing'. Another is the recourse to '⊃' and quantification to avoid the vernacular 'if–then', with the problems of cause and modality to which it gives rise. And the classic case is Russell's theory of descriptions.[1]

This is what Quine later came to call *regimentation*: the replacement of ordinary language, in which deductions fall under no codifiable laws, or in some cases only convoluted laws, by the artificial language of formal logic, which has been purpose-built to streamline formal deduction. I see regimentation as philosophy's core activity.

Before we move on to anti-philosophy argument #3, let me insert three clarifications.

First, there is a terminological glitch that we need to be aware of. Quine tended to use the word 'science' broadly, to include the whole diverse web of sentences that together tell us something about experience. So, for Quine, any part of common sense that plays a role in predicting or explaining experience was part of science. I, on the other hand, have been using 'science' more narrowly, to designate the portion of the web that is at least somewhat systematic, and perhaps even professional. So, for me, science is in contrast to common sense, though both are parts of total theory. I will persist in my usage, as I believe it to be the standard one, but it is important to be attuned to Quine's broader usage, because otherwise some of his remarks come across as narrowly scientistic in ways that are hard to explain.

Second, when I distinguish (i), the project of improving the less rigorous sciences, from (ii), the project of improving common sense, I do not mean to suggest that they are mutually exclusive. The projects overlap. Wherever science has not yet crystallized into equations, we find it using the same linguistic constructions as common sense; and, for the sake of a smooth-running total theory, we would probably like it and common sense to move towards a single logical language. Therefore, each time we find a way to paraphrase some idiom from the colloquial to the logical language, as a contribution to (ii), we are incidentally finding a way to contribute to (i). And of course the logical laws are also part of the overlap.

And third, since one cannot write the words 'regimentation' and 'language' in the same sentence without sensing that the combination will trigger Orwellian nightmares in some readers, I hasten to recall a lesson from the end of Chapter 5: endorsing a sufficiently logically explicit theory officially is one thing and speaking it in company is another. Our epistemology requires the former, but it does not dictate what we utter in any given social situation. That will depend on a range of extra epistemological factors, which almost always preclude, e.g. 'the avoidance, by means of quantification theory, of the misleading substantive "nothing"'. In other words, when your practice of regimentation leads you to sentences in the robotic argot of formal logic, you aren't supposed to blurt them out over dinner. Hold them in reserve, and only vocalize them if and when serious questions of justification arise.

Now I come to the last of my three arguments that purport to show how our epistemology destroys philosophy. I have so little sympathy with this one that I struggle to state it fairly, but the gist is as follows:

> It is interesting to see that you have shrunk the scope of philosophy down to the semantic analysis of ordinary language, but that creates two problems for you. First, ordinary language is a real-world phenomenon whose study requires dedicated field work: you cannot do it properly from an armchair. And second, even if you do discover something about what certain statements of common sense mean, that won't take you far. You won't know whether the formal-language sentences that you come up with are true, because you don't know whether the ordinary-language statements that you started with were true. You burned that bridge when you rejected the norm of theoretical conservatism.

There is much to disagree with here, but the root of it is the assumption that we are engaged in semantic analysis. Quinean regimentation does not aim to produce output that is the semantic equivalent of its input, nor does it aspire to reveal some 'logical form' or 'deep structure' lying below the surface of its input. So, with all due respect to hard-working field linguists, their quest is not ours. Our quest is to *improve upon* what is said in ordinary language, where improvement is measured against the very same epistemic norms that determine what we are entitled to assert.[2] It follows that, by the time we have decided that a certain sentence in the formal language is a good regimentation of some sentence of common sense, we may assert the formal sentence without further ado. A further corollary is that some items of common sense will not have any good regimentations. The overall regimentation of common sense will deal with those items by discarding them. Over to Quine:

> Nor let it be supposed that [formal logic's] philosophical relevance must consist in a point-by-point application to the recorded speech behavior of the man in the street. Philosophy is in large part concerned with the theoretical, non-genetic underpinnings of scientific theory; with what science could get along with, could be reconstructed by means of, as distinct from what science has historically made use of. If certain problems of ontology, say, or modality, or causality, or contrary-to-fact conditionals, which arise in ordinary language, turn out not to arise in science as reconstituted with the help of formal logic, then those philosophical problems have in an important sense been solved: they

have been shown not to be implicated in any necessary foundation of science. Such solutions are good to just the extent that (a) philosophy of science is philosophy enough and (b) the refashioned logical underpinnings of science do not engender new philosophical problems of their own.

… Russell's '$(\imath x)$' is to the vernacular 'the x such that' as '$\supset$' is to the vernacular 'if–then'; in neither case do we have a *translation*, but in both cases we have an important means of *avoidance* for scientific purposes. And in both cases we therefore have solutions of philosophical problems, in one important sense of this phrase.[3]

Let me be frank: this passage is one of my favourites. In it I see Quine giving free rein to his non-conservative best self. 'Non-genetic', 'reconstructed', 'reconstituted', 'refashioned', 'as distinct from what science has historically …': these are fighting words against theoretical conservatism, and I cheer for every one of them. Nevertheless, I can see how the passage might be puzzling. If the improvements on common sense are 'non-genetic', then a reader might well wonder how common sense is involved at all. How does the quest to improve upon common sense differ from ignoring common sense and starting over?

The answer is that, as we improve upon common sense, we depend on common sense to keep us informed about the experiences that will support the incoming theory. That includes our own past experiences, when their only remaining traces are preserved in our common sense, and it includes the experiences of others, when we learn about them indirectly via everyday testimony. But do not mistake this answer for theoretical conservatism, for we know that it is possible to use an old theory as a conduit of information about experience without accepting any obligation to agree with the old theory. We know it is possible because we have done it once already. If I may quote from my own Chapter 4:

Notice that we do not ignore [classical mechanics]. We allow it to teach us something, indirectly, about some old empirical data, which in turn informs our search for the simplest empirically correct theory. In that way we give it its due. And in the same way we should give our own testimony its due; but whether we end up agreeing with it or not will vary case-by-case according to the sum of available evidence. Let us judge each theory on its merits.

If another example is wanted, then think of the data that Galileo inherited from earlier astronomers. Much of it was, we may assume, given in geocentrism-laden terms, yet it carried the traces of past experience. Galileo could use those traces, and ensure that his heliocentrism squared with them, without buying into conservatism about geocentrism.

Summarizing this chapter so far: we have met with three attempts to show that our epistemology rules out all of philosophy, and we have seen off all three by describing a philosophical activity that none of them could impugn. That activity is called 'regimentation'; its goal is to create a theory that covers the same experiential ground as common sense, but with a higher epistemic score, especially on the axis of logical explicitness; and its method is the replacement of ordinary-language idioms by other idioms more conducive to the goal.

◆

'Oh, all right then'; the anti-philosopher retreats, 'you have found an opening for some philosophical activity, but only a paltry amount. No matter whether you call it "analysis" or "regimentation", the replacement of natural language by formal notation is a topic that fits into the first few weeks of an introductory logic course. Even you have called it "low-hanging fruit". So you don't have much of a subject left now, do you?' At this point the anti-philosopher might go on to quote Quine against me; specifically the words 'little difficulty' in this passage:

> By developing our logical theory strictly for sentences in a convenient canonical form we achieve the best division of labor: on one hand there is theoretical deduction and on the other hand there is the work of paraphrasing ordinary language into the theory. The latter job is the less tidy of the two, but still it will usually present little difficulty to one familiar with the canonical notation. For normally he himself is the one who has uttered, as part of some present job, the sentence of ordinary language concerned; and he can then judge outright whether his ends are served by the paraphrase.[4]

Please do forgive me while I repeat, for this slow learner (the anti-philosopher, not Quine), that my use of 'low-hanging' was in reference to regimentation's experiential requirements, not to its intellectual difficulty. In fact its intellectual difficulty is immense. One cannot get a proper sense of it from the outside, so subsequent chapters will look inside; but meanwhile I offer this summary: a good regimentation of common sense will allow chains of formal deduction that traverse all parts of the regimented theory, and we can only achieve that if we design some aspects of the new theory on a system-wide basis. Quine was right that the regimentation of an individual sentence presents little difficulty – but only after the great architectural decisions have been made. Similarly, the Logic 101 lecturer need not spend long on the regimentation of individual sentences – but only because she has made an assumption that the great architectural decisions will have been made by someone else.

Earlier I gave a rough demarcation of science as that which, in addition to conforming to our three epistemic norms, is 'at least somewhat systematic, and perhaps even professional'. By that standard, regimentation could come to count as science, if I am right that it involves the making of 'great architectural decisions' and that 'its intellectual difficulty is immense'. In that event, and to the extent that regimentation is philosophy's core activity, philosophy would not merely be continuous with science; it would be substantially a *part* of science, albeit an armchair-based part. But the rise and rise of regimentation is a topic for Chapters 8–12. Right now, there is some less pleasant business awaiting our attention.

◆

In Chapter 2, a passage from Huw Price alerted us to the revival, from the 1950s onwards, of unapologetic metaphysics. I shall not repeat my deplorations of metaphysics, but there may be some benefit in raking over the mistakes that led to its resurgence.

Here is Price, continuing from the previously quoted passage:

> If [a philosopher] were to ask where the battle against metaphysics was lost in twentieth century philosophy, he would do well to turn his attention to a skirmish between [Carnap] and Quine in the early 1950s. In philosophy, as in less abstract conflicts, single engagements are rarely decisive, but this particular clash does seem of special significance. By the late 1940s, Carnap's position seems to represent the furthest advance of the anti-metaphysical movement, at least on one of its several fronts. The fact that the position was never consolidated, and the ground lost, seems to owe much to Quine's criticism of Carnap's views. Ironically, Quine's criticism was friendly fire, for ... Quine, too, was no friend of traditional metaphysics. But the attack was no less damaging for the fact that it came from behind, and its effect seems to have been to weaken what – at that time, at any rate – seems to have been Quine and Carnap's common cause.[5]

And Price goes on to say why, in his view, 'this metaphysical rebirthing myth is in large part bogus'. While I cannot agree with the specific diagnosis in Price's paper,[6] I do agree about the bogusness. Metaphysicians have misused the early Quine, and I would like to offer a diagnosis of my own.

Let me distinguish three steps that were taken in close succession close to 1950. *Step 1*: Quine made some decisions about how to deploy variables and quantifiers within a formalized total theory. *Step 2*: Quine reached out to a wider philosophical audience by doing the opposite of regimentation, viz. paraphrasing his findings from logical notation into English (whence it was translated into other natural languages). *Step 3*: That wider audience, including some with little or no interest in formalization, carried on the vernacular discussion in its own terms.

Was step 1 metaphysical? It depends on the details. It is certainly possible to use variables and quantifiers to construct metaphysical sentences, i.e. sentences that complicate one's theory while offering nothing of epistemic value in return; but one can also use variables and quantifiers for legitimate theorizing. The next chapter will say more about all this. For now, we can perhaps agree that, in step 1, Quine at least *aimed* for simplicity (while insisting on logical explicitness), so the project of step 1 was not a metaphysical project.

Step 2, Quine's regression to *sermo humilis*, was an example of the social practice that I have called 'backsliding'. At the end of Chapter 5, I explained that backsliding is not a proper object of epistemic criticism, so I would not accuse Quine of metaphysics at step 2. Nonetheless, he courted misunderstanding by not clearly signalling what he was doing.

Having arrived at, say, '$\exists x$ (x is a number)', Quine might have thought it harmless to express it as 'Numbers exist'; and, to be sure, it was harmless, as long as he was addressing logicians who could be counted on to hear in those words the existential quantification and nothing more or less. However, when he turned to audiences that were preoccupied with such questions as 'Are you saying that numbers are real things?', 'Are you a Platonist?' and 'Are you a small-"r" realist or a capital-"R" Realist?', Quine could have spared philosophy a great many dead ends by clarifying his position as follows: 'I'm not going to defend or explain "Numbers exist", because it was a throwaway line. All I was getting at was "$\exists x$ (x is a number)". That is the sentence that I claim is warranted, because of the part it plays in a logically explicit total theory, and I'll be happy to take your questions on that topic.'

Regrettably, though, the early Quine made an opposite move. Rather than playing down the parallels between English and the existential quantifier, he played them up, by proclaiming that certain English idioms do and certain English idioms do not carry 'ontological commitment'; e.g.:

> To be assumed as an entity is, purely and simply, to be reckoned as the value of a variable. In terms of the categories of traditional grammar, this amounts roughly to saying that to be is to be in the range of reference of a pronoun. Pronouns are the basic media of reference; nouns might better have been named propronouns. The variables of quantification, 'something', 'nothing', 'everything', range over our whole ontology, whatever it may be; and we are convicted of a particular ontological presupposition if, and only if, the alleged presuppositum

has to be reckoned among the entities over which our variables range in order to make one of our affirmations true.⁷

and, most memorably:

> A curious thing about the ontological problem is its simplicity. It can be put in three Anglo-Saxon monosyllables: 'What is there?'⁸

It is important for students of Quine to understand that that was a mistake, and that he corrected it later, e.g.:

> We give content to the ontological issue when we regiment the language of science strictly within the framework of the logic of truth functions and objectual quantification.⁹

and:

> Ordinary language is only loosely referential, and any ontological accounting makes sense only relative to an appropriate regimentation of language. The regimentation is not a matter of eliciting some latent but determinate ontological content of ordinary language. It is a matter rather of freely creating an ontology-oriented language that can supplant ordinary language in serving some particular purposes that one has in mind.¹⁰

and:

> The common man's ontology ... is vague in its scope; we cannot ... tell in general which ... things ... to count him as assuming. Should we regard grammar as decisive? Does every noun demand some array of denotata? Surely not; the nominalizing of verbs is often a mere stylistic variation. But where can we draw the line?
>
> It is a wrong question; there is no line to draw. Bodies are assumed, yes; they are the things, first and foremost. Beyond them there is a succession of dwindling analogies. Various expressions come to be used in ways more or less parallel to the use of the terms for bodies, and it is felt that corresponding objects are more or less posited, *pari passu*; but there is no purpose in trying to mark an ontological limit to the dwindling parallelism.¹¹

But those remarks came in 1977 and 1981 – too late to prevent the storm that was brewing *ca.*1950. Back then, the word got out that Quine believed that numbers exist (along with sets and physical objects, but not properties or *possibilia*), and after that there was no stopping step 3, the outbreak of metaphysics; for who could deny philosophers the right to join a debate that Quine had started? And so metaphysics carries on to this day, all because of a game of Chinese whispers that began with Quine.

And it is not just metaphysics that carries on. Sometimes the whole three-step process is repeated, more or less. I am thinking in particular of the way that David Lewis fuelled the metaphysics of modality. First there was step 1':

> Instead of formalizing our modal discourse by means of modal operators, we ... could stick to our standard logic (quantification theory with identity and without ineliminable singular terms) and provide it with predicates and a domain of quantification suited to the topic of modality.[12]

Then came step 2':

> I advocate a thesis of plurality of worlds, or *modal realism*, which holds that our world is but one world among many. ... The worlds are something like remote planets; except that most of them are much bigger than mere planets, ...
>
> The other worlds are of a kind with this world of ours. ...
>
> Nor does this world differ from the others in its manner of existing. I do not have the slightest idea what a difference in manner of existing is supposed to be.[13]

And step 3', obdurate modal metaphysics, decoupled from formal logic, is all around us still.

Was Lewis's step 1' metaphysical? As with Quine's step 1, it depends on the details. I am inclined to think that 1' was metaphysical though 1 was not, but those are matters for Chapters 8 and 15. If we assume, for the space of this paragraph, that 1' was legitimate, then Lewis can hardly be faulted for 2'. Counterpart theory is complicated, and if left in formal notation it would have been impenetrable to many. To drive it home Lewis needed to be vivid, and to be vivid he needed to be vernacular. (E.g. in the last-quoted passage, Lewis drives home that he uses the same physical predicates across his whole domain of quantification, and that he has only one type of existential quantifier.) But then, as surely as 3 followed 2, 3' followed 2'.

Hume used to dream that he could separate metaphysics books from others at running speed,[14] but developments such as 1–3 and 1'–3' have forced us to walk slowly. These days, a volume that reads like traditional metaphysics might be exactly what it seems, or it might be an informal sketch of a proposal for formal discourse; and we might have no way of telling which of those it is, short of calling up the author and asking her intention. And then, if we find that it is a sketch of a proposal for formal discourse, that is not the end of the matter. We must ask, *What* is being proposed for formal discourse? Would the proposal add complexity to our formal theory, while offering nothing of epistemic value in return? If so, then the proposal is metaphysics, and the volume can be nothing but a sketch of metaphysics.

◆

This chapter has reflected on a few kinds of philosophy, but there is endless variety, and not much that I can say about the subject as a whole. The only points I shall make about philosophy in general are: (i) in every case, I would evaluate a philosophical theory against my usual epistemic norms (Chapters 3–5) and (ii) let anyone who wants to work outside those norms suggest an alternative set, but I would challenge her to find another set that she can live with on a full-time basis (Chapters 1–2).

8

Adapting to predicate logic

To regiment common sense is to decide what to put in its place. It is an open-ended project, involving countless micro-decisions of the form 'Let me put *this* formal-language sentence in place of *that* item of common sense', with each micro-decision requiring a formal sentence that is epistemically warranted. But a sentence is never warranted in isolation. Epistemic warrant is a property of a total theory, and an individual sentence is warranted only insofar as our total theory is more warranted with it in than with it out. So a micro-decision is never truly micro: we choose a formal sentence with an eye on the emerging formal theory in which it will play its part.

We aspire to a formal theory that is simple, but we need to be realistic on that score. Common sense is a behemoth, millennia in the making, so any theory that replaces it is almost certain to be a machine of many parts. And we would like a theory that is highly logically explicit; i.e. wherever one of its parts can be deduced from another, we want those parts to be connected via stated logical laws. A theory with that combination of features is unlikely to come together without planning, and so, in addition to the micro-decisions, there must be macro-decisions: decisions about the formal theory's architecture.

This chapter ponders a few of the macro-decisions. The topic is far greater than the space allocated to it, so the treatment will be partial and superficial, and the decisions, perforce, uncertain. But the decisions themselves are not my highest priority. Mainly I want to illustrate how our epistemology applies to the decision-making process. The decisions themselves matter in one respect, though: they are the points at which we can cross-check our decision-making process against Quine's, and thereby gauge the likelihood that his process was driven by the same set of norms as is driving our process.

◆

Topping the list of macro-decisions is the choice of logic. There are many candidates; however one of them, the classical first-order predicate calculus with identity (hereafter *predicate logic* and occasionally *standard predicate logic*), enters the contest with an advantage. Predicate logic serves the needs of mathematics, and with it the sciences that are expressed mathematically, and there appears to be a near-consensus that it is the simplest logic that can perform that function. Those points indicate that it is a good choice of logic for mathematics and the mathematical sciences; and that, in turn, is a good reason to choose it as the logic of a regimented common sense, since doing so would allow chains of deduction to cross seamlessly from one part of the finished formal theory to the other.

So we have a good reason to regiment common sense into predicate logic – but not a conclusive reason. Other considerations could defeat it. Quine noted one such vulnerability:

> Revision even of the logical law of the excluded middle has been proposed as a means of simplifying quantum mechanics; and what difference is there in principle between such a shift and the shift whereby Kepler superseded Ptolemy, or Einstein Newton, or Darwin Aristotle?[1]

And I agree; but at present another vulnerability worries me more: we might find ourselves *unable* to regiment common sense completely into predicate logic.

Now, to be clear, a regimentation can be complete without including a replacement for every sentence of common sense. Some of the old sentences may be discarded outright, and deservedly so. Yet the discarding has its limits. Wherever traces of past experience are embedded in the old theory, we must hold onto enough of the old theory to keep them embedded, until we have developed the new theory to a stage where the same traces are embedded there instead. And there is no guarantee that we can always do that, since the language and laws of predicate logic are in some ways quite different from the language and informal logic of common sense.

So, as I choose predicate logic as the target logic for regimentation, I do so tentatively. How sound the choice turns out to be will depend on how well we can adapt to predicate logic's exotic ways.

◆

Take, for instance, the handling of *time*. The language of predicate logic is tenseless, so if we choose it then we must decide how to replace the tenses that pervade most natural languages. Fortunately, a solution is well known, viz. the four-dimensional view, in which time is treated like any of the spatial dimensions (so 'Sue ate an apple and Joe will eat a peach' is rendered similarly to 'Sue eats an apple south of here and Joe eats a peach north of here'). Alternatively, we could back out of the decision to use standard predicate logic, and switch to a logic that has tenses built into it. That option, too, has been well explored.

Happily, the issue between tensed logic and the four-dimensional view does not turn on matters of detail: we need only pay attention to what is at stake. On one side, tensed logic more faithfully reflects the pattern of the source language, and arguably it makes less of a demand on us to change our world view. On the other side, the four-dimensional view leads to a simpler theory in the end. For us non-genetic regimenters, who neither aim for analysis nor keep score by theoretical conservatism, but who value simplicity in our formal theory, this is no real contest. I hand over to Quine to declare the winner:

> Our ordinary language shows a tiresome bias in its treatment of time. Relations of date are exalted grammatically as relations of positions, weight, and color are not. This bias is of itself an inelegance, or breach of theoretical simplicity. Moreover, the form that it takes – that of requiring that every verb form show a tense – is peculiarly productive of needless complications, ... Hence in fashioning canonical notations it is usual to drop tense distinctions.[2]

♦

If the handling of time was easy, the same cannot be said of our next exercise: the handling of *objects*. This one is made difficult by two intersecting subtleties that are present in English (and, I presume, other natural languages), but not in predicate logic.

The first subtlety is the way that referential idioms in English grade off, from the clearly literal to the clearly figurative. Between one extreme (*'There are twelve* eggs in the box', '*Some* eggs are in the box') and the other (*'It* is raining', 'I did it for your *sake*'), there is a spectrum of debatable or indeterminate examples, including, in no particular order, *'There are twelve* characters in the play (five of whom really exist)', *'There are twelve* prime numbers less than 40', 'Wollongong and Gijón have *something* in common', 'Wollongong and Gijón have *twelve things* in common', '*Some* possible aircraft will never be built' and 'You can leave in *a huff*'. In predicate logic, by contrast, there is only one referential idiom: the bound objectual variable, and it admits no shades of grey. Quine described the situation this way:

> My point is not that ordinary language is slipshod, slipshod though it be. We must recognize this grading off for what it is, and recognize that a fenced ontology is just not implicit in ordinary language. Scientists and philosophers seek a comprehensive system of the world, and one that is oriented to reference even more squarely and utterly than ordinary language. Ontological concern is

not a correction of a lay thought and practice; it is foreign to lay culture, though an outgrowth of it.[3]

As regimenters aiming for predicate logic, we are firmly within the 'scientists and philosophers' camp. We must decide, for each category of vaguely purported entity, *shall we include it in the domain of our bound variables, or not?*

One option is to decide, as a matter of policy, only to use bound variables in cases where the expression to be regimented is well towards the literal end of the spectrum; but it is worth noting that nothing we have said so far foists that policy upon us, and nor is it foisted by the fact that most people who read '∃' pronounce it as 'there exists'. We could break from that convention and choose some other vernacular reading or none. As long as our deductions conform to the stated laws of predicate logic, our official theory will have a high degree of logical explicitness, and that will allow the norms of simplicity and empirical correctness to apply to it directly. So, no matter what we decide to quantify over, we will be able to assess our official theory on its merits – all three of them – without ever a backward glance to ordinary language.

In fact, a plausible argument can be made for the opposite policy, viz. to use bound variables even when the expression to be regimented is quite near the figurative end of the spectrum. The argument is as follows. The figurative or quasi-figurative cases, or many of them, are parts of common sense that bear their share of its collective empirical load, so we had better regiment them somehow; and, since predicate logic does not provide any quasi-referential idioms, we might have to shoehorn its one referential idiom into the job.

The debate does not end there. The side that favours using variables only in the more literal cases has a countermove, but for that I must explain the second of the two intersecting subtleties of English that I mentioned a moment ago.

When some expression falls in the soggy middle of the literalness spectrum, we English speakers often exercise subtle judgement in deciding what may and may not be asked about the so-called (or perhaps not even so-called) entity. Thus take the example of fictional characters. Take Hamlet. On the one hand we probably count him in a tally of Shakespeare's characters, and we might ask whether he is wise and answer yes or no; but on the other hand we do not even ask whether Hamlet keeps a goldfish. We do not *wonder* whether Hamlet keeps a goldfish, nor do we *try to work out* whether Hamlet keeps a goldfish; and if we catch someone engaging in such flights of fancy we pull her up with a curt, 'He's not real, you know', for we can sense that there is nothing good to be gained here, and that the patient is teetering on the edge of 'How many angels can dance on the head of a pin?'

Such is the unformalized wisdom of common sense. Predicate logic, by contrast, is unblinkingly bivalent; so if we decide to include fictional characters in the domain of our variables, and if 'keeps a goldfish' is one of our predicates, then, like it or not, we are committed to Hamlet's either keeping or non-keeping of a goldfish.

Fictional characters are only an example; similar points could be made about many of the grey cases. E.g. in the following passage, Quine's sights are on the category of *possible objects*; and, while he does not directly mention logic, he shows us what happens when he pursues bivalence with a logician's pertinacity:

> Take, for instance, the possible fat man in that doorway; and, again, the possible bald man in that doorway. Are they the same possible man, or two possible men? How do we decide? How many possible men are there in that doorway? Are there more possible thin ones than fat ones? How many of them are alike? Or would their being alike make them one? Are no *two* possible things alike? Is this the same as saying that it is impossible for two things to be alike? Or, finally, is the concept of identity simply inapplicable to unactualized possibles? But what sense can be found in talking of entities which cannot meaningfully be said to be identical with themselves and distinct from one another? These elements are well-nigh incorrigible. By a Fregean therapy of individual concepts, some efforts might be made at rehabilitation; but I feel we'd do better simply to clear [this] slum and be done with it.[4]

So here is the argument for frugal quantification: it avoids opening a doorway, in the presence of bivalent logic, to certain apparently metaphysical questions: a doorway that we would rather keep shut, for the sake, ultimately, of simplicity.

◆

Which argument prevails, then: the previous one for liberal quantification, or this? There is no one answer; it comes down to cases. I have spoken somewhat airily of a literalness spectrum, but, on closer inspection, different cases turn out to display a variety of special features that allow one argument to prevail in some cases and the other to prevail in others.

Take numbers. Shall we quantify over them? Arguing for the affirmative, it may be said that quantifying over numbers allows us to regiment a good common-sense sentence like 'I have as many cups as saucers' as '$\exists x$ (I have exactly x cups and I have exactly x saucers)'. That example does not clinch the point, however, since we can also regiment 'I have as many cups as saucers' in other ways. (E.g. start by paraphrasing it as 'There is a pairing of my cups with my saucers that leaves no cup or saucer behind', and then carry on the regimentation from there.) In fact, I am not sure whether there is any truly commonsensical sentence that can *only* be regimented using quantification over numbers.

Let us remember, though, that in regimenting common sense we are adding to a formal theory that already includes mathematics, wherein quantification over numbers is already under way. E.g. in the mathematical definition of 'limit', which is at the core of the differential and integral calculi, the definiens quantifies over numbers. (In fact it quantifies over numbers into a quantification over numbers into a quantification over numbers.) So, for as long as we retain standard mathematics, numbers are in the domain of our quantifiers, and that puts them at our disposal when we regiment mundane remarks about domestic crockery.

Now the contrary argument. By quantifying over numbers, mathematics opens the door to a dazzling array of number-theoretic questions, including many whose answers are never applied in empirical science, and do not increase our total theory's score against any of the epistemic norms; so isn't mathematics guilty of the sort of metaphysical doorway-opening that we are determined to oppose?

One is tempted to reply as follows: 'No, the answers to abstruse mathematical questions are not metaphysical because, unlike metaphysics, they do not add complexity to our theory, and the reason they do not add complexity is that (i) they are *theorems*, i.e. deductive consequences of the axioms of mathematics; (ii) theorems add nothing to the compact presentation of our theory; and (iii) the complexity of our theory is to be judged by the complexity of its compact presentation alone (Chapter 3).'

I say one is tempted to reply that way. It is not correct though, because (i) is not true in general. Gödel proved that no consistent system of axioms generates answers to every yes/no question about numbers, so there will always be questions left over; questions whose answers are not theorems of the system.

We should, I think, acknowledge that such questions are a mark against quantification over numbers, in the same way that the question 'Does Hamlet keep a goldfish?' is a mark against quantification over fictional characters: they lure us away from theoretical simplicity. But there is one more consideration. Simplicity judgements, in our epistemology, are always comparative; so complexities in mathematics, as unwelcome as some of them are, are only grounds for rejecting mathematics if we have some alternative way of doing science that is less complex overall – and currently we do not. As things stand, then, I find myself suspiring with Quine, 'I see nothing for it but to make our peace with the situation'.[5] We must carry on quantifying over numbers.

◆

And what, now, about possible objects: shall we quantify over them too? We saw how Quine argued against it, but David Lewis argued in great detail that we should. Lewis's view was that possible objects are parts of possible worlds, possible worlds are physical things like our world, and we should quantify over all the worlds and their parts – for the following reason:

> We have only to believe in the vast realm of *possibilia*, and there we find what we need to advance our endeavours. We find the wherewithal to reduce the diversity of notions we must accept as primitive, and thereby to improve the unity and economy of ... total theory, the whole of what we take to be true. What price paradise? If we want the theoretical benefits that talk of *possibilia* brings, the most straightforward way to gain honest title to them is to accept such talk as the literal truth. It is my view that the price is right, if less spectacularly so than in the mathematical parallel. The benefits are worth their ontological cost. Modal realism is fruitful; that gives us good reason to believe that it is true.[6]

The 'endeavours' to which Lewis referred include regimentations of counterfactual conditionals, modal adverbs, the 'because' of causation and ascriptions of propositional attitudes. He found ingenious ways to regiment all of these into standard predicate logic, but each regimentation relied on quantification over possible objects.

In some ways I find Lewis's attitude congenial. I agree that we can be justified in expanding our domain of quantification when the expansion buys system-wide 'unity and economy' – i.e. simplicity – and I agree that our acceptance of mathematics is a precedent for that type of major purchase. However, I also agree with Lewis's proviso:

> Provided, of course, that [the theoretical benefits] cannot be had for less.[7]

Here Lewis was alluding to a theory known as 'ersatzism' (which Chapter 15 touches on); but, if we want to know whether the theoretical benefit of simplicity can be had for less, then we ought to interrogate all possible means to that end. In particular, we should see whether we can simplify our theory by discarding modal adverbs, counterfactual conditionals, etc. outright, or by replacing them with simpler constructs that make no pretence at being analyses of the originals. Lewis did not explore those options, and I can only surmise that the reason he did not was because they offend against his deep theoretical conservatism.

We saw some of that conservatism in Chapter 4, and here is another sample – one in which Lewis described his regimentations as 'analyses':

> In trying to improve the unity and economy of our total theory, by providing resources that will afford analyses, for instance of modality as quantification over worlds, I am trying to do two things that somewhat conflict. I am trying to *improve* that theory, that is to change it. But I am trying to improve *that* theory, that is to leave it recognisably the same theory we had before.[8]

And here, for contrast, is Quine the non-conservative, writing after Lewis but eager to exclude from regimentation the same limbs of common sense that Lewis worked so hard to accommodate:

> Much remains ... that cannot be regimented to fit the structure of predicate logic. 'Because' cannot, nor 'necessarily', nor 'possibly', nor the strong 'if–then' of the contrary-to-fact conditional. There is no place for the idioms of propositional attitude: '*x* believes that *p*', '*x* regrets that *p*', and so on. ...
>
> Despite such exclusions, all of austere science submits pliantly to the Procrustean bed of predicate logic. Regimentation to fit it thus serves not only to facilitate logical inference, but to attest to its conceptual clarity. What does not fit retains a more tentative and provisional status.[9]

For my part, I agree with Quine about the tentative and provisional status of 'because', 'necessarily', 'possibly' and the counterfactual conditional, though I would put the rationale slightly differently. For me, the tentativeness is not grounded in a conviction that these idioms 'cannot be regimented to fit the structure of predicate logic'. It is, rather, a product of my current cluelessness over whether and how to regiment them.

Consider 'necessarily'. More specifically, consider the uses of this adverb that express 'alethic necessity', i.e. the kind of necessity that Lewis and others elaborate as truth in all possible worlds; and, for definiteness, take the simplest case, i.e. whole sentences of the form 'Necessarily *p*' (rather than, say, 'Some *F*s are necessarily *G*'). The first thing I would like to know about such sentences is whether they add anything of epistemic value to any informal theory that already includes the sentence *p*. If they do not, then they are metaphysical and should be discarded outright. And if they do add something of epistemic value, then I would next like to know what that something is, so that we can look for the formal replacement that achieves the same benefit at least cost.

I do not have the answers, but I think I know what answers would look like. We saw in Chapter 3 how various theoretical sentences, from 'All swans are white' to heliocentrism and others, made our theory simpler by serving as premises in the deduction of many other sentences that (i) we could not deduce otherwise (or could not deduce as systematically otherwise) and (ii) we could not discard without feigning amnesia about past experience. Similarly, if some sentence of the form 'Necessarily *p*' is of benefit to total theory, then presumably it serves as a premise in the deduction of other, more conspicuously empirical, sentences that we cannot deduce as well without it. I would like to know what those other sentences are, and how 'Necessarily *p*' contributes to their deduction.

These requests might be described as a demand for empirical criteria of (*de dicto*) necessity, which is not far from the very Quinean demand for empirical criteria of analyticity (even if that side of Quine is beyond the scope of this book). However, I should emphasize that I am not seeking empirical definitions, nor empirical 'necessary and sufficient conditions'. I only wish to know what contribution is made, by sentences of the form 'Necessarily *p*', to the informal deduction of empirical consequences. And let me emphasize, also, that I require this information not only for the purpose of deciding *whether* to regiment these sentences; but also for deciding *how* to regiment them. Without it, I could not regiment them even as an exercise; for the exercise would be: 'Find the simplest replacement that allows formal deduction to hit some set of empirical targets, without knowing which targets.'

My cluelessness about the most basic modal sentences extends, naturally enough, to more difficult examples, involving iterated and *de re* modalities. And I am similarly clueless about assertions of counterfactuals and causation, insofar as they assert something more than material implications and concomitances. That is to say, I do not know what, of epistemic value, they add to a theory that already makes good use of material implications and concomitances. Thus it can be seen that my cluelessness engulfs most of the idioms whose regimentation is at issue between Lewis and Quine.

Most, but not all.

Part Three

Case study: Propositional attitude ascriptions

In thus writing off modal logic I find little to regret.
Regarding the propositional attitudes, however, I cannot be so cavalier.

W. V. Quine[1]

9

Destination and horizon

In Part One we identified and upheld three Quinean epistemic norms. In Part Two we applied those norms to some central philosophical questions, and were led to answers that closely tracked Quine's. Now it is time to leave the nest and strike out on our own. In this part we shall do some fresh theorizing, and watch how the three norms guide our way.

For any sentence p and anyone's name S, there are several English sentences that we can form by concatenating S, a psychological verb, the word 'that', and p. There is 'S believes that p', 'S desires that p', 'S perceives that p' and so on. For historical reasons these are called *propositional attitude ascriptions*, and historically they have proven tough to regiment. Many philosophers have tried their hands at regimenting them, and in this part we shall try ours.

That is not to say, however, that we shall be working the same problem that exercised the others. On the contrary, we shall apply *our* epistemic norms (Chapters 3–5) by means of *our* conception of regimentation (Chapters 7–8); and so, to the extent that others' sights were on other goals, such as conformance to a conservatively biased epistemology, or a conception of regimentation as semantic analysis, or the unearthing of an ontology implicit in ordinary language, we can fairly be said to have shifted the goalposts.

Michael McDermott, on the other hand, is a philosopher whose goals have significant overlap with ours. He pursues his in 'A Russellian Account of Belief Sentences', which, though I disagree with it on several key points (including its conclusion), is the primary influence on the thoughts that follow.

Recall that to regiment ordinary-language sentences, in our sense of 'regiment', is to find formal-language sentences that increase the epistemic merit of our theory, and increase it in a specific way: where the old sentences served as premises, leading via informal logic to conclusions that carry empirical information, the new sentences should serve as premises leading to the same empirical information via formal logic. Therefore our eye must always be on the inferences. When we come to such well-worn questions as 'How can we make propositional attitude ascriptions extensional?' and 'Which parts of a propositional attitude ascription can be replaced by variables bound to quantifiers outside the ascription?', we must be guided by the need to fit ascriptions into formal inferences; and not just any formal inferences, but specifically formal inferences that deliver the same empirical information as is delivered by informal inferences from propositional attitude ascriptions in English.

What are these informal inferences, and what empirical information do they deliver? The answers are not hard to find. Every day, as we deal with people and animals, and sometimes even machines, we ascribe propositional attitudes to them, and from the ascriptions we draw conclusions about visible, tangible interactions between those subjects and their environments.

It will be convenient to describe the subject–environment interactions that we draw conclusions about as *behaviour*; but only on the proviso that we construe that term broadly enough to include passive behaviour. E.g. given a premise that S now has certain beliefs about the murderer's clothing (along with other premises), we might conclude that S was present at the scene of the crime, facing the murderer, with eyes open, etc. Then we must count S's presence at the scene and so forth as behaviour, even if it didn't involve S *doing* anything.

It is often said that attitude ascriptions *explain* behaviour, and indeed many of them do; but I shall not set much store by that, because some informal inferences from ascriptions to behaviour are not explanatory – e.g. the inference about the witness does not *explain* her presence at the scene etc. – and I am interested in formalizing the non-explanatory inferences as much as the explanatory ones.

These inferences, whether explanatory or not, are sometimes redundant, because sometimes we can reach the same conclusions about behaviour via other paths, e.g. by reasoning from patterns in behaviour alone, or from physiological data about the subject's brain. There might even come a day when such alternative routes are available in all cases, and then we might decide to simplify our total theory by eliminating propositional attitude ascriptions altogether.[1] In the actual present, however, a great many propositional attitude ascriptions are non-redundant, and so the counsel of our epistemology is to regiment them.

◆

If the destination of our inquiry is an adequate regimentation of propositional attitude ascriptions, then we will not have arrived until we can write out a formal replacement for any non-redundant informal deduction in which a propositional attitude ascription participates. As things stand, however, I do not see how to go that far, so I had better put some space between the ambition of this part and the destination of the inquiry. The most I can promise here is to take us some way towards an adequate regimentation; or rather, to take us some way along what seems to be the way, since I cannot rule out the possibility that the road we set out on is bound for a dead end, somewhere further than I can see, that will one day turn us back and force us to retrace even these early steps.

How far shall we go? Far enough to sketch some chains of formal reasoning that stretch from ascriptions to behaviour, taking in such diverse elements as the subject's good and bad reasoning, her rational action and her acquisition of beliefs from her senses. That combination should be enough to teach us some valuable lessons about the structure of regimented ascriptions. Yet our mission will be significantly curtailed, both in breadth, i.e. the range of informal discourse that we attempt to regiment, and in depth, i.e. how near we get to the genuine formal discourse that we ultimately seek.

I count seven curtailments: five of breadth and two of depth.

Curtailment #1. I exclude anything that depends on professional psychology. I shall stick to regimenting what I know (along with everyone else), which is folk psychology: the part of common sense that deals with mental states. (I note in passing that the use of the phrase 'philosophy of psychology' for inquiries such as this can be misleading, because it suggests a connection with the science of psychology, even when no such connection exists.)

Curtailment #2. The only propositional attitude ascriptions that I shall regiment are ascriptions of belief and desire; not ascriptions of intention, perception or others. E.g. given that a subject desires some outcome, and believes that a certain action will bring about that outcome, one might infer that the subject will perform the action – and *that* is a kind of inference that I shall formalize, rather than a more sophisticated chain of inference in which an ascription of intention plays an intermediary role. Likewise I shall formalize inferences that link reports of a subject's visual stimulation (a kind of passive behaviour) to ascriptions of her belief, where a more sophisticated theory might have interposed ascriptions of perception.

Curtailment #3. I exclude the subject's *verbal* behaviour. In particular, there will be no attempt to regiment inferences from what the subject believes to what she says or vice versa. This policy might be surprising, especially if your first thought, when trying to find out what someone believes, is 'Just ask her.'

Just asking her certainly seems straightforward, but, when you try to spell out all the steps, it is far too difficult. That is because, even assuming that the subject gives a straight answer, the inference from 'S sincerely asserts the sentence "..."' to any belief ascription (or vice versa) involves figuring out what S's words mean;

and meaning is, to put it mildly, a philosophical minefield. I don't know whether there will ever be a warranted and explicit theory of meaning, but I venture to say that the chances will be improved if we wait until the theory of belief has been developed further than it will be in these pages.[2]

And anyhow, even if we had a first-rate theory of meaning, there would still be reason to specialize in regimenting the fragment of folk psychology that does without verbal behaviour. That is because there is a class of cases where we make propositional attitude ascriptions though no verbal behaviour is available to us – whether because the subject lacks the power of speech or because she happens not to be using it or because we only see her on silent film – and in all of those cases we would like to be sure that we are living within our limited epistemic means (rather than, say, relying on verbal behaviour that we merely imagined[3]).

Curtailment #4. As a consequence of Curtailment #3, and of living within our means, we shall not attempt to regiment ascriptions with highly sophisticated content.

I do not know how far it is possible to go in the direction of ascribing sophisticated content while excluding verbal behaviour. Donald Davidson's opinion was that we could not ascribe belief in a largest prime,[4] and Quine's was that we could not ascribe beliefs about ancient history;[5] and both may be right. If such beliefs make a difference to non-verbal behaviour then it ought to be possible, but, if not, then presumably it is neither possible nor desirable. In any case, we shall not be going that far today – but nor shall we let the difficulty of high-end cases put us off ascribing what content we can.

Curtailment #5. I exclude ascriptions of degrees of belief (e.g. 'S suspects that p', 'S is nearly certain that p') and degrees of desire (e.g. 'S marginally prefers that p', 'S fervently wishes that p'). That is to say, I shall only regiment ascriptions that treat belief and desire as all black or white. In the long run this curtailment is indefensible, but I make it to limit the scale of the present exercise, and perhaps it will not be too hard to rectify later. (Many other authors have incorporated degrees of belief etc. into their regimentations, and perhaps that is a feature of their regimentations that could be imported into ours.)

Curtailment #6. When we come to idioms whose regimentations are obvious (e.g. 'some', 'and', 'or', 'before', 'after'), I shall leave them alone rather than dragging us through the predictable final manoeuvres into logical notation. Also I shall leave 'if ... then ...' alone, because, though its replacement is controversial, I can tell you now that I would use the '⊃' of material implication. And I shall leave quotations alone, on the understanding that they are to be replaced by definite descriptions of character sequences in the manner of Tarski[6] (e.g. the quotation

' 'dog' ' is to be replaced by the description 'dee^oh^gee', where 'dee', 'oh' and 'gee' are names of letters and '^' is the concatenation operator).

Curtailment #7. When we come to idioms whose regimentations are problematic, but so broadly problematic as to present no more difficulty to regimenters of folk psychology than to regimenters of, say, folk meteorology, then I shall leave them alone rather than open any cans of universal worms.

The idioms I have in mind here are those of probability and statistics. One approaches a subject with an understanding of how *most* subjects tick, and one supposes that the present subject is *likely* to fit the common patterns. That is what one does in folk psychology, anyhow, and I do not imagine that we can be any more categorical, or any more certain, when we move to a regimented system. So we cannot simply drop statistical and probabilistic sentences; but if we cannot simply drop them then we ought to regiment them, which would include formalizing the logical connections among them. And, while we are at it, we ought to say something enlightening about what it takes for a body of probabilistic sentences to conflict with experience. We *ought* to do these things, as part of regimenting common-sense propositional attitude ascriptions – but no more than we ought to do them as part of regimenting common sense about the weather, or common sense about cooking. And so doing them (even if I knew how) would divert us from our special topic to the general philosophy of probability.

So I shall leave the word 'probably' alone, along with 'usually', 'almost always', etc.; and I shall get by with egregiously crude forms of statistical-probabilistic inference, such as the proportional syllogism ('Most Fs are G; a is F; so probably a is G.'). But, whenever I draft a generalization, whether statistical or categorical, I shall take scrupulous care of the *variables*, especially the ones that occur in attitudinative contexts when bound to quantifiers outside, because, in the end, those variables are what will dictate the structure of our regimented ascriptions.

♦

With these preliminary remarks out of the way, let me proceed without further ado to other preliminary remarks. There are three conspicuous ways in which common-sense propositional attitude ascriptions differ from any sentences in the language of predicate logic; which is to say, there are three characteristics that our regimentation, whatever it turns out to be, will have to change.

First, there is the way that sentences *nest* within sentences; e.g. 'Snow is white' within 'John believes that snow is white'. Predicate logic allows sentences to nest within sentences, but only in a small handful of ways: there are the sentential operators ('__ and __', '__ or __', 'not __', 'if __ then __') and there are the quantifiers ('for all _, _', 'for some _, _'). Nowhere in this handful do we find 'John believes that _'; so we will have to drop that phrase and use something else instead.

The most obvious way to do this is by making two simultaneous replacements: (i) replace the attitudinative verb ('believes' or 'desires') with a two-place predicate[7] (for which we can reuse the old spelling: 'believes' or 'desires'); and (ii) replace the 'that'-clause (e.g. 'that snow is white') with a definite description of an object of some sort. Then the question becomes 'An object of what sort?' (It is sometimes phrased as 'What are the objects of the attitudes?', and I have no quarrel with that wording, provided we are clear that it is still a question about the regimented ascriptions, not the vernacular ones. We are asking what sort of objects are to be described in the second place of the newly minted two-place predicates.)

The second conspicuous difference between vernacular propositional attitude ascriptions and any sentence of predicate logic is that the former are often not *extensional*. I defer to Quine to define extensionality:

> I shall call two closed sentences *coextensive* if they are both true or both false. Two predicates or general terms or open sentences are coextensive, of course, if they are true of just the same objects or sequences of objects. Two singular terms are coextensive if they designate the same object. And finally to the point: an expression is *extensional* if replacement of its component expressions by coextensive expressions always yields a coextensive whole.[8]

And again, to illustrate how a vernacular propositional attitude ascription can fall short:

> The clarity and convenience conferred by extensionality are evident: free interchangeability of coextensive components *salva veritate*. When in particular those components are singular terms, indeed, their interchangeability would seem mandatory from any point of view; for this is simply the substitutivity of identity. Still, 'Tom believes that Cicero denounced Catiline' and 'Tom believes that Tully denounced Catiline' might be respectively true and false despite the identity of Cicero and Tully.[9]

It is striking that Quine chose, for his example, a belief about ancient history: the very topic about which he opined that any ascription of belief must depend on the subject's verbal behaviour (see Curtailment #4). Presumably this was coincidence rather than a deliberately drawn connection, but I find it no less instructive for that. It shows that one's intuitions about the truth or falsity of propositional attitude ascriptions can depend on subjects' verbal behaviour, even when one does not pause to note the dependency. In the context of the current exercise, where we seek to isolate ascriptions from verbal behaviour (Curtailment #3), that gives us stronger than usual grounds to distrust pretheoretical intuitions.[10]

Now the third conspicuous difference: the vernacular idioms of propositional attitude ascription, unlike expressions in predicate logic, are *ambiguous*. They have one sense, just noted, in which substitutivity of identity fails. That is the *de dicto* sense. But, as Quine reminds us, 'a further complication is that usage cannot be depended on to follow this *de dicto* line either'.[11] Vernacular propositional attitude ascriptions also have a sense in which substitutivity of identity succeeds, and that is the *de re* sense. For an example of the latter, suppose that Catiline had a dog, Fidus, who would tremble and cower behind Catiline's toga whenever Cicero came near. On that basis we might be willing to accept 'Fidus believed that Cicero was dangerous' and, if so, we should be equally willing to accept 'Fidus believed that Tully was dangerous'. It would be unreasonable to assent to one of these ascriptions and withhold assent from the other, since the choice between the names 'Cicero' and 'Tully' is obviously ours alone (the dog played no part in it) and *we* know that they are names of a single individual. Give your ears a moment to adjust to this way of speaking, and they might even accept 'Fidus believed that the author of *In Catilinam I–IV* was dangerous'.[12]

Once the *de dicto/de re* divide is appreciated, it may be felt that the *de re* ascriptions should reduce to the *de dicto* ones. Sometimes the reduction is seen as vital to the defence of *de re* ascriptions, and then any failure of the reduction is seen ipso facto as a discredit to the *de re*. This line of thinking, however, has me reaching for another Latin phrase – '*petitio principii*' – because *de re* ascriptions are being judged by a test that assumes *de dicto* ascriptions are the preferred standard. It leaves us to wonder why *de dicto* ascriptions were granted that status, and it leaves me to nurse a suspicion that it had something to do with verbal behaviour, real or imagined;[13] but I digress. I come neither to praise the various vernacular ascriptions nor to bury them, but only to flag some of their features that have no place in the formal theory to be sketched below.

10

Sententialism

By 'sententialism', I mean the proposal to replace attitudinative verbs with two-place predicates that relate a subject to a *sentence*. In this chapter, I would like us to try being sententialists.

For readability's sake, let us spell our two-place predicates 'believes' and 'desires', and let us use infix notation. So a regimented propositional attitude ascription will look like this:

(4) Tom believes 'Cicero denounced Catiline'.

I shall call this a *sentential ascription*, and call the sentence that is the object of the attitude ('Cicero denounced Catiline', in this case) the *content sentence*.

A well-known benefit of sententialism is that it rescues extensionality. E.g. even if we assert (4) while denying 'Tom believes 'Tully denounced Catiline' ' (and at this stage I take no position on whether we should), that is no violation of extensionality because, by the time the regimentation is complete, the quotations will have dissolved into Tarskian descriptions of character sequences (see Chapter 9, Curtailment #6), so the terms that had occurred between quotation marks will not occur in the ascriptions at all.[1] 'Cicero', for example, will not occur in the fully regimented version of (4), so extensionality will not tell us that we can substitute 'Tully' for it.

Nonetheless, if we are going to take sententialism on board then we need to be cautious, because it comes to us with baggage, some of which needs to be left at the kerb. E.g. in the sententialism of Carnap's *Meaning and Necessity*, the belief predicate had a definition that mentioned (i) the subject's dispositions to assent to sentences, and (ii) a relation of 'intensional isomorphism' between sentences. (Intensional isomorphism is, roughly, sameness of structure plus sameness of meaning of corresponding components.) Clearly we cannot accept Carnap's definition, nor anything like it – but nor do we need to. We can pursue sententialism without any definition of belief (nor any definition of desire). Definition, after all, has never been one of our demands.

Still, we need to remain cautious. It is one thing to reject an official association of sentential ascriptions with verbal behaviour and semantics, but a similar association exists at an intuitive level, and the intuitive association needs to stay at the kerb too. It is the same intuition that Quine acknowledged, along with the possibility of transcending it, in that most Quineanly non-conservative phrase, 'unnatural without being therefore wrong':

> We may treat a mouse's fear of a cat as his fearing true a certain English sentence. This is unnatural without being therefore wrong. It is a little like describing a prehistoric ocean current as clockwise.[2]

Can we cure ourselves of the intuition that makes a mouse attitudinizing an English sentence seem unnatural? Probably not. I do not recommend trying it. What I would suggest instead is that we reduce its sway on us, through the discipline of addressing the question that we ought to be addressing, which is: *Can sentential ascriptions contribute to formal reasoning that leads to conclusions about non-verbal behaviour?*

◆

To their credit, sentential ascriptions can be slotted fairly smoothly into some important segments of that formal reasoning, viz. the segments that track attitude–attitude interactions.[3] Here, e.g. is a possible step of our reasoning about a step of Sophie's deductive reasoning:

(5) Sophie believes 'Socrates is a human'.
(6) Sophie believes 'All humans are mortal'.
(7) For any subject s, name n and general terms f, g, usually, if s believes $n^\frown$' is a '$^\frown f$, and s believes 'All '$^\frown f$'s are '$^\frown g$, then s comes to believe $n^\frown$' is '$^\frown g$.

(8) ∴ Probably, Sophie believes 'Socrates is mortal'.

Similarly, we can reason about inductive reasoning, taking this generalization as a premise:

(9) For any subject s and general terms f, g, often, if s believes 'All observed '$^\frown f$'s are '$^\frown g$, then s comes to believe 'All '$^\frown f$'s are '$^\frown g$.

We can even reason about fallacious reasoning, using this:

(10) For any subject s and sentences p, q, occasionally, if s believes q and s believes 'If '$^\frown p^\frown$' then '$^\frown q$, then s comes to believe p.

And we can reason about interactions between a subject's beliefs and her desires; e.g. by using this generalization, adapted from Paul Churchland:[4]

(11) For any subject s and sentences p, q, usually, if s desires q and s believes 'If '⌐p⌐' then '⌐q, then either s desires p or there is some sentence r such that s desires r and s believes 'If '⌐p⌐' then it is not the case that '⌐r.

In these examples I have chosen English as the *content language*, i.e. the language of the content sentences, but that policy creates some unhelpful complications; e.g. (7) only applies in cases where the term f is a common noun that takes the plural suffix 's', so we would need to add clauses to cover subjects who believe 'All *men* are mortal' or 'All *women* are mortal'. Banal inconveniences of this sort will be rife unless we streamline the syntax of the content language. I shall not pursue that line of improvement now, though, because sententialism has two loose ends that are significantly harder to tie off. I shall turn to those, but, as I do, let us keep in mind that the content language is not settled, so we can adjust it as needed as we go.

◆

We have envisaged steps of deduction that proceed from sentential ascriptions to other sentential ascriptions, and I have called those steps important; but their value to us depends on their being segments within longer deductions that tell us something about the subject's behaviour. So there must be other steps, somewhere, that bridge the attitude–behaviour gap. I would like to see some of those *bridging* steps. I am especially interested in the ones that step from sentential ascriptions to reports of behaviour, rather than in the opposite direction, but in the long run we need both, and the issues I raise in this chapter are the same for both.

That is one loose end, and now the other. I assume that the content language, no matter which way we streamline its syntax, will continue to use *terms*, and that our regimented psychology must decide, en route to making a sentential ascription, which term the content sentence will use in each term position. For that purpose, the patterns of argument that we have envisaged provide some help, but not enough. E.g. the argument (5)–(8) delivered a content sentence that used the terms 'Socrates' and 'mortal', but only after we already had the content sentences 'Socrates is a human' and 'All humans are mortal'. So our problem is pushed back: how did the regimented psychology choose the terms for those sentences? Perhaps part of the answer is that we got (6) by applying law (9) – but only after we had the content sentence 'All observed humans are mortal'. So how did we choose the terms for *that* sentence? And so on. Let me cut to the chase.

For each content-language term *t*, there must have been a step in our regimented psychological reasoning where we put *t* into a content sentence for the first time. I would like to see some of these *term-introducing* steps.

In this connection someone is bound to mention the 'Language of Thought' hypothesis, which says that subjects' brains store sentences in a 'mentalese' language, just as computers store strings of symbols in a machine language, only with this difference: the mentalese language is yet to be discovered. The hypothesis is as may be, but it alone, without the hypothesized language, does not solve our present conundrum: it does not tell us how to choose content-language terms here and now.[5]

We can make some progress on the second loose end (term choice) by revisiting the first (bridging), because, though it strains the metaphor to say so, the two loose ends are intertwined. To see how, let us consider a couple of situations that call for bridging steps. Take Beth,[6] who faces a bat while awake, with eyes open, in good light, etc.; for short: *Beth looks upon a bat*. A folk psychologist would infer that Beth probably believes that there's a bat in her vicinity. And take Fidus,[7] who retreats behind environing objects whenever Cicero is nearby; for short: *Fidus avoids Cicero*. A folk psychologist would infer that there's a fair chance that Fidus believes that Cicero is dangerous. How shall we, as sententialists, regiment these two steps of informal reasoning?

Here is one way:

(12) Beth looks upon a bat.
(13) For any subject *s*, usually, if *s* looks upon a bat, then *s* comes to believe 'There's a bat'.

---

(14) ∴ Probably, Beth believes 'There's a bat'.

(15) Fidus avoids Cicero.
(16) For any subject *s*, fairly often, if *s* avoids Cicero, then *s* believes 'Cicero is dangerous'.

---

(17) ∴ There is a fair chance that Fidus believes 'Cicero is dangerous'.

These are bridging steps, but they draw us back to the problem of term introduction, in this form: How did we choose the terms that occur quoted in (13) and (16)? E.g. how did we decide that bat-viewing subjects usually believe 'There's a bat' rather than believing, say, 'There's a Fledermaus'? Or, for that matter, why didn't we choose 'schmat' or some other made-up word that does not exist in our own vocabulary? If, instead of (13), our law had been 'For any subject s, usually, if s looks upon a bat, then s comes to believe 'There's a schmat'', then our conclusion would have been 'Beth believes 'There's a schmat' '; and, provided we made the same change uniformly in all our laws that mention the term 'bat', our entire regimented psychology could have proceeded with 'schmat' in its content sentences in place of 'bat', and it would have worked just as well. Likewise, we could have done just as well by saying that Cicero-avoiding subjects believe 'Schmicero is dangerous' (with corresponding changes elsewhere); so on what basis did we choose to say (16)?

These are not, strictly speaking, compulsory questions. We *could* say that, though any of these term choices would have been arbitrary, it's also the case that any of them would have been good enough, and therefore we don't need to fix the arbitrariness. And besides, aren't we destined to make arbitrary choices sooner or later anyway; e.g. won't we eventually have to pick a symbol for *conjunction* in the content language, be it 'and', '∧', '&' or some new squiggle? So why baulk arbitrarily at the arbitrariness of 'bat' or 'Cicero'?

In fact, arbitrariness is not the true bugbear here. Our epistemic norms don't mention arbitrariness, so I have nothing against it per se. But complexity is another matter. Consider the complexity, not just of the sentences (12)–(17), but of the emerging formal theory to which they belong. Since that theory has special laws to cover subjects who look upon bats and subjects who avoid Cicero, presumably it will also have special laws to cover subjects who look upon cats, subjects who look upon rats, subjects who avoid Clitheroe and subjects who avoid Lisarow.[8] While we acknowledge that folk psychology is complicated, and we might expect its regimentation to have hundreds or even thousands of laws, *this* multiplication is surely too much to abide. We should strive to bring these many similar, special laws under fewer, more general laws, since doing so would, in the terminology of Chapter 3, reduce the size of our theory's compact presentation. More general laws would, moreover, let us do explicitly what folk psychology does without a second thought, viz. apply the general patterns to new cases for which we have not yet confirmed any relevant special law.

I assume that the more general laws that apply to Beth and Fidus will take these forms:

(18) For any subject s, general term g and kind k such that ..., usually, if s looks upon a member of k, then s comes to believe 'There's a ⌢g.
(19) For any subject s, name n and object o such that ..., fairly often, if s avoids o, then s believes n⌢' is dangerous'.

And I assume, further, that whatever fills the blanks in (18) and (19) will be pretty much[9] the same as what fills the blanks in other bridging laws of similar generality, e.g.:

(20) For any subject s, general term g and kind of action k such that ...,
often, if s can do k and s desires 'I do '⌒g, then s does k.

(21) For any subject s, name n and object o such that ..., usually, if s believes n⌒' is dangerous', then s avoids o.

along with sundry others.

The missing clauses will, presumably, say something that relates subjects, terms in the content language, and things in the non-psychological world (objects or kinds), so the phrase *'mental representation'* seems to fit. Not that the phrase achieves anything, other than to label a relation that is still at large; but if we could find that missing relation, then laws (18)–(21) and others in the same mould would let us formalize inferences that are at once bridging and term-introducing.

◆

Our two loose ends have merged into a single question: 'What is mental representation?' 'What is ...?' questions in philosophy are notoriously slippery – they can be requests for semantic analysis, or for explication, or for assertions of mere identity, necessary identity or 'ontological ground', or they can be confused expressions of several of these at once – but in the present case the purpose is refreshingly clear. When we ask 'What is mental representation?', we are seeking a way to fill the blanks, in laws (18)–(21) and others like them, that will allow us to apply those laws to actual cases. Various answers to 'What is mental representation?' may serve various other purposes, but any answer that does not let us put our laws to work is not an answer for us.

Take, for instance, *causal theories of reference*, which say that an occurrence of a term designates a certain thing, or denotes each thing of a certain kind, iff the term-occurrence is connected to the thing or kind via an appropriate causal chain. Those theories cannot solve our problem, even if we grant *arguendo* that a clear specification of 'appropriate causal chain' is at hand, because we need to pin down instances of the representation relation *before*, and *en route to*, pinning down occurrences of terms. A causal theory would have us argue: 'Beth denotes bats by 'bat', because the occurrences of 'bat' in the sentences Beth believes or desires are connected to bats by an appropriate causal chain' – but we cannot argue that way, because we have not yet worked out that there *are* any occurrences of 'bat' in the sentences that Beth believes or desires. We are still looking for a principle to tell us whether Beth believes 'There's a bat' or 'There's a schmat' or something else.

Similar remarks apply to *informational theories of reference*,[10] which say, approximately, that a term designates a certain thing, or denotes each thing of a certain kind, iff occurrences of the term are appropriately correlated with presences of the thing or kind. Again granting *arguendo* that the details are at hand, these theories cannot help us in our current bind because they require that term occurrences be divined *en route* to divining reference, and we need to do it the other way around.

Similar remarks do not apply, however, to the *disquotational theory of reference*. This theory's pronouncements require no prior knowledge of what any subject believes or desires. They are recognizable, rather, by a certain echoic quality, e.g.:

(22) 'bat' denotes each bat.
(23) 'duck' denotes each duck.
(24) If Cicero exists, then 'Cicero' designates Cicero.
(25) If Tully exists, then 'Tully' designates Tully.

In general, the disquotational theory endorses any sentence of the form ' '__' denotes each __', where both blanks are replaced by the same general term; and it endorses any sentence of the form 'if __ exists, then '__' designates __', where all three blanks are replaced by the same name.[11]

There is a puzzle about *how* the disquotational theory can deliver the results it does, since they are not instances of any generalization that we can formulate (unless we are confused about the use–mention distinction). One solution is to add *logical* laws that explicitly license the assertion of any sentence that fits one of the disquotational forms. I am reluctant to add logical laws, especially ones that the physical sciences seem not to need,[12] but they might be worth having if they let us get ahead with a regimented psychology. So let us tentatively suppose them added, so we can use the disquotational theory of reference and see what it buys us.

The disquotational theory allows us to have psychological laws such as

(26) For any subject s, general term g and kind k such that g denotes each member of k, usually, if s looks upon a member of k, then s comes to believe 'There's a '⌢g.
(27) For any subject s, name n and object o such that n designates o, fairly often, if s avoids o, then s believes n⌢' is dangerous'.

with 'denotes' and 'designates' understood disquotationally. Then we can have bridging, term-introducing steps of regimented psychological reasoning such as

(28) Beth looks upon a bat.

(29) 'bat' denotes each bat.

(26) For any subject s, general term g and kind k such that g denotes each member of k, usually, if s looks upon a member of k, then s comes to believe 'There's a '⌒g.

---

(30) ∴ Probably, Beth believes 'There's a bat'.

(31) Fidus avoids Cicero.

(32) 'Cicero' designates Cicero.

(27) For any subject s, name n and object o such that n designates o, fairly often, if s avoids o, then s believes n⌒' is dangerous'.

---

(33) ∴ There is a fair chance that Fidus believes 'Cicero is dangerous'.

And that is how we can introduce 'bat', rather than 'Fledermaus' or 'schmat', and 'Cicero', rather than 'Schmicero', into the content language: disquotation ensures that the terms we put into it are terms that we use ourselves when we describe the subject's behaviour.[13]

11

From sententialism to Russellianism

In Chapter 10 we tried to be sententialists, and we made some headway. We framed usable laws to cover attitude–attitude interactions, and usable laws to cover bridging steps that also introduce terms into the content language. Of course the laws we actually saw were only a sample, and a viable replacement for commonsense propositional attitude psychology would need more; but would a greater volume of laws suffice, or should we change the theory in more fundamental ways?

To get clearer on the question, let me define a family of propositional attitude psychologies that Chapter 10's sketch typifies. I call these *disquotational-sententialist* (DS) psychologies. A DS psychology is a regimented propositional attitude psychology that meets the following three conditions:

DS1: It is sententialist.
DS2: Each of its ascriptions can be reached from reports of behaviour via serial application of its psychological laws.
DS3: Each of its psychological laws is of one of the following types:
a. *Bridging laws that are also term-introducing laws.* These cover interactions between attitudes and behaviour, and they let us introduce terms into content sentences that might not have been in any content sentence before; but the introductions are always subject to the introduced term meeting a single condition. That condition is either of the form 'n designates o' or of the form 'g denotes each member of k', where 'designates' or 'denotes' is understood disquotationally, n or g is the name or general term being introduced, and o or k is an object involved in the behavioural side of the attitude-behaviour interaction, or a kind to which such an object belongs.
b. *Formal laws of attitude-attitude interaction.* These never mention behaviour, and only mention content-language terms by way of

formal patterns. So they allow terms that occur in some lot of content sentences to turn up in another content sentence; but these laws are blind as to *which* terms are involved, and they never let us place a term into a content sentence if it was not in at least one content sentence already.

And now the question, which will occupy us for this chapter and the next, is whether we would do better to have a psychology that is not DS.

Here in Chapter 11 we consider departures from DS that promote simplicity, and in Chapter 12 we shall consider departures that let us regiment more of folk psychology, thereby increasing the logical explicitness of our total theory. Regrettably, the two chapters' improvements are mutually incompatible, so they will be in competition, not just with DS, but with each other.

Before we depart from DS psychologies at all, though, let us observe four of their properties.

Property one: *No vacuous names*. In a DS psychology, we can never make an ascription $a[n]$ in which the content sentence contains a name n that is vacuous by our lights. E.g. we can never assert 'Sandra believes 'Santa Claus will come' ', nor 'Sandra desires 'Santa Claus is feeling generous' '. [Proof: The only way a name can enter the content language is via application of DS3(a) laws, and DS3(a) laws are all conditional on the name designating something (specifically: something with which the subject has interacted).]

Property two: *No null general terms*. Content sentences can never contain a general term with null extension. [Proof: The only way a general term can enter the content language is via application of DS3(a) laws, and DS3(a) laws are all conditional on the name denoting each member of some kind that has at least one member (specifically: a member with which the subject has interacted).]

Property three: *Uniform substitutivity of co-designating names*. If we can assert an ascription $a[n]$ in which the content sentence contains (one or more occurrences of) a name n that designates an object o, and if n' is another name that designates o, then we can also assert an ascription $a[n']$ that differs from $a[n]$ only by the uniform replacement of n by n'. E.g. if we can assert 'Fidus believes 'Cicero is dangerous' ', then we can assert 'Fidus believes 'Tully is dangerous' '.

[Proof: Since we can assert $a[n]$, DS2 assures us that we can reach $a[n]$ by a chain of applications of psychological laws; and DS3 assures us that, within that chain, (i) n could only have entered the content language via an application of a DS3(a) law (or entered multiple times via multiple applications of DS3(a) laws), and (ii) every other ascription whose content sentence contains n must have come via an application of a DS3(b) law. Now, at each place where n appeared via an application of a DS3(a) law, it must have done so on the strength of n's designating o; but n' also designates o; so we can make the same move with n' in place of n. And then, in every place where n appeared via an application of a DS3(b) law, n' will take the place of n – all the way to $a[n']$.]

Property four: *Uniform substitutivity of coextensive general terms.* If we can assert an ascription $a[g]$ in which the content sentence contains (one or more occurrences of) a general term g that denotes all and only the members of a kind k, and if g' is another general term that denotes all and only the members of k, then we can also assert an ascription $a[g']$ that differs from $a[g]$ only by the uniform replacement of g by g'. E.g. if we can assert 'Tom believes 'Fidus was cordate' ', then we can assert 'Tom believes 'Fidus was renate' '. [The proof is the previous proof modified as follows: substitute 'g' for 'n', 'g'' for 'n'', 'k' for 'o', and 'denotes all and only the members of' for 'designates'.]

♦

Notice what we have *not* proven. We have not proven the general substitutivity, within content sentences, of co-designating names or of coextensive general terms. E.g. we have not proven that if we can assert 'Fidus believes 'Cicero loves Cicero' ' then we can also assert 'Fidus believes 'Cicero loves Tully' ', because there the substitution is not uniform. Similarly, we have not proven that if we can assert 'Tom believes 'All cordate things eat cordate things' ' then we can also assert 'Tom believes 'All cordate things eat renate things' '.

Since we have not proven the more general substitutivity principles, the only way we can have them in our system is by adding them as new hypotheses. Let us say that a propositional attitude psychology is DS+ iff it is DS and it also contains the hypotheses of general substitutivity of co-designating names and of coextensive general terms.

Now I submit that, if we are going to have a DS psychology, then we should add the hypotheses of general substitutivity, and thus make it DS+. This is for a combination of two reasons. On one hand, DS+ psychologies are open to simplifications that we shall soon see. And on the other, I see no significant downside: in view of DS's proven principles of uniform substitutivity, I do not see that we lose anything of value by adding general substitutivity. E.g. given that a DS psychology will not let us say both 'Tom believes 'Cicero denounced Catiline' ' and 'Tom does not believe 'Tully denounced Catiline' ', it gives us no obvious means to regiment folk psychology's discourse about attitudes *de dicto*; so, as things stand, I see no sacrifice in making 'Cicero' and 'Tully' interchangeable inside content sentences.

It may be of some interest that, in any DS+ psychology, content-language names occupy *purely referential positions* in ascriptions. 'Purely referential position' is Quine's phrase so I am applying his criterion: substitutivity of identity.[1] It is unusual for a position between quotation marks to be purely referential, but Quine assures us that he means his definition to apply even in that setting.[2] (Of course these purely referential positions last only for as long as we keep the quoted content sentences intact, i.e. as long as we hold off executing the Tarskian transformation promised in Chapter 9's Curtailment #6.)

♦

It has seemed to many that, whenever terms are intersubstitutable within a context, they must be alike in reference within that context;[3] but that is not the case in a DS+ psychology. In a DS+ psychology, the content-language terms 'Cicero' and 'Tully' are intersubsitutable in the context of an ascription, but they occur quoted in that context, so they designate distinct letter sequences. Similarly with 'cordate' and 'renate'. DS+ psychologies are, therefore, somewhat odd.

Oddness is not, as a rule, something we need to fix, but on this point I think it is worth making an effort to join the mainstream, to see whether it leads to genuine gains – and we can always back out if it does not. So let us try to restructure our ascriptions in such a way that intersubstitutable terms are always alike in reference.

We can achieve this if we can pull every occurrence of those terms that is inside quotation to outside. But that will leave blanks in content sentences where these occurrences used to be. Very well: they will no longer be content sentences but *content predicates*; and we will no longer be sententialists but *Russellians*.

There are several ways to manage the details. One version has 'believes' and 'desires' as multigrade predicates, and uses prefix notation, e.g.:

believes(Fidus, '___ is dangerous', Cicero)[4]

desires(Hannibal, 'I find a ___', cordate-kind)

Another achieves an incremental gain in readability through a sort of infix notation,[5] with the attitudinative verb and 'of':

Fidus believes '___ is dangerous' of Cicero.

Hannibal desires 'I find a ___' of cordate-kind.

And a third has 'believes' and 'desires' as two-place predicates,[6] relating a subject to a sequence:

Fidus believes <'___ is dangerous', Cicero>.

Hannibal desires <'I find a ___', cordate-kind>.

But the differences among the versions are small compared to what they have in common. None of them involves mentioning (as opposed to using) terms; none of them employs the disquotational theory of reference (nor any theory of reference); and, as a result, all enjoy three pleasing features. First: they allow us to say, by way of quantification, that subjects have attitudes that we cannot ascribe individually; e.g. we can say 'There is an object x such that x has no name and believes (Fidus, '__ is dangerous', x)'.[7] Second: bridging laws are no longer burdened with the duty of term introduction, so they can be less cluttered; e.g. instead of (26) and (27) we can have:

(34) For any subject s and kind k, usually, if s looks upon a member of k, then it comes to pass that believes(s, 'There's a __', k).[8]

(35) For any subject s and object o, fairly often, if s avoids o, then believes(s, '__ is dangerous', o).[9]

And third: with the disquotational theory of reference out of the way, we dodge the concern about extending logic in ways not seen in physical science (Chapter 10).

But it's not all good news. While our restructuring engenders simplicity with one hand, it endangers simplicity with the other. For the same considerations that led us to pull 'Cicero' out of one content sentence, leaving a blank, and to pull 'cordate-kind' out of another content sentence, leaving a blank, would have us do both at once in the case of Galen, who believes that Cicero is cordate; thus:

believes(Galen, '__ is __', Cicero, cordate-kind)[10]

and similarly we could – and would – have content predicates with three or more blanks, followed by lists of three or more non-linguistic items. Then all of our formal reasoning about attitudes would need to keep track of the correspondence between the various blanks inside content predicates and the various items listed after them.

The difficulty would be most acute when we reasoned about attitude–attitude interactions. In the same way that sententialist laws like (7) and (9)–(11) let us form new content sentences by combining and permuting parts of old content sentences, their Russellian counterparts would let us form new content predicates by combining and permuting parts of old content predicates; but then, to keep the correspondence straight, the Russellian laws would have to effect parallel combinations and permutations of parts of old lists.

Were we to pursue this course, we would probably need to drop the undifferentiated blanks in content predicates and move to *variables*. That would give us open sentences, rather than predicates, and then we could, following

Quine,[11] use the 'such that' operator, 'ə', to build predicates out of the open sentences. I shall elaborate no further, however, because there is another course, laid out by David Kaplan and Quine (though not endorsed by Quine),[12] that avoids these encumbrances entirely.

◆

We previously said that a sentence is a sequence of *characters*. Let us now consider a more liberal sort of sequence, in which each element is a character (e.g. 'c') or an object (e.g. Cicero) or a kind (e.g. cordate-kind). Call these more liberal sequences *hybrids*. (The terminology is imperfect. A hybrid, in the ordinary sense of the word, is a mixture; but our definition allows, as special cases, homogenous hybrids, e.g. hybrids whose elements are all characters.) Tarski's operator '⌢' already expresses sequence concatenation, so we can continue its use even when the sequences to be concatenated are hybrids.

The Kaplan–Quine idea is to regiment 'believes' and 'desires' as two-place predicates that relate a subject to a hybrid, in such a way that ascriptions look like this:

Fidus believes Cicero⌢' is dangerous'.
Hannibal desires 'I find a '⌢cordate-kind.
Galen believes Cicero⌢' is '⌢cordate-kind.

Then bridging laws can look like this:

(36) For any subject s and kind k, usually, if s looks upon a member of k, then s comes to believe 'There's a '⌢k.
(37) For any subject s and object o, fairly often, if s avoids o, then s believes o⌢' is dangerous'.

And laws of attitude–attitude interaction can be as simple as this:

(38) For any subject s, object o and kinds k, l, usually, if s believes o⌢' is '⌢k, and s believes 'All '⌢k⌢' are '⌢l, then s comes to believe o⌢' is '⌢l.
(39) For any subject s and kinds k, l, often, if s believes 'All observed '⌢k⌢' are '⌢l, then s comes to believe 'All '⌢k⌢' are '⌢l.
(40) For any subject s and hybrids p, q, occasionally, if s believes q and s believes 'If '⌢p⌢' then '⌢q, then s comes to believe p.
(41) For any subject s and hybrids p, q, usually, if s desires q and s believes 'If '⌢p⌢' then '⌢q, then either s desires p or there is some hybrid r such that s desires r and s believes 'If '⌢p⌢' then it is not the case that '⌢r.

One kink in this scheme is that characters, or character sequences, cannot figure in attitudes in the same way that Cicero does. E.g. if Andrew, a highly selective logophobe, considers the word 'and' to be dangerous, then, as much as we might say 'Fidus believes Cicero⌢' is dangerous' ', we cannot say 'Andrew believes 'and'⌢ ' is dangerous' ', because to do so would be to ascribe to Andrew a belief of the ill-formed homogeneous hybrid 'and is dangerous'.[13] We might be able to solve that problem,[14] but for now let us bookmark it and keep moving. We are, after all, only exploring this style of ascription. If we are tempted to keep it, we can return to the problem then.

◆

Comparing our hybridized version of Rusellianism with DS+, the advantages that either side can claim over the other are so far fairly minor. On the side of hybrids: they let us simplify bridging laws, they let us avoid the disquotational theory of reference with its debatable foundations, and they let us acknowledge the existence of attitudes that we lack the vocabulary to ascribe individually. On the side of DS+: it does not have the problem of logophobic Andrew.

The more weighty advantages are ones that all the theories, and all the versions of theories, sketched in the previous chapter and this, have in common. All are extensional. All allow us to frame laws of attitude–attitude interaction, including laws about many varieties of reasoning. And they all seem to work, more or less. That is to say, they are not obviously broken, in the way that a sententialist psychology would be broken if it had no bridging laws, or if it had a circular dependence on a theory of linguistic meaning, or if it had a circular dependence on a theory of mental representation.

On the other hand, all of these theories have a weighty disadvantage, which is that they work only *roughly* – and in some ways more roughly than folk psychology.

E.g. take this law from Chapter 10:

(13) For any subject s, usually, if s looks upon a bat, then s comes to believe 'There's a bat'.

This will mislead us in cases where the subject looks upon an albino bat, or a bat that presents a silhouette that is more crow-shaped than bat-shaped. That is not to say that the law is false: its use of 'usually' prevents that. Nor is it to say that we do not want rough laws, such as (13) or the even rougher (26) or (36). On the contrary, there are situations where all we know is that the subject looked upon a bat – we don't know its colour or the shape of its silhouette – and then a rough law is the only sort of law we can use. The problem, rather, is this: there are *some* times when we ought to be able to do better. Sometimes we do know about more proximal causes, and then folk psychology allows us to use that information to say, e.g. 'Although subjects who look upon bats usually believe that there's a bat nearby, the present case is an exception, because this bat is not presenting the appearance of a bat'. Or, conversely, if a crow presents the appearance of a bat, folk psychology lets us say, 'Although we don't usually expect subjects who look upon crows to believe that there's a bat nearby, the present case is an exception, because this crow is presenting the appearance of a bat'. These are informal inferences that we cannot yet regiment, because, so far, our bridging steps only bridge to *distal* objects and kinds.

This roughness reaches its degenerate extreme in cases where folk psychology ascribes attitudes about Santa Claus. There is never a distal Santa Claus to bridge to, which is why laws of types DS3(a) and DS3(b) could never lead us to 'Sandra believes 'Santa Claus will come' ', and why this chapter's streamlining made it impossible even to formulate a corresponding Russellian ascription. Yet we should have some regimentation of 'Sandra believes that Santa Claus will come', because, as a piece of folk psychology, it contributes to informal inferences that tell us, e.g. that Sandra is likely to hang up a stocking.

There is also a kind of roughness in cases where folk psychology ascribes attitudes about Hesperus (the morning star) that, according to folk psychology, are not attitudes about Phosphorus (the evening star). Because Hesperus and Phosphorus are, as a matter of astronomical fact, a single object (also known as the planet Venus), we currently lack the means to regiment both 'Gottlob believes that Hesperus is wet' and 'Gottlob does not believe that Phosphorus is wet'. The best we can do is to pick the one that gives the better rough fit for Gottlob's behaviour, regiment that one and do without the other.[15] And the case is similar with Hannibal: we must choose whether to regiment 'Hannibal wants to find a cordate thing' or to regiment 'Hannibal does not want to find a renate thing': we cannot do both.

12

Sententialism with non-designating names

Take the problem of regimenting common-sense ascriptions of attitudes about Santa Claus. We could not solve it with a DS, DS+ or Russellian theory, so I propose that, in this chapter, we take a step back. Let us be sententialists again, as we were in Chapter 10, but this time let us depart as needed from the features that defined DS and enabled the developments in Chapter 11.

Take the following piece of common-sense reasoning: 'Sandra is likely to hang up a stocking because she believes that Santa Claus will come.' As sententialists who are no longer wedded to DS, we can try regimenting it this way:[1]

(42) Sandra believes 'Santa Claus will come'.
(43) Sandra believes 'If Santa Claus will come, then I will get a present if I do stocking-hanging'.
(44) Sandra desires 'I will get a present'.
(45) For any subject s, sentences p, q, general term g, and kind of action a, such that g denotes each member of a, usually, if s believes p and s believes 'if '$\frown p\frown$' then '$\frown q\frown$' if I do '$\frown g$, and s desires q, then s does a.

---

(46) ∴ Probably, Sandra does stocking-hanging.

(with 'denotes' understood disquotationally); but then we run into the question of how, within the regimented psychology, we could have arrived at (42) and (43).

To their credit, (42) and (43) help us to deduce (46); but we could have deduced (46) just as well if we had chosen 'Schmanta Schlaus', or any other made-up name,[2] and deployed it everywhere in place of 'Santa Claus'. So on what basis did we choose 'Santa Claus'? Perhaps we deduced (42) and (43) from other ascriptions, together with some laws of type DS3(b); but only if those other ascriptions mentioned the name 'Santa Claus' too. So the question really is: On what basis did we choose 'Santa Claus' the first time?

In Chapter 10, I posed a similar question about 'Cicero', and we pondered whether we could legitimately pick a content-language term on no basis at all, i.e. arbitrarily. I came down against it, but it is important to remember the reason. There we had a special law ((16)) that simultaneously introduced the name 'Cicero' and bridged to behavioural reports that mentioned the man Cicero; and the only way we could have avoided an intolerable multiplication of similar special laws was by finding a general principle for term-picking. In the case of 'Santa Claus', however, we do not face that problem, because it is eclipsed by a greater problem, viz. a lack of any applicable term-introducing laws, even special ones.

For, consider how folk psychology first decides that Sandra has attitudes about Santa Claus. Almost certainly, it makes some informal inference from reports of verbal behaviour, i.e. from reports of things Sandra was told and of things she subsequently said, or from reports of things that most children her age are told and of things they subsequently say – but we are not ready to regiment those inferences (Curtailment #3), so we cannot say what laws are involved. Another, though less likely, possibility is that folk psychology decides that Sandra acquired beliefs about Santa Claus by abductive reasoning from her beliefs about arrivals of presents, departures of milk and cookies, and so on. But abductive reasoning is not well understood: we lack generalizations about it even in folk-psychological terms, so we are not well placed to frame regimented laws about it.

Faced with this paucity of laws, we cannot expect to deduce ascriptions like (42) and (43) from laws and reports of behaviour. So either we stay the course set in Chapter 10, and avoid ascriptions whose content sentences contain 'Santa Claus', or we break from DS2 and accept some such ascriptions without deducing them. The latter plan adds complexity to our theory where it hurts, i.e. its compact presentation (Chapter 3), but I propose to go ahead and do it anyway. As long as we can deduce enough true behavioural reports *from* those ascriptions, by way of arguments like (42)–(46), the ascriptions will confer a net simplification.

They will not, however, confer any more net simplification than various alternative sets of ascriptions would have, i.e. ones in which 'Schmanta Schlaus' or some other name takes the place of 'Santa Claus' in all the content sentences. So I see no epistemic grounds to prefer one of these sets to another. I choose the set with 'Santa Claus'; you may choose differently.

◆

Now let me vary the example, but only slightly. Suppose folk psychology tells us that Pete will lock his dog indoors because Pete believes that postman Pat will come; and suppose that the folk-psychological reasoning is such that we are tempted to regiment it as follows:

(47) Pete believes 'Pat will come'.
(48) Pete believes 'If Pat will come, then I will get a letter if I do dog-locking'.
(49) Pete desires 'I will get a letter'.
(45) For any subject s, sentences p, q, general term g, and kind of action a, such that g denotes each member of a, usually, if s believes p and s believes 'if '⌢p⌢' then '⌢q⌢' if I do '⌢g, and s desires q, then s does a.

(50) ∴ Probably, Pete does dog-locking.

And suppose, further, that Pat is a real person, and that we have no evidence for any reports of Pete's behaviour that mention Pat (e.g. we have no evidence for 'Pete avoids Pat'). That is to say, although Pat exists, we have no more behavioural evidence about Pete vis-à-vis Pat than we had about Sandra vis-à-vis Santa.

Then, just as we had no basis for choosing between 'Santa Claus' and any made-up name in Sandra's case, we have no basis for choosing between 'Pat' and any made-up name in Pete's case. You could choose the name 'Pschmat' and, provided you deployed it consistently across all the content you ascribe to Pete, I would have no reason to rate your lot of ascriptions as better or worse than the lot in which the content sentences contain 'Pat' – at least not yet.

But the story of Pete continues. What we have just described is day one. On day two, we learn of interactions between Pete and Pat that let us apply some laws of type DS3(a), to deduce new ascriptions that definitely mention the name 'Pat', e.g.:

(51) Pete avoids Pat.
(19) For any subject s, name n and object o such that n designates o, fairly often, if s avoids o, then s believes n⌢' is dangerous'.

(52) ∴ There is a fair chance that Pete believes 'Pat is dangerous'.

Yet on day two we also have other ascriptions, legacies from day one, in which, depending on the choice we made then, the content sentences contain either 'Pat' or 'Pschmat'. Which would we rather have?

It depends on the details of the case, but in typical situations we will do better if the legacy ascriptions deploy the same name as the new ascriptions, i.e. 'Pat', so that the legacy ascriptions and new ascriptions can operate together in further deductions under laws of type DS3(b). (E.g. if we have the legacy ascription (47) and the new ascription (52), then, given some unremarkable further premises, we might expect Pete to keep all of his pets indoors.) If, on the other hand, the legacy ascriptions mention the name 'Pschmat', then things will run less smoothly. We will need either to revise the legacy ascriptions, i.e. decide on day two that we were wrong on day one, or else keep the legacy ascriptions and add an ascription of identificatory belief: 'Pete believes 'Pat = Pschmat''. Apart from the ascription of identificatory belief raising what seems to be the spurious question of *when* Pete acquired the belief, the ascription itself is a bit of extra complexity that we would rather be without.

It seems likely, then, that 'Pat' is a more durable choice than 'Pschmat' on day one: it is a choice that we are less likely to revise in the future. That is not an epistemic reason on day one, but the epistemic reasons that we have on day one lead to indifference, so we might as well let durability be our guide.

I have been assuming that Pat exists, but the arguments are essentially the same if we aren't sure whether Pat exists or not. The argument for epistemic indifference between the names 'Pat' and 'Pschmat' does not depend on Pat's existence, and the future-directed argument for preferring 'Pat' depends only on the *chance* of Pete's interaction with Pat – a chance that remains even if Pat's existence is uncertain.

The lower the probability of Pat existing, the weaker the future-directed argument; but even the weakest of arguments can tip the scales. Indeed, we could follow this line of thought all the way to Sandra and 'Santa Claus'. If there is a chance, however slight, that we will one day decide (i) that Santa Claus exists, and (ii) that Sandra interacts with Santa Claus in a way that activates a bridging law that introduces the name 'Santa Claus' into a content sentence via disquotation, then that chance gives us a wafer-thin reason to prefer the name 'Santa Claus' in the content sentences that we ascribe to Sandra today.

◆

Early in Chapter 11 we proved, for DS psychologies, this principle of uniform substitutivity of co-designating names:

> If we can assert an ascription $a[n]$ in which the content sentence contains (one or more occurrences of) a name n that designates an object o, and if n' is another name that designates o, then we can also assert an ascription $a[n']$ that differs from $a[n]$ only by the uniform replacement of n by n'.

However, the proof in Chapter 11 relied on DS2, which this chapter has not maintained. So we must scratch that proof, and start from scratch on the question of whether to uphold the uniform substitutivity of co-designating names.

I begin with two observations. First, the principle in question concerns only designating names, with 'designating' understood disquotationally. It says nothing about either vacuous names of the familiar sort, such as 'Santa Claus', or names that are outside our own vocabulary, such as 'Pschmat'. And second, in each of our examples so far, when we bring a designating name n into the content language, we do so in one of only two ways. Either

(a) n occurs in the content sentence of an ascription that we hypothesize, rather than deduce, and we choose n on the forward-looking grounds that it makes our ascription interoperable with possible ascriptions that we reach in way (b),

or

(b) n occurs in the content sentence of an ascription that we deduce using a DS3(a) law.

Now, whenever we bring n into a content sentence in way (b), we can also make the same move with n' in place of n. We saw this in Chapter 11 and it still holds. E.g. let us suppose that the name 'Mr Isserie' is co-designating with 'Pat'. Then, on day two of the Pete story, when we deduce (52) from (51) and (19), we can also deduce (54) from (53) and (19):

(53) Pete avoids Mr Isserie.
(19) For any subject s, name n and object o such that n designates o, fairly often, if s avoids o, then s believes $n^\frown$' is dangerous'.

---

(54) ∴ There is a fair chance that Pete believes 'Mr Isserie is dangerous'.

And, given this point, it follows that, whenever we bring n into a content sentence in way (a), we can also make *that* same move with n' in place of n. E.g. on day one of the Pete story, when we choose the name 'Pat' (rather than 'Pschmat') in the hypothesized ascriptions (47) and (48), for the sake of interoperability with possible ascriptions like (52), we have just as much reason to choose 'Mr Isserie' (rather than 'Pschmat' or 'Mr Schmisserie', etc.), and thus hypothesize:

(55) Pete believes 'Mr Isserie will come'.
(56) Pete believes 'If Mr Isserie will come, then I will get a letter if I do dog-locking'.

for the sake of interoperability with possible ascriptions like (54).

So if we assume – and I see no reason not to[3] – that (a) and (b) are the only ways that designating names enter the content language, then it follows that, at any site where a designating name n enters, a co-designating name n' may be uniformly substituted for it. And if we further assume – as we did in Chapter 11 and I see no reason not to – that the only way a name propagates from one ascription to another is via applications of DS3(b) laws, then the principle of uniform substitutivity of co-designating names is proved.

In retrospect, we may be glad to have this principle, because it lets us simplify our theory's compact presentation. For recall how, having hypothesized (47) and (48), we decided that we should also hypothesize (55) and (56). That would have constituted a double complexity within the compact presentation; but, now that we have the principle of uniform substitutivity of co-designating names, we are spared the doubling. As soon as the compact presentation includes, say, (47) and (48), uniform substitutivity ensures that (55) and (56) appear outside the compact presentation, as its deducible consequences.

◆

So the principle of uniform substitutivity of co-designating names stays. And what, now, of *general* substitutivity of co-designating names?

In Chapter 11 we adopted that principle for a combination of two reasons: it opened the door to Russellianism, which was arguably a simplification, and it seemed harmless. In the present context, however, Russellianism is not such a drawcard, for we can find ourselves asserting:

(47) Pete believes 'Pat will come'.

when we are not sure whether Pat exists, and under those circumstances we are in no position to assert the corresponding Russellian ascription:

(57) believes(Pete, '__ will come', Pat).

If, at a later date, we become sure that Pat exists, then we *could* decide to assert (57); but, if we did, would we recant (47)? Or would we keep (47) along with (57) and try to articulate the links between them? Surely the simplest plan is to keep (47) and avoid the Russellian ascription altogether.

In declining Russellianism we lose our motive for the general substitutivity of co-designating names. That principle still seems harmless, though, so I register no opinion as to whether we should retain it.

◆

The uniform substitutivity of co-designating names, I have said, is staying. However, it would land us in a contradiction if we asserted both 'Gottlob believes 'Hesperus is wet' ' and 'Gottlob does not believe 'Phosphorus is wet' ', because, unbeknownst to Gottlob, Hesperus (the morning star) and Phosphorus (the evening star) are both the planet Venus. Therefore, when folk psychology asserts both 'Gottlob believes that Hesperus is wet' and 'Gottlob does not believe that Phosphorus is wet', we are barred from regimenting those statements in the most obvious way.

Happily, we have an alternative. We can make up two names outside our own vocabulary – 'Schmesperus' and 'Schmosphorus', let us say – and deploy those, instead of 'Hesperus' and 'Phosphorus', respectively, throughout the content we ascribe to Gottlob. Then we have:

(58) Gottlob believes 'Schmesperus is wet',
(59) Gottlob does not believe 'Schmosphorus is wet',

and no contradiction, because, unlike 'Hesperus' and 'Phosphorus', 'Schmesperus' and 'Schmosphorus' are non-designating (like 'Pschmat'), and a fortiori non-co-designating.

As always, though, we must keep our eye on the inferences.

Perhaps folk psychology reasons thus: 'Gottlob believes that Hesperus is wet; Gottlob believes that Hesperus is a planet; Gottlob believes that Hesperus is visible early in the morning; Gottlob wants to see a wet planet; therefore Gottlob is likely to get up early in the morning.' It is a straightforward exercise to regiment all that, putting 'Schmesperus' in place of 'Hesperus' everywhere and supplying some obvious suppressed premises, so let us skip it for a more challenging example.

Take a case where the folk's reasoning mentions the planet itself. This news just in: 'Gottlob was looking at Venus through his good telescope at 7 a.m., when Venus exploded.' As soon as folk psychology receives this report of Gottlob's passive matinal behaviour, it infers that Gottlob probably believes that Hesperus has exploded; but folk psychology still maintains, as it always has, that Gottlob does not believe that Phosphorus has exploded.

It is easy enough to regiment the conclusion. We can say with reasonable confidence:

(60) Gottlob believes 'Schmesperus has exploded'.

and still maintain:

(61) Gottlob does not believe 'Schmosphorus has exploded'.

But now we come to the hard question: What is the inference, within our regimented psychology, that takes us from the behavioural report to (60)?

We can frame the following law:

(62) For any subject s, name n and planet p such that n designates p, usually, if s looks at p through a good telescope when p explodes, then s comes to believe n⌢' has exploded'.

but this does not help. (62) could lead us to 'Gottlob believes 'Venus has exploded' ' (as well as to 'Gottlob believes 'Hesperus has exploded' ' and to 'Gottlob believes 'Phosphorus has exploded' '), but (62) could never lead us to (60). Nor is it helpful to constrain (62) by inserting conditions of some sort between the 'if' and the 'then'. Such extra conditions cannot alter the fact that the law only delivers ascriptions whose content sentences use a designating name – i.e. ascriptions that are not (60).

A more promising strategy is to reason about some more proximal stimulus; perhaps some pattern of illumination in the morning sky. Whatever the details, let us call the chosen proximal stimulus 'X'. Then the strategy is 'divide and conquer'. One half of our reasoning will be astronomical, arguing from Venus's exploding to the occurrence of X, and the other half will be psychological, arguing from the occurrence of X to (60). The astronomical part will make free use of the name 'Venus', but neither use nor mention 'Schmesperus', while the psychological part will neither use nor mention 'Venus', but freely mention the name 'Schmesperus'. In particular, the psychological part will draw on ascriptions of Gottlob's background beliefs, such as 'Gottlob believes 'Schmesperus appears in the morning' ', which support the inference to (60) but cast no doubt on (61).

◆

That strategy could work, but it raises the question, 'Why stop there?', for 'divide and conquer' could also conquer other problems, outside of the so-called Frege cases.

At the close of Chapter 11 we observed that laws that link a subject's attitudes to distal stimuli are *rough*, i.e. prone to exceptions (though their use of 'usually' protects them from being false). We saw exceptions due to *illusion*, where a proximal stimulus is not caused by the distal stimulus that usually causes it. And there is a similar source of exceptions on the output side, which we might call *misadventure*: where a proximal action does not cause the distal action that it usually causes. Why do we put up with all this? Imagine, instead, a regimented psychology in which bridging laws mention only *proximal* inputs and outputs. Imagine, in a word, that bridging laws are all *narrow*. Illusion and misadventure would never create exceptions to those laws, so why not simply decide to do psychology that way?

I can see the appeal of that policy, and I would endorse it if I thought that we could make it work. Unfortunately, however, we are often unable to apply narrow bridging laws, because the behavioural data that we actually have is often distal. For instance we might be told, with no details of azimuth, elevation or time of day, that Marcia was looking at Mars, through a good telescope, when Mars exploded.

With only that information, folk psychology infers that Marcia probably believes that Mars has exploded. Granted, there might have been an illusion, leading Marcia not to believe that Mars has exploded; but folk psychology is willing to take that risk, duly acknowledged with 'probably'. And we regimenters, being no better informed than the folk on the topic of Marcia's proximal stimulus, should take that risk too. So we have:

(63) Marcia looked at Mars through a good telescope when Mars exploded.

(62) For any subject s, name n and planet p such that n designates p, usually, if s looks at p through a good telescope when p explodes, then s comes to believe $n^\frown$' has exploded'.

---

(64) ∴ Probably, Marcia believes 'Mars has exploded'.

Naturally we should be less rough when the data allows it. If we do receive relevant details of Marcia's proximal stimulus, then it behooves us to divide and conquer, much as we envisaged doing in the Gottlob case. In Marcia's case, however, it never behooves us to coin a made-up name. When our reasoning about Marcia uses information about a proximal stimulus, then it doesn't matter whether we choose 'Mars' or 'Schmars'; but when it bridges to Mars itself, then we have to choose 'Mars'; *ergo* we should choose 'Mars' from day one.

◆

In the Gottlob case, what we lack is a regimentation of the *rough* inference. So, if we cannot identify a proximal stimulus, we have no logical path to (60).

It is a price we pay for being so damned good at astronomy. If only we were not burdened with the information that Hesperus = Phosphorus, then we could, within our regimented psychology, assert both 'Gottlob believes 'Hesperus is wet' ' and 'Gottlob does not believe 'Phosphorus is wet' ', and be in no danger of deducing a contradiction. We would have no need to coin 'Schmesperus' and 'Schmosphorus', and we could regiment folk psychology's rough reasoning in the most obvious way:

(65) Gottlob looked at Hesperus through a good telescope when Hesperus exploded.

(62) For any subject s, name n and planet p such that n designates p, usually, if s looks at p through a good telescope when p explodes, then s comes to believe $n^\frown$' has exploded'.

---

(66) ∴ Probably, Gottlob believes 'Hesperus has exploded'.

Of course I am not proposing that we abandon 'Hesperus = Phosphorus'. I merely note that, as things stand, that equation is preventing us from regimenting a rough psychological inference. Or in other words, 'Hesperus = Phosphorus' is precluding the combination of a rough psychological inference and logical explicitness.

We can also put it this way: As things stand, logical explicitness is precluding the combination of a rough psychological inference and 'Hesperus = Phosphorus'.

If only we were not burdened with the drive for logical explicitness, then we could hold a rough psychology in one hand and 'Hesperus = Phosphorus' in the other, and we could stop the two from sparking a contradiction. For our psychology would use native folk ascriptions, linked to each other and to behavioural reports only via an informal logic that invests us, its human conductors, with the discretion to treat occurrences of 'Hesperus' in 'that'-clauses as sometimes transparent and sometimes opaque. In exercising our discretion we could be guided, as we often are, by our uncodified talent for sensing impending absurdity and then stopping short of it. And all of that could work. In fact, it does.

Still, I do not propose that we abandon the drive for logical explicitness. See Chapters 5 and 7.

Part Four

Paths not taken

But you more knowing justly shun
The error into which they run; ...
And in the place of monk, elect
Voltaire your conscience to direct.

Voltaire[1]

13

The 'Two Dogmas' argument

In Quine's 'Two Dogmas of Empiricism', the opening lines explain the title and set the crosshairs:

> Modern empiricism has been conditioned in large part by two dogmas. One is a belief in some fundamental cleavage between truths which are *analytic*, or grounded in meanings independently of matters of fact, and truths which are *synthetic*, or grounded in fact. The other dogma is *reductionism*: the belief that each meaningful statement is equivalent to some logical construct upon terms which refer to immediate experience. Both dogmas, I shall argue, are ill-founded.[1]

And argue Quine does, for most of the paper, against several attempts to draw the analytic–synthetic distinction, and against reductionism. By exposing the errors of previous empiricists, that much of the paper provides a valuable service, and will continue to do so for as long as there are those who find the old errors tempting. And of course the back pages provide something that I find even more valuable, viz. Quine's own version of empiricism, which has (with minor amendments) become the cornerstone of this book.

'Two Dogmas' spawned a vast literature on the analytic–synthetic distinction, pro and con, but this chapter is not about that. For the sake of the argument here I simply grant Quine's thesis that the distinction is illusory. Nor is this chapter about the positive contribution in Quine's §6, on which I effused sufficiently in Chapter 3. This chapter is, rather, about the connection: it is about how Quine moves from the negative part of 'Two Dogmas' to the positive part.

Prima facie there is something fishy[2] about resting a new philosophy on criticisms of an earlier view. One feels that it ought to be possible to persuade a reader who never held the earlier view in the first place; yet such a reader will find that the main argument of 'Two Dogmas' passes her by. Is it because there is a premise somewhere that she does not accept? This is unclear.

I shall argue that Quine's reasoning, in 'Two Dogmas' and other works from around the same time, depends, not just on rejecting the earlier empiricism, but also on retaining something of what was behind it, and that what is retained is untenable in light of what is rejected. But, before I make those points, we need to catch up on some background reading.

◆

Traditional empiricists, whose starting point is sense data and whose first challenge is to defend talk of physical objects in space, have often made surprising claims about what physical-object talk *means*. In particular, some have said that it is *synonymous* with sense-data talk. This helps their cause, or would if it were true, because then they could get from sense data to physical objects without abduction or any other inference that they might be sceptical about. The tactic goes back at least as far as George Berkeley:

> By sight I have the ideas of light and colours with their several degrees and variations. By touch I perceive for example hard and soft, heat and cold, motion and resistance ... Smelling furnishes me with odours; the palate with tastes, and hearing conveys sounds to the mind in all their variety of tone and composition. And as several of these are observed to accompany each other, they come to be marked by one name, and so to be reputed as one thing. Thus, for example, a certain colour, taste, smell, figure and consistence having been observed to go together, are accounted one distinct thing, signified by the name *apple*.[3]

And others followed suit;[4] but they lacked the means to prove their key semantic claims.

It was only in the early twentieth century, when the resources of modern logic came on stream, that a proof appeared possible. In that environment, focus shifted from natural to artificial languages. The goal was to construct a language that would speak of space and occupants of space, but in which every linguistic element was clearly defined, and defined in such a way that whoever read the definitions could see that everything said in the language boiled down to sense data. Russell epitomized the program when he wrote:

> The supreme maxim in scientific philosophizing is this:
>
> *Wherever possible, logical constructions are to be substituted for inferred entities.*[5]

Meanwhile the concept of *definition* was liberalized. Russell famously introduced 'contextual definition', where a phrase is defined by showing, not how to replace it *in situ*, but how to transform the enclosing sentence to make the phrase in question disappear. At that stage a claim of synonymy could still be made, but only of synonymy between two *sentences*: the original one and the transformed one. Yet that was not liberal enough to complete the project, even sketchily, and so Carnap, in *Der Logische Aufbau der Welt* (The Logical Structure of the World, and hereafter the *Aufbau*), went further. The linguistic rules for his 'thing language' – i.e. his language for assigning colours to space-time points – did not say how to translate a single thing-language sentence into a single sentence about sense data. They were instructions, rather, for asserting many thing-language sentences at once, given many sense-data sentences. In this sense Carnap's linguistic rules were *holistic*, as opposed to *reductionistic*.

At this point, the word 'synonymy' seems no longer to fit, and nor does the word 'definition'; but still Carnap viewed his rules as linguistic conventions, so we can see his tactic, like Berkeley's, as an attempt to avoid what Russell called 'inferred entities'.[6] Indeed, Russell's 'supreme maxim' became the motto of Carnap's *Aufbau*, and Carnap himself wrote:

> The introduction of new ways of speaking ... does not need any theoretical justification.[7]

In Carnap's philosophy, we come to a warranted theory of the world by answering questions of two sorts. First there are *external questions*, i.e. questions about which system of linguistic rules to follow;[8] and then, once the rules are chosen, there are *internal questions*, i.e. questions about what to say according to those rules.

How should we answer external questions, according to Carnap? One consideration is that we want to show (not merely plead) that everything we are going to say will be linked by nothing but linguistic rules to nothing but sense data. To that end, we should choose a language whose rules are all laid out, in detail and in writing. Call this principle *total linguistic explicitness*. And a second consideration is pragmatism. At this stage we are choosing a language, not attempting to describe reality, so we have a great deal of freedom.[9] Nevertheless, a language is a tool, so we would be wise to choose the one that we can use most efficiently. Call this principle *external pragmatism*. It is a principle that favours simplicity.

Now, supposing that we choose a language like the one Carnap chose in the *Aufbau*, how will it have us answer internal questions? One feature of that language is that its rules are not mere definitions of terms; they include a complete set of instructions for deduction. So our deductions must all obey that set of rules. Call this *total logical conformance*. And a second feature is the so-called principle of least action.[10] This is a linguistic rule that has us assign colours to space-time points so as to reduce, as far as possible consistently with sense data, the motion and acceleration attributed to things. The historical value of this rule lies in its suggestiveness of the following nearby alternative: assign colours to space-time points so as to reduce, as far as possible consistently with the sense data, the complexity of the sentences needed to fix the positions of all the things.[11] Call this *internal pragmatism*.

♦

Now that we have caught up with Quine's predecessors, let us reopen our copies of 'Two Dogmas', beginning with §§1–4.

Here we see Quine criticizing, as circular or question-begging, certain facile attempts to define 'analytic', viz. in terms of essence, logic, synonymy, state-descriptions, definition, substitution, necessity and semantical rules. Though I find these sections persuasive, they do not prove that 'analytic' can never be defined. For all I know, 'analytic' might be defined in terms of *belief*, one day when we have a well-developed theory of belief that does not lean on any of the disputed concepts.[12] But it is not my purpose here to debate Quine's view of the analytic–synthetic distinction. I simply grant that view in order to see what follows.

In §5 Quine criticizes one more purported definition of 'analytic'. Definitions of 'analytic' are still not my topic, but I shall say a little about this argument of Quine's, if only to forestall confusion with the arguments that are my topic.

This argument, which fills most of Quine's §5, runs as follows. Carnap's linguistic rules, being holistic, do not provide translations of individual thing-language sentences into sentences about sense data; nor do they in any way map individual thing-language sentences to ranges of sense data; *ergo* they do not support a purported definition of 'analytic' that might be built on top of such a translation or such a mapping.

The argument is sound, but redundant. For, while Quine is correct to observe that Carnap, with his sketches of holistic linguistic rules, differs from the pre-Carnapians who envisaged reductionistic linguistic rules, let us also observe this similarity: both assume that we already understand the notion of linguistic rules. If that assumption were true, then analyticity could be defined directly: an analytic sentence is one that has a proof from linguistic rules alone. But the assumption is not true: we no more already understand the notion of linguistic rules than we already understand the notion of analyticity. (Indeed Quine made this point in his §4.) So the weakness in Carnap's position is not that it, unlike its predecessors, won't let us build the analytic–synthetic distinction on top of it; the weakness is that it, like its predecessors, is built on top of something tantamount to the analytic–synthetic distinction.[13]

♦

And finally, now, to my actual topic: the reasoning that propels Quine from the negative theses in §§1–5 of 'Two Dogmas' to the positive proposals in its §6.

Quine never sets this reasoning out in premise/conclusion form, but it appears to run as follows. We begin with a Carnapian[14] position, including (i) the purported distinction between external and internal questions, (ii) adherence to total linguistic explicitness and external pragmatism when answering external questions and (iii) adherence to total logical conformance and internal pragmatism when answering internal questions. But the analytic–synthetic distinction is illusory; so there is no distinction between revising an analytic sentence, i.e. changing one's linguistic rules, and revising a synthetic sentence, i.e. working within one's linguistic rules. So the distinction between external questions and internal questions is illusory, and the distinction between two ways of answering must be illusory too. Therefore we should fuse the principles of total linguistic explicitness and total logical conformance, and fuse the principles of external and internal pragmatism.

I would like this to be a sound argument, because its conclusion is close[15] to the normative epistemology that this book promotes. Fusing total linguistic explicitness and total logical conformance would produce the norm that my Chapter 5 called 'total logical explicitness', and fusing the two pragmatisms would produce an all-purpose pragmatism, equivalent to a conjunction of the norms that my Chapter 3 called 'empirical correctness' and 'simplicity'.

Is it a sound argument, though? I am at a loss to say, because, while I have presented it as clearly as I can, I am still not sure what the argument is. What, for instance, is its first premise? I wrote 'We begin with a Carnapian position, including (i) ..., (ii) ... and (iii) ...'; but is that position, with its three inclusions, a *premise*? It cannot be a premise of the usual sort, because Quine neither agrees with it nor wants us to agree with it. Is it, then, a *reductio* premise, assumed temporarily for the purpose of proving it false? Apparently not, because Quine's conclusion is not a simple negation of Carnapianism. In fact Quine's conclusion comes as close to Carnapianism as anyone could, without an analytic–synthetic distinction.

On reflection, it seems to me that Quine relies on two arguments, not one. There is an argument against accepting the whole Carnapian position, which is quite straightforward:

Carnapianism, as a whole, can only be true if there is an analytic–synthetic distinction.

There is no analytic–synthetic distinction.

───────────────

∴ It is not the case that Carnapianism, as a whole, is true.

And there is a separate argument for staying close to Carnap, which is anything but straightforward. Let us see what we can find.

Carnap's position originally seemed attractive because it held the promise that linguistic convention, rather than any problematic inference, would close the epistemic gap from experience to physical objects. Quine cannot say flat out that he wants to preserve that feature, because he does not recognize any such thing as linguistic convention, in contrast to substantive theory. So, instead of saying it flat out, he says it equivocally, or metaphorically, or with qualifications that might be denials. Take, e.g., this remark from §4 of 'Two Dogmas':

> It is obvious that truth in general depends on both language and extralinguistic fact. The statement 'Brutus killed Caesar' would be false if the world had been different in certain ways, but it would also be false if the word 'killed' happened rather to have the sense of 'begat'.[16]

Can we pin down what Quine is calling obvious here? Apparently it is obvious that truth depends on language; but what is *language*? Quine said a great deal about *languages* earlier, in his §4, but here he is using the mass noun, not the common noun; and in any case he goes on to deny that there is a separable 'linguistic component':

> Thus one is tempted to suppose in general that the truth of a statement is somehow analysable into a linguistic component and a factual component. Given this supposition, it next seems reasonable that in some statements the factual component should be null; and these are the analytic statements. But, for all its a priori reasonableness, a boundary between analytic and synthetic statements simply has not been drawn. That there is a distinction to be drawn at all is an unempirical dogma of empiricists, a metaphysical article of faith.[17]

So it is by no means obvious what he was calling obvious.[18]

Quine's whispered conventionalism also appeared in other works, e.g. *Methods of Logic*:

> Physical objects, if they did not exist, would, to transplant Voltaire's epigram, have to be invented.[19]

'Posits and Reality':

> Unless we change meanings in midstream, the familiar bodies around us are as real as can be; and it smacks of a contradiction in terms to conclude otherwise.[20]

Word and Object:

> On the face of it there is a certain verbal perversity in the idea that ordinary talk of familiar physical things is not in large part understood as it stands, or that the familiar physical things are not real, or that evidence of their reality needs to be uncovered. For surely the key words 'understood', 'real' and 'evidence' are too ill-defined to stand up under such punishment. We should be depriving them of the very denotations to which they mainly owe such sense as they make to us. It was a lexicographer, Dr Johnson, who demonstrated the reality of a stone by kicking it; and to begin with, at least, we have little better to go on than Johnsonian usage.[21]

And, best of all, in 'Carnap and Logical Truth':

> Now I am as impressed as anyone with the vastness of what language contributes to science and to one's whole view of the world; and in particular I grant that one's hypothesis as to what there is ... is at bottom just as arbitrary or pragmatic a matter as one's adoption of a new brand of set theory or even a new system of bookkeeping. ... But what impresses me more than it does Carnap is how well this ... attitude is suited also to the theoretical hypotheses of natural science itself, and how little basis there is for a distinction.
>
> The lore of our fathers is a fabric of sentences. ... It is a pale gray lore, black with fact and white with convention. But I have found no substantial reasons for concluding that there are any quite black threads in it, or any white ones.[22]

I am as impressed as anyone with Quine's poetry, but behind it I have found no literal argument for the extent of his (or my) proximity to Carnap on epistemology.

14

Naturalized epistemology

Our epistemology is naturalistic in several senses of the word. It avoids mention of a sensory realm unknown to physical science (Chapter 3); it eschews a priori claims, including a priori metaphysics and a priori semantic analysis (Chapter 3, Chapter 7); it allows findings of fact to influence the choice of epistemic norms (Chapters 1–2); and the norms that it applies to philosophical theories are none other than the norms that it applies to science of all kinds (Chapters 6–7).

For me that is naturalism enough, but there are other ways of defining 'naturalism' that would make our position count as non-naturalistic. If, for instance, one defined 'naturalism' as a norm of *replicating the practice of scientists*, then we would not be naturalists, for we have no such norm;[1] but nor would we want to be, because naturalism so defined would be terminally unscientific. Science cannot solve its epistemological problems by asking 'What would a scientist do?', so the norm in question would be one for non-scientists only.

Our epistemology is also non-naturalistic in the following, more controversial, sense: it is not a part of our theory of reality, i.e. not a part of the theory that it counsels us to accept. It is informed by natural science, but it sits outside natural science. If that sounds impossible, as it might, to anyone who has succumbed to a false dichotomy between epistemology as 'first philosophy' and epistemology as 'working from within',[2] then an analogy with ethics might help. Medical ethics, environmental ethics and military ethics take scientific and social facts as input, but they take them from across the fact–value divide; and that is what I see normative epistemology doing.

When we turn to Quine's writings on naturalism, we can find much with which to agree. E.g. take this passage:

> In *Theories and Things* I wrote that naturalism is 'the recognition that it is within science itself, and not in some prior philosophy, that reality is to be identified and described'; again that it is 'abandonment of the goal of a first philosophy prior to natural science' (pp. 21, 67). These characterizations convey the right

mood, but they would fare poorly in a debate. How much qualifies as 'science itself' and not 'some prior philosophy'?

> ... If I saw indirect explanatory benefit in positing sensibilia, possibilia, spirits, a Creator, I would joyfully accord them scientific status too, on a par with such avowedly scientific posits as quarks and black holes. ...
>
> ... My point in the characterizations of naturalism that I quoted is just that the *most* we can reasonably seek in support of an inventory and description of reality is testability of its observable consequences in the time-honored hypothetico-deductive way.³

Here I have only minor quibbles. I would like to see 'the ... hypothetico-deductive way' elaborated as compliance with our three norms, and I would like to see greater acknowledgement of Quine's own contributions than can be read into the phrase 'time-honored'; but, apart from those points, I concur with this statement of naturalism.

Serious disagreement only sets in when Quine includes *epistemology* within 'science itself', where 'reality is to be identified and described'. That inclusion thesis, in its several versions, and my disagreements with each version, are the topics of this chapter.

◆

Here is one version of the inclusion thesis:

> Science itself tells us that our information about the world is limited to irritations of our surfaces, and then the epistemological question is in turn a question within science: the question how we human animals can have managed to arrive at science from such limited information.⁴

I have nothing against Quine attending to that kind of question, as he did in chapter III of *Word and Object*, most of *The Roots of Reference*, and many later works. That inquiry is not the topic of this book, but it may be part of natural science, and that is all very well. I do not even mind that Quine stretched the word 'epistemology' to cover it. I do protest, though, at his attempts to monopolize the word 'epistemology', as if to make his non-normative epistemology the only kind:

> Naturalism does not repudiate epistemology, but assimilates it to empirical psychology.⁵

> [I]t may be more useful to say rather that epistemology still goes on, though in a new setting and a clarified status. Epistemology, or something like it, simply falls into place as a chapter of psychology and hence of natural science.⁶

Why not settle for psychology?[7]

Why not settle for psychology? Because psychology describes good and bad theorizing alike, and we want to tell them apart, so that we can practise one and not the other.

I am taking this first version of the inclusion thesis at face value, i.e. as a plot to do away with normative epistemology and to put in its place the mere description of current practice. Others, however, have understood it differently: as a strain of normative epistemology that *defers* to current practice. Thus Sander Verhaegh writes:

> As some scholars have recognized, Quine ... adopts an immanent, *deflationary theory of justification*, i.e. a theory which does not seek a substantive extrascientific explanation for the justification of our statements beyond their being included in or excluded by our inherited world theory.
>
> Although Quine's project has a significant descriptive component, his epistemology remains normative because it appeals to such a deflationary notion of justification – a notion according to which facts about how we *actually* construct theory from evidence coincide with facts about how we *should* do this.[8]

If Verhaegh's interpretation is right,[9] then Quine's first attempt at naturalized epistemology stamps 'Approved' on every theory that we actually construct, or perhaps on every method of theorizing that we actually follow. That is not normative epistemology in the sense that I have been using the term, though; it is not a system of principles that we can put to work, to guide us through genuine quandaries about how to theorize. And we need an epistemology that is normative in that sense; hence we need to look elsewhere.

◆

Fortunately, Quine was not wedded to his first attempt. By 1974 he was making his way to a position that did not merely describe current practice and did not merely defer to it either:

> Mostly in this book I have speculated on causes, not justifications. ... I asked how, given our stimulations, we might have developed our corporeal style of talk. One could ask, in the same spirit, how we developed our religious talk, and our talk of witchcraft ... In short, I have speculated on causes and not on values. Sheep are caused and goats are caused, and they are caused in similar ways.
>
> ... How then should we settle our ontology? ...
>
> ... That last question is little less than the general question of scientific method: the question how best to develop an inclusive scientific theory. We want

to maximize prediction; that is, we want a theory that will anticipate as many observations as possible, getting none of them wrong.[10]

Though he retained the motto 'naturalized epistemology', subsequent writings reaffirmed that Quine had found a way for naturalized epistemology to *evaluate* practices of theorizing:

> Naturalization of epistemology does not jettison the normative and settle for the indiscriminate description of ongoing procedures. For me normative epistemology is a branch of engineering. It is the technology of truth-seeking, or, in more cautiously epistemological term, prediction.[11]

And he subsequently settled on prediction, rather than truth, as the terminal parameter:

> Normative epistemology gets naturalized into a chapter of engineering: the technology of anticipating sensory stimulation.[12]

So, according to this second version of Quine's inclusion thesis, epistemology can judge theories *instrumentally*, as better or worse predictors of sensory stimulation.[13]

Judgements of that sort will cut no ice, of course, unless one's audience agrees that predicted stimulation is the goal. If one cannot get agreement on that point, what is left to say then? Can one dig deeper, and give reasons why prediction should be prized? Quine says no:

> When I cite predictions as the checkpoints of science, I do not see that as normative. I see it as defining a particular language game, in Wittgenstein's phrase: the game of science, in contrast to other good language games such as fiction or poetry. A sentence's claim to scientific status rests on what it contributes to a theory whose checkpoints are in prediction.[14]

So one can withhold scientific status from theories that mispredict, but only for purposes of classification; it is not to be meant as a rebuke. Ultimately, on this view, criticism is not possible:

> There is no question here of ultimate value, as in morals; it is a matter of efficacy for an ulterior end ... The normative here, as elsewhere in engineering, becomes descriptive when the terminal parameter is expressed.[15]

Let us agree to use 'engineering' as a name for the study of efficacy of means to ends; i.e. the study of instrumental value. Stimulatory prediction is an end, and I do not object to anyone studying the efficacy of means to it. But, when

Quine equates that 'chapter of engineering' with normative epistemology, then I have four objections.

Objection #1 concerns ends. Theories serve ends other than prediction, as Quine was aware:

> [The purposes] of the science game are understanding, control of the environment, healing, and, in some cases, mental exhilaration, pride of achievement, and even fame, if not fortune. Prediction is only occasionally the purpose.[16]

And yet epistemology always makes prediction trump, in the following sense: when a theory has failed one of the 'checkpoints ... in prediction', the rules of epistemology *forbid* us from retaining the original theory whole. We *must* reject at least some part of it, even if doing so sacrifices elegance, human contentment, or some other happy outcome. And epistemology is surely right to take this line; Quine and I are in agreement there. My objection is that, if epistemology were a branch of engineering as Quine says it is, then its single-mindedness would appear peculiar, even reckless; for what would make the epistemologist any better than a reckless mining engineer – one who always puts ore tonnage ahead of cost, safety and environmental impact?

Of course it would not be reckless to *study* a rarefied branch of engineering, in which theories are assessed purely as sensory predictors, in abstraction from every other concern. That would be like studying just the ore-shifting capacity of various mining machines. But there would still be a mystery, viz.: Why do we base real decisions directly on the former abstraction and not the latter?

Objection #2 concerns means. There are some means of accurately predicting experience that no epistemologist would consider, but when one views epistemology as engineering, one is hard-pressed to explain or excuse its very reasonable dismissal of those means.

Suppose, e.g. that in a certain university the chaplain preaches to a group of research scientists every Sunday on metaphysical topics: an invisible seraphim, the transubstantiation of the Eucharist and so on. Somehow these sermons promote diligence, temperance and emotional stability in the daily lives of the congregation, and the result is that many scientific projects flourish. Indirectly, the chaplain's words have contributed to the betterment of prediction. Any epistemologist worthy of the name would decry the contribution, calling it merely causal as opposed to rational; but when did an engineer ever decry 'merely causal' means to her ends?

Objection #3 may be put as an inversion of objection #2: not only does epistemology sometimes overlook discourse that improves prediction; it sometimes looks favourably on discourse that makes no appreciable difference to prediction. I submit the following passage as a sample:

> Consider Carnap's clarification of measure, or impure number, where he construes 'the temperature of x is $n°C$' in the fashion 'the temperature-in-degrees-Centigrade of x is n' and so dispenses with the impure numbers $n°C$ in favour of the pure numbers n. There had been, we might say, a two-place predicate 'H' of temperature such that '$H(x, α)$' meant that the temperature of x was $α$. We end up with a new two-place predicate 'H_C' of temperature in degrees Centigrade. '$H(x, n°C)$' is explained away as '$H_C(x, n)$', ... 'H' had applied to putative things $α$, impure numbers, which came to be banished from the universe.[17]

Tradesmen and scientists have for centuries been able to measure things, to record the results using numerals, and to predict further measurable results by manipulating the numerals, i.e. calculating. Such useful practices as these have not waited for philosophers to invent, and subsequently eliminate, bindable variables that take impure numbers as values. If tomorrow morning every philosophical essay on variables were lost than measurement would go on as before, furnishing data for computations that would yield predictions as before. So why do we bother with the variables? Why do we bother deciding whether impure numbers are in their domain or not? What do we hope to gain from a fenced ontology?

In Chapter 8, I gave my answer: variables and a fenced ontology (either with or without the impure numbers) are worthwhile as a means to logical explicitness. They enable the codification of laws, so that predictive deductions can be spelled out fully in premise/conclusion form – something that I find valuable for its own sake.

Not that the spelling out is without fringe benefits. Sometimes it adds to the reliability of inferences, or to their efficiency. Sometimes it reveals a parity of reasoning with another problem or another branch of science, where one might have been at a nonplus. These bonuses do engender better predictions, and so the drive for logical explicitness will hold a certain degree of interest for a prediction-seeking engineer. But *her* interest will always be pegged to the prospect of the bonuses. When the prospect looks faint, as it did in the passage above and it does in much of logic and philosophy,[18] then the engineer will reveal herself to be no epistemologist, for her interest will turn to impatience.

And objection #4 is just this: I do not yet see how this instrumentalism is meant to proceed. I do not yet see how 'the normative ... becomes descriptive when the terminal parameter is expressed'. E.g. take this normative remark:

(67) Newton was warranted in accepting his laws of mechanics.

What descriptive remark does this 'become', when we express that the terminal parameter is prediction? It cannot be:

(68) Newtonian mechanics predicts many observations, getting none of them wrong.

because (68) has been disproven, while (67) remains very plausible. (The experiments that disproved (68) were irrelevant to (67); they showed nothing about Newton's evidentiary situation, and they came too late to influence it.) Nor can it be:

(69) It seemed likely to Newton that his laws of mechanics would predict many observations, getting none of them wrong.

because (69) says less than (67); (69) could be true even if Newton believed his theory on superstitious grounds. We might try replacing (67) with:

(70) Newton had good reason to expect that his laws of mechanics would predict many observations, getting none of them wrong.

and this is closer to the sense of (67); but here the normative has not become descriptive, on account of the phrase 'good reason'.

◆

Just now I have been reading Quine's 'normative naturalized epistemology' as an instrumentalism of the most direct kind – a good theory is one that predicts successfully – but perhaps more nuance is called for. Perhaps the 'normative naturalized epistemology' evaluates, not theories themselves, but methods of theorizing; and perhaps it evaluates a method, not by the actual predictions of any one theory, but by the method's overall tendency to produce theories that deliver successful predictions. This would be a second version of instrumentalism, hence a third version of the inclusion thesis, and it seems to be Quine's message here:

> Naturalized epistemology on its normative side is occupied with heuristics generally – with the whole strategy of rational conjecture in the framing of scientific hypotheses. In the present pages I have been treating rather of the testing of a theory after it has been thought up …; so I have passed over the thinking up, which is where the normative considerations come in. Ullian and I did go into it somewhat in *The Web of Belief*, listing five virtues to seek in a hypothesis: conservatism, generality, simplicity, refutability, and modesty. Further counsel is available anecdotally in the history of hard science. In a more technical vein, normative naturalized epistemology tangles with margin

of error, random deviation, and whatever else goes into the applied mathematics of statistics.[19]

This would explain why Quine sometimes wrote of conservatism as if it was on par with simplicity. It is not that he accorded conservatism the same status as I accord to simplicity, but rather the reverse: he accorded simplicity the same status as I accord to conservatism, viz. the status of a means to an end.[20] (Beware of terminological pitfalls. Where I distinguish norms from heuristics, Quine at this stage was counting everything but prediction as a heuristic, and he was identifying norms with heuristics.)

Moreover, this version would provide an answer to objection #4. We could replace (67) with:

(71) Newton arrived at his laws of mechanics by following methods that tend overall to produce empirically successful theories.

However, it is not clear that this version provides any answer to objections ##1–3. Also there is another objection: it seems to me that both the direct and indirect instrumentalisms are inconsistent with the view of predictions as *checkpoints*.

At any stage in our theorizing, we have past and present experience on one hand and the prospect of future experience on the other. As epistemologists we ought to declare our attitude to both. I declared mine in Chapter 3:

> When our theory leads us to expect experience to go a certain way, and actual experience does not comply, we understand that, somewhere along the line, the theory is at fault. …
>
> The experiences that count here are experiences (ours or others') that we already know about, not experiences that we are yet to discover. Naturally we have an interest in predicting the future, but, in each moment, as we contemplate our choices, we must go on what we have.

When Quine wrote of checkpoints he seemed to agree, because a checkpoint does not check our theory until we reach it. (Future experience *will* check our theory, but by then it will be present or past experience.) However, if Quine and I agree on that point, then what are we to make of his words 'purpose' and 'end', or 'terminal parameter' and 'engineering'?

Thus suppose we face a choice among three theories (or, if you prefer, three methods) *A*, *B*, *C*, such that

- *A* would have us report past experience accurately, but it stands a high chance of having us mispredict some future experience,

- *B* would have us misreport some past experience, but it stands a lower chance than *A* of having us mispredict any future experience, and
- *C* would have us report past experience accurately, *and* it stands the same chance as *B* of having us mispredict future experience; but *C* is more complex than *A* or *B*.

If we were *engineers*, whose *purpose* or *end* or *terminal parameter* is accurate prediction, then, since *B* and *C* are better instruments than *A*, and *B* is simpler than *C*, we would choose *B* now. But that is the wrong choice, since *B* has failed a checkpoint. So what is left of the claim that epistemology is engineering?

♦

I look to epistemic norms as a way to decide *which theory to accept*, and so far I have assumed that Quine's instrumentalisms were directed to that question. Accordingly I have read the direct instrumentalism as telling us *to accept* whichever theory is the best instrument of prediction, and I have read the indirect instrumentalism as telling us *to accept* whichever theory is produced by methods that tend to produce the best instruments of prediction. But the following passage suggests that Quine sought norms to answer a different question: not 'What to accept?' but 'What to *test*?':

> For a richer array of norms, vague in various degrees, we may look to the heuristics of hypothesis: how to think up a hypothesis worth testing. This is where considerations of conservatism and simplicity come in, and, at a more technical level, probability and statistics.[21]

I agree that we must at times decide which hypothesis to test, and Quine may be right about how we should decide; but that is not my topic. All I wish to say about it is that, even if we become experts in choosing testworthy hypotheses, the question 'What to accept?' does not go away. Even in the best of cases, where we correctly identify all the testworthy hypotheses and then, through a series of tests, reject all of them but one, that does not settle whether we should accept the one. It is a separate question.

Or, to come at the point another way, imagine a scientist who has in her laboratory some apparatus for measuring the effect of physical quantity x on physical quantity y, *ceteris paribus*. She can vary x at will and measure y but, no matter how many $<x, y>$ pairs she collects in this way, there are infinitely many possible laws of the form '$y = f(x)$' that fit the whole collection. Eventually we may say 'Choose the simplest!', but that had better not be advice about which law to *test*, because the experiments that would test the simplest law are the same experiments as would test all the others, viz. setting x to untried values and measuring y. But then what could our interjection be, except advice about what to accept?

♦

In this chapter I have criticized Quine's several attempts to find normative epistemology inside the web of theory that it commends to us, but all along I have been puzzled as to what motivated those attempts. When he wrote on moral values, Quine had no trouble acknowledging 'the deep old duality of thought and feeling, of the head and the heart, the cortex and thalamus, the words and the music';[22] so what made him so allergic to the other deep duality, the duality of epistemic norms and theory?

Here he cites two motivations:

> Naturalism has two sources, both negative. One of them is despair of being able to define theoretical terms generally in terms of phenomena, even by contextual definition. ... The other negative source of naturalism is an unregenerate realism, the robust state of mind of the natural scientist who has never felt any qualms beyond the negotiable uncertainties internal to science.[23]

I concur with both points, but for me they do not motivate the inclusion thesis; they motivate something else. We should hold philosophers' descriptions of reality to the same standards as scientists' descriptions of reality, and thus we should find a system of norms that we can apply even-handedly to both. In this book I have argued that Quine, in his practice as a describer of reality, excelled in following the same norms that he would expect a scientist to follow. That, for me, is the naturalism that Quine's motivations motivate.

If he had gone on to find his epistemic norms inside his theory of reality, that would have been an interesting further development, but he did not. Quine looked into his theory of reality, expecting to find his epistemic norms, and turned up a series of other things instead.

15

Attitudes to sets of *possibilia*

In Chapter 9 I proposed that we regiment common-sense propositional attitude ascriptions by simultaneously (i) recasting their attitudinative verbs as two-place predicates and (ii) replacing their 'that'-clauses with definite descriptions of objects of some sort. Chapter 9 left open the question 'Objects of what sort?', to which Chapter 10 was quick to answer 'Sentences', and we carried on from there; but we could have made a different choice.

It is sometimes said that vernacular 'that'-clauses refer to propositions. It is also sometimes said that propositions are sets of possible worlds. Taken separately, I find each statement difficult to evaluate, but in combination they suggest a coherent answer to Chapter 9's question. That answer is: replace the 'that'-clauses by definite descriptions of sets of possible worlds.

I understand that answer, and I reject it. David Lewis argued that, as objects of the attitudes, sets of possible worlds do not work as well as sets of possible individuals do, and I defer to Lewis's arguments on that point.[1] So my attention turns to Lewis's alternative plan. Should we replace 'that'-clauses by descriptions of sets of possible individuals? That is the question for this chapter.

◆

According to Lewis, this is what a subject believes:

> a class of possible individuals – call them the believer's *doxastic alternatives* – who might, for all he believes, be himself. Individual X is one of them iff nothing that the believer believes, either explicitly or implicitly, rules out the hypothesis that he himself is X.[2]

E.g. if Errol believes $\{x \mid x \text{ is tall}\}$ – the set of all possible individuals who are tall – then Errol believes that he himself is tall. Notice, though, that if this is the case then Errol doesn't believe that he is dark, because being dark would distinguish him from some members of $\{x \mid x \text{ is tall}\}$, viz. the fair ones. Nor does Errol believe that he is handsome, because being handsome would distinguish him from some members of $\{x \mid x$ is tall$\}$, viz. the ugly ones. So the ascription 'Errol believes $\{x \mid x$ is tall$\}$' is not a regimentation of 'Errol believes that he is tall'. It is a regimentation of 'Errol believes that he is tall, and that is all that Errol believes'.

If Errol believes that he is tall *and* believes that he is dark *and* believes that he is handsome, and that is all he believes, then the correct thing to say, on Lewis's view, is 'Errol believes $\{x \mid x$ is tall and x is dark and x is handsome$\}$'. A subject has just one set of doxastic alternatives; not one set per belief that folk psychology ascribes to him.

If Errol believes that he is tall, but we do not know what else he believes, then we cannot say exactly which set he believes; we can only say 'All members of the set that Errol believes are tall'; or more briefly: 'All Errol's doxastic alternatives are tall'. That leaves us free to add 'Moreover, all his doxastic alternatives are dark' etc. as we find out more about Errol.

As it is for belief, so it is for desire. A subject desires a set of possible individuals. 'Errol desires $\{x \mid x$ is tall$\}$' regiments 'Errol wants to be tall, and that is all he wants'. 'Errol desires $\{x \mid x$ is tall and x is dark and x is handsome$\}$' regiments 'Errol wants to be tall and wants to be dark and wants to be handsome, and that is all he wants'. 'All members of the set that Errol desires are tall' regiments 'Errol wants to be tall'.

As we have the phrase 'doxastic alternative' for each member of the set that a subject believes, it will be convenient to coin the phrase '*orectic alternative*' for each member of the set that a subject desires. Then our regimentation of 'Errol wants to be tall' is 'All Errol's orectic alternatives are tall'; and we are free to add 'Moreover, all his orectic alternatives are dark' etc. as we find out more.

What I have just given is an oversimple sketch of Lewis's theory. The theory that Lewis actually held is three amendments away.

Firstly, Lewis recognized that belief and desire admit of degree, and he expressed that by saying that a subject divides his credence among different sets of doxastic alternatives. I have no objection to that aspect of the theory, but for brevity's sake I shall set it aside and continue to limit my attention to cases where belief and desire are all black and white (Chapter 9's Curtailment #5).

Secondly, subjects sometimes hold mutually inconsistent beliefs, or fail to believe some of the deductive consequences of their beliefs, and Lewis held that the deductively deficient mind is best viewed as fragmented. Let me set that aside too, but only for a while. I shall return to it.

Thirdly, the regimentation of individual folk ascriptions is not as straightforward as my examples about Errol suggest. Different cases call for different treatments. Here are some of the variations:

- Many folk ascriptions ascribe non-egocentric attitudes, e.g. 'Fred believes that all things decay'. We must recast such an ascription into egocentric form, e.g. 'Fred believes that he inhabits a world wherein all things decay', before proceeding further, e.g. to 'All Fred's doxastic alternatives inhabit worlds wherein all things decay'.
- Some folk ascriptions contain names of things other than the subject, e.g. 'Ralph believes that Ortcutt is a spy'. We cannot say 'All Ralph's doxastic alternatives inhabit worlds wherein Ortcutt is a spy', because Ortcutt does not exist in any worlds but ours. (Lewis's rejects trans-world identity.[3]) One alternative is to say 'All Ralph's doxastic alternatives inhabit worlds wherein a counterpart of (the actual) Ortcutt is a spy', with the counterpart relation understood as a type of similarity.
- Some folk ascriptions contain vacuous names, e.g. 'Sandra believes that Santa brings presents'. We cannot say 'All Sandra's doxastic alternatives inhabit worlds wherein a counterpart of the actual Santa brings presents', because there is no actual Santa. One alternative (though not one that we would choose, given Chapter 9's Curtailment #3) is 'Each of Sandra's doxastic alternatives is in a position to say truly, "Santa brings presents", and Sandra and her alternatives more or less understand what this sentence means.'

Lewis acknowledged these variations among others, and suggested that there might be still more.[4]

Nothing in our epistemology requires uniformity in the regimentation of folk ascriptions. It only requires a regimented psychology to account for the same observational data as folk psychology does – i.e. the behavioural data – and Lewis seemed to share this view:

> If the content of belief, as given in terms of the subject's doxastic alternatives, is not tied in any uniform and straightforward way to the truth of ordinary language ascriptions of belief, how is it tied down at all? I would say that it is tied down mainly by belief–desire psychology. We suppose that people tend to behave in a way that serves their desires according to their beliefs.[5]

And he gave an example,[6] in which a system of attitudes is ascribed based on the 'fit' between, on one hand, the attitudes, given in terms of doxastic and orectic alternatives, and, on the other hand, the subject's action. Moreover, Lewis acknowledged that belief–desire psychology involves more than the fit of attitudes to action: the ascribed attitudes should fit the passive behaviours that cause them⁷ as well as the active behaviours that they cause.⁸ Needless to say, I find all of this congenial.

◆

To accept Lewis's psychology, we must include sets of possible objects, and a fortiori possible objects themselves, in the domain of our quantifiers. For those who will not quantify over *possibilia*, Lewis's psychology is off limits.

In Chapter 8, I expressed a reluctance to quantify over *possibilia*, so is Lewis's theory off limits to me? Not quite. My reluctance was tentative. It was the result of not seeing what, of epistemic value, quantification over *possibilia* could offer; and I am open to education on that topic. If I can be shown that the best theory to account for observed behaviour is one that quantifies over *possibilia* (and sets thereof), then I might be persuaded, because in that event I will understand what the quantification buys.

Furthermore, if a Lewisian psychology succeeds in accounting for observed behaviour, then it might shed light on *which* possible objects we should quantify over. E.g. suppose we are unsure whether to quantify over possible entities that are green but not extended. If we have a Lewisian psychology up and running, then we can see how it works with, and then without, so quantifying. Perhaps 'with' lets the psychology account for behaviour that it cannot account for when we say 'without'; or perhaps there is no difference in behavioural coverage and 'without' makes the total theory simpler. In either case, we will have found a basis on which to choose. Thus a worked-out Lewisian psychology might provide what Lewis called 'principles of plenitude' (although the principles of plenitude that it provides might be different from any that Lewis investigated).⁹

◆

Lewisian ascriptions are extensional, i.e. their truth-values do not change when we substitute coextensive general terms or co-designating names. However, since we have taken to quantifying over possible objects, many general terms that would once have counted as coextensive do not count as coextensive now. E.g. 'cordate' and 'renate' are not coextensive, because some possible creatures are cordate but not renate or vice versa. So extensionality does not take us from:

(72) All Hannibal's orectic alternatives find a cordate thing.

to:

(73) All Hannibal's orectic alternatives find a renate thing.

Also we must take care with names. It is almost certainly a mistake to say:

(74) All Tom's doxastic alternatives inhabit worlds wherein Cicero denounced Catiline.

because Cicero and Catiline do not exist in any worlds but ours. We might be persuaded to say:

(75) All Tom's doxastic alternatives inhabit worlds wherein some counterpart of Cicero denounced some counterpart of Catiline.

in which case extensionality would indeed license the inference to:

(76) All Tom's doxastic alternatives inhabit worlds wherein some counterpart of Tully denounced some counterpart of Catiline.

but that just shows that we should only say (75) when we mean to regiment an ascription of belief *de re*. (Lewis had other proposals for regimenting ascriptions of attitudes *de dicto*.[10])

Some philosophers (the 'linguistic ersatzists') have identified possible worlds with linguistic entities, e.g. set-theoretic constructs of some sort with sentences or other linguistic items at their base. Lewis, however, made no such identification. According to Lewis, a subject's doxastic and orectic alternatives are physical beings, rather like the subject herself, and the worlds that they inhabit are physical worlds, rather like the world that the subject (and we) inhabit. This is Lewis's notorious modal realism.

Strange though it may seem, modal realism is helpful to us in two significant ways. Firstly, it allows us to ascribe attitudes without mentioning terms, so our psychological reasoning can operate with none of what Chapter 10 called 'term-introducing steps'. And secondly, the physicality of subjects' environments facilitates what Chapter 10 called 'bridging steps', i.e. steps of reasoning that take us from attitude ascriptions to reports of behaviour or vice versa. E.g. in place of Chapter 10's (12)–(14) and (15)–(17) we can have:

(77) Beth looks upon a bat.
(78) For any subject s, usually, if s looks upon a bat, then all s's doxastic alternatives are looking upon bats.

(79) ∴ Probably, all Beth's alternatives are looking upon bats.

(80) Fidus avoids Cicero.
(81) For any subject s, fairly often, if s avoids Cicero, then all s's doxastic alternatives inhabit worlds wherein the counterpart of Cicero is dangerous.

(82) ∴ There is a fair chance that all Fidus's doxastic alternatives inhabit worlds wherein the counterpart of Cicero is dangerous.

and the special laws (78) and (81) are readily generalized to:

(83) For any subject s and kind k, usually, if s looks upon a member of k, then all s's doxastic alternatives are looking upon members of k.
(84) For any subject s and object o, fairly often, if s avoids o, then all s's doxastic alternatives inhabit worlds wherein the counterpart of o is dangerous.

In Chapter 10 I referred to bridging steps and term-introducing steps as sententialism's two loose ends, and tying them off, in one way or another, kept us busy throughout Chapters 10–11. But if we accept Lewis's theory, including his modal realism, then there is nothing to tie off. Bridging steps are straightforward and there are no terms for term-introducing steps to introduce.

In Chapter 12 we saw other kinds of cases, where, as sententialists, we needed to mention non-designating names such as 'Santa Claus' and 'Schmesperus' in order to regiment various folk-psychological inferences. As Lewisians we would need to tackle those cases in other ways. I suspect it could be done, but I shall not pursue it here because I think I see a larger obstacle to accepting a Lewisian psychology.

◆

Observe the folk psychology of deduction: 'Sophie believes that Socrates is a human, and she believes that all humans are mortal; and then, at some time t, she deduces from those beliefs a belief that Socrates is mortal.' Folk psychology does not say much about the mechanism, but it does say loud and clear that something has changed: it says, 'Before t, Sophie didn't believe that Socrates is mortal, and after t she does.' And this is valuable information; it can help us to explain differences in Sophie's behaviour, post-t versus pre-t. Therefore a regimented psychology should also acknowledge some change of belief at t.

My focus is on cases where we know nothing about the subject's verbal behaviour. This is Chapter 9's Curtailment #3: I only consider cases where we do not know what language the subject speaks or writes, nor whether she speaks or writes at all. Some will say that we should not attribute deduction in such cases, so let me address that claim straight away, with the help of an example from Lewis Carroll.[11]

Consider the following folk ascriptions:

(85) Carl believes that no kitten that loves fish is unteachable.
(86) Carl believes that no kitten without a tail will play with a gorilla.

(87) Carl believes that kittens with whiskers always love fish.
(88) Carl believes that no teachable kitten has green eyes.
(89) Carl believes that no kittens have tails unless they have whiskers.

If Carl is an experienced trainer of kittens, and has always succeeded with the ones that love fish, and has made ichthyophagy a sufficient condition for entry to his kitten-training school, then folk psychology will count that bundle of behaviour as evidence for (85) – and it is all non-verbal. Similarly we could describe non-verbal behaviour that would count as evidence for each of (86)–(89). Furthermore, certain kinds of non-verbal behaviour would count as evidence for

(90) Carl believes that no kitten with green eyes will play with a gorilla.

E.g. Carl inspecting a kitten's eyes before admitting it to the gorilla cage, and excluding the green-eyed ones, might be evidence for (90). Clearly this is different from the behaviour that would be evidence for (85)–(89).

Thus we could have ample evidence for (85)–(89) and lack evidence for (90). Indeed, we could have ample evidence for (85)–(89) and have ample evidence *against* (90): perhaps Carl never looks at a kitten's eyes before admitting it to the gorilla cage (though he always looks for a tail then, and he looks at eyes before commencing training). If that is the case then folk psychology will say that (85)–(89) are true and (90) is false.

Nonetheless, the belief that (90) ascribes is a deductive consequence of the beliefs that (85)–(89) ascribe. So, if (85)–(89) are true and Carl is smart, then, at some time t when he is sitting quietly, a change might come over Carl such that, from t onwards, he inspects kittens' eyes before letting them into the gorilla cage, etc. Then folk psychology will say, 'Before t, Carl didn't believe that no kitten with green eyes will play with a gorilla, and after t he does.'

Can we tell the same story in Lewis's terms? If we regiment (85)–(89) in the most obvious way:

(91) All Carl's doxastic alternatives inhabit worlds wherein no kitten that loves fish is unteachable.
(92) All Carl's doxastic alternatives inhabit worlds wherein no kitten without a tail will play with a gorilla.
(93) All Carl's doxastic alternatives inhabit worlds wherein kittens with whiskers always love fish.
(94) All Carl's doxastic alternatives inhabit worlds wherein no teachable kitten has green eyes.
(95) All Carl's doxastic alternatives inhabit worlds wherein no kittens have tails unless they have whiskers.

(96) All Carl's doxastic alternatives inhabit worlds wherein no kitten with green eyes will play with a gorilla.

then we run into trouble, because (91)–(95) entail (96). To be clear: this is not an entailment of a belief by other beliefs; it is an entailment of a belief *ascription* by other belief *ascriptions*. The ascription (96) was true from the moment that (91)–(95) were true. So what changed at *t*?

Lewis was aware of a range of challenges in this vicinity, and he responded:

> The use of classes of *possibilia* to specify content is supposed to be discredited by the way it imputes logical omniscience. Not so. We have seen several ways for someone to fall into inconsistency, either by holding impossible beliefs or by holding possible beliefs that conflict with one another.[12]

Our cases do not involve *inconsistent* beliefs, so some of the remedies that Lewis was alluding to here do not help us. Note, also, that our cases do not involve a subject's attitudes to language, and that our puzzle is not about how to explain folk ascriptions, but about how to describe a subject's changing mental state directly in terms of doxastic alternatives. Consequently, when we scan Lewis's menu of remedies, we find several that clearly cannot help us, and only one that looks like it might:

> Consider an everyday failure to draw a conclusion from several premises that one believes. Stalnaker (*Inquiry*, chapter 5) has shown how this can be explained as a case of compartmentalised thinking. Take the simplest way to believe something: a proposition holds throughout your doxastically accessible worlds. Suppose that you believe that P, also you believe that Q, and P and Q jointly imply R in the sense that every world that is both a P-world and a Q-world is also an R-world. We may even suppose that *none* of your doxastically accessible worlds is an R-world. How can this be? – The answer is that you may be thinking double, with P and Q in different compartments. You believe that P by believing it in one system; that one gives you doxastically accessible worlds where P holds but Q and R do not. You believe that Q by believing it in the other system; that one gives you doxastically possible worlds where Q holds but P and R do not. Thus you believe P and you believe Q, though in both cases half-heartedly; but you whole-heartedly disbelieve the conjunction of P and Q, and you whole-heartedly disbelieve R. You fail to believe the consequence of your two premises taken together so long as you fail to take them together.[13]

Transplanting this idea from Stalnaker's theory to Lewis's, the claim is as follows: A logically deficient subject has multiple sets of doxastic alternatives, each set being one compartment of her fragmented mind. E.g. Sophie before *t* had compartments C1 and C2. All the doxastic alternatives in C1 inhabited worlds wherein Socrates is a human, but not all of them inhabited worlds wherein all humans are mortal, and not all of them inhabited worlds wherein Socrates is mortal. Meanwhile all the doxastic alternatives in C2 inhabited worlds wherein all humans are mortal, but not all inhabited worlds wherein Socrates is a human, and not all inhabited worlds wherein Socrates is mortal. Now we *can* say what changed at *t*. C1 and C2 merged into a single compartment C3. Merging is by intersection, so all members of C3 inhabit worlds wherein Socrates is human *and* inhabit worlds wherein all humans are mortal *and* (consequently) inhabit worlds wherein Socrates is mortal.

Perhaps this much is manageable; but, if we accept the Stalnaker–Lewis idea that deduction is the merging of compartments, we cannot stop here. Every deduction will reduce the number of compartments by at least one, so if a subject is going to spend next week performing a thousand deductions, then the number of her compartments will be reduced by at least one a thousand times over. Ergo she must have at least a thousand and one compartments now. This doctrine might be called 'the complexity of simpletons' because, the more deductions a subject has yet to draw, the more compartments she must have; or it might be called 'the genius of singletons', because only a subject who has drawn all possible deductions from her beliefs can have a single compartment. Can we accept all this?

I think not, or at least not yet. Earlier in this chapter we observed the ease with which Lewis's theory let us regiment bridging steps, e.g. as (77)–(79) and (80)–(82); but then we were using the phrase 'all *s*'s doxastic alternatives' with no regard to compartments. If we now say that typical subjects have compartments in the thousands, then we need to rewrite those bridging steps; but how? Not like this:

(97) Beth looks upon a bat.
(98) For any subject *s*, usually, if *s* looks upon a bat, then, for some compartment *c*, all *s*'s doxastic alternatives in compartment *c* are looking upon bats.

---

(99) ∴ Probably, for some compartment *c*, all Beth's alternatives in compartment *c* are looking upon bats.

This will not do because its conclusion is too indefinite. If we are to reason about deductions in the way we have just been envisaging, then we will need some ascription like 'All Beth's alternatives in compartment C3829 are looking upon bats'. The step from (97) and (98) to (99) does not deliver that, and right now I cannot conceive of any bridging step that would.

That is not to say that Lewis's theory, or something like it, will never be developed into a successful regimentation of folk psychology. It might, but, for those who attempt it, the moral of this chapter is as follows. Belief ascriptions must fit into both bridging steps and an account of deduction, so we should not optimize them for one of those parts of our theory to the neglect of the other. We should all strive to merge our compartments.

16

The mythical given

Could a theory to be linked to a person's senses, in such a way that the theory changes in response to sensory input? Yes, of course it could. It is a conspicuous fact that most people's theories change in response to present sights, sounds and smells, and whatever does happen could happen. Next question please.

The next question is normative: granted that it could, *should* a theory be linked to a person's senses, in such a way that it changes in response to sensory input? Again, yes. The empiricism that we chose in Chapters 3–5 commits us to 'yes', but even apart from that, 'yes' to the second question seems almost as obvious as 'yes' to the first. Why would anyone dispute it?

To understand the controversy, we must understand that empiricists invariably go further than answering 'yes' to the preceding two questions, and that it is in the going further that they run the risk of going wrong. But empiricism per se is not destined to go wrong. In this chapter we shall see some of the traps that fellow empiricists have walked into, and check that we have not walked into the same or similar ourselves.

◆

In normative epistemology, how you go depends on how you begin, and one traditional beginning is the question 'What supports my beliefs?' The normative word here is 'support': if x supports y, in the relevant sense, then x is a good reason for y, in contrast to a bad reason or mere cause.

Apparently some beliefs are supported by one or more other beliefs, but if that were the only kind of support then there would be either an infinite regress or a circle. A traditional empiricist solution to this traditional problem runs as follows: 'Some beliefs are supported by one or more other beliefs, and some beliefs are supported by experience directly.' Call this *foundational empiricism*.

Foundational empiricism postulates a special class of beliefs that are supported by experience directly, but what are they? Are they beliefs about experience, or beliefs about ordinary things? Are any of them false? Could they be? Is one always aware of these beliefs, when one has them? Are there enough of them to represent the whole truth about one's experience, or do some truths about experience go unbelieved? These are dangerous questions, because they can lure the normative epistemologist beyond the business of sorting the justified beliefs from the unjustified, into dubious speculation about what beliefs there are. Moreover, ever since Wilfrid Sellars coined the phrase 'Myth of the Given',[1] the idea that experience directly supports any beliefs at all has come under fire; thus Davidson: 'Nothing can count as a reason for holding a belief except another belief.'[2] Even the assumption that there are beliefs has been questioned; thus Stich: 'It is too early to say whether folk psychology has a future.'[3] All in all, then, you and I can be glad that we are not tasked with explaining or defending foundational empiricism, having arrived, in Part One, at a position that is quite different from it.[4] Let me count four differences.

First, while foundational empiricism trains its normative scrutiny on beliefs, our normative scrutiny is directed only to theories and, derivatively, to accepted sentences. (In Part Three we took a normative stance towards various candidate belief ascriptions, but never towards the beliefs themselves.)

Second, while foundational empiricism postulates a relation of support that holds between one or more beliefs and another belief, our Quinean empiricism has no analogue of that relation. A totality of experience can support a total theory, yes; and in the special case of formal deduction we can make clear sense of the idea that premises support a conclusion; but, outside of that special case, we do not postulate a relation of support that holds between a set of sentences and a single sentence. Our standard of justification is holistic: a total theory is justified for person(s) A iff it is the simplest sufficiently logically explicit total theory available to A that is empirically correct vis-à-vis the totality of experience available to A; and, derivatively, a sentence is justified for A iff it is part of the total theory that is justified for A. On this view, when we cite some list of sentences as premises in an inductive or abductive argument with conclusion c, those sentences do not justify c; their role is, rather, to prompt some cohort of readers or listeners to apprehend that c is justified, for themselves, according to the holistic standard just defined. And the same holistic standard applies in cases where no premises are cited, such as when we adopt a system of mathematical axioms, or a system of ontology, or even a system of deductive logic.

Third, while foundational empiricism postulates a relation of support that holds between experience and a belief, our epistemology has no analogue of that relation either. That is to say, we do not postulate a relation of support that holds between experience and a single sentence. Of our three norms, the two that mention experience are the norm of empirical correctness and the norm of sufficient logical explicitness, and they mention it only as a source of constraint on theory acceptance.

And fourth, I disagree with foundational empiricism on a more primal level, independent of the particular epistemology we chose in Chapters 3–5. Whereas foundational empiricism is purpose-built to fill a demand for support, my view, from Chapter 1, is that the purpose of normative epistemology is to guide decisions. To home in on this difference, let us pretend for just a moment that beliefs are the objects of our normative scrutiny, and assume that there is a category of beliefs that the believer is literally unable to give up. Then I would say that these beliefs are beyond the proper scope of norms.[5] They are the points at which no decision, either to believe or not to believe, can have any effect, so any energy spent treating them normatively, e.g. by inquiring into their support, is misdirected. It is lost motion, to say nothing of lacking a virtue that Reinhold Niebuhr called 'the serenity to accept the things I cannot change'.[6]

◆

Whatever traps foundational empiricism may have wandered into, at the nexus of experience and belief, we can be sure that our holistic empiricism has not followed in its exact footsteps. But might it, perhaps, run into some analogous hazard, or indeed some other hazard, at the nexus of experience and theory?

I have been using 'experience' as a term of folk psychology, rather than of any regimented psychology. To reason about experience, in this sense, requires informal logic, and, though we have not entirely renounced informal logic, we know that it conceals presuppositions and commitments (Chapter 5). So let us dig deeper into our uses of the term 'experience'.

In our suite of norms, the two that mention experience are the norm of empirical correctness and the norm of sufficient logical explicitness, each of which only mentions it in the context 'conflict with experience'. So conflict, not support, is the nexus we need to examine.

Conflict is not confined to conflict between an individual's theory and the same individual's experience. On the contrary, *our* theory can be in conflict with *other people's* experience. Suppose, for instance, that our ancient history tells us that a certain civilization was flourishing at a certain place on Earth in a certain year BCE, and that, throughout that year, the whole civilization saw nothing noteworthy in the sky. Now suppose that our astronomy tells us that a certain comet cast light as bright as the sun's onto that place for several days and nights of that year. If we hold our ancient history fixed, then we can informally deduce that the ancient people experienced an ordinary sky all year. Meanwhile we can informally deduce from our astronomy that they did not experience an ordinary sky all year. So, while we continue to hold our ancient history fixed, we can say that *our* astronomy generates a conflict with *their* experience, and so we ought to revise our astronomy.[7]

This fragment of normative reasoning is redundant, though, because we can also come to revise our astronomy via a straightforward, non-normative argument. Again holding our ancient history fixed, we can (i) deduce that the ancients' experience was thus and so, (ii) deduce that if our astronomy is all true then their experience was not thus and so, and then (iii) deduce by modus tollens that our astronomy is not all true.

As a possible further improvement, we might one day formalize this non-normative argument. To do so would require a regimented psychology which, if it follows any of the leads proposed in Chapters 10–12, will include laws that bridge between ascriptions of the ancients' attitudes and descriptions of the (distal or proximal) inputs that caused those attitudes. At that point, the term 'experience' would drop out.

So we could, at least in principle, eliminate a fragment of informal normative reasoning about conflict with experience, and replace it with formal, non-normative reasoning that is free of the interesting words 'conflict' and 'experience'. Shall we, therefore, congratulate ourselves that, in the long run, these words give us nothing to worry about? No; that would be premature, for two reasons.

The first is that we might not be able to repeat the elimination for every example. The prospect of elimination in the comet example depends on the fact that a single total theory (ours) that conflicts with experience (because it includes our astronomy) also contains a verbal account of the experience with which it conflicts (because it includes our ancient history); but we have not established that the same holds for every instance of conflict with experience. We need to consider a wider range of conflicts.

The second reason is that, within the scope of the comet example, the elimination only applies to one step of our reasoning, and there are more steps to look into. Our decision to revise astronomy depends also on our decision to hold ancient history fixed, which comes down to a cost–benefit analysis: if replacing our current ancient history with an empirically correct, sufficiently logically explicit rival that is consistent with our current astronomy would add more complexity than would be added by replacing our current astronomy with an empirically correct, sufficiently logically explicit rival that is consistent with our current ancient history, then we should keep the ancient history; and if not, not. Which way we go will depend *(inter alia)* on numerous further decisions about which theories are empirically correct and sufficiently logically explicit, hence numerous further decisions about which theories lead, formally or informally, to conflicts with experience. So again: we need to consider a wider range of conflicts.

◆

Now let us consider *synchronous intrasubjective conflict*, i.e. conflict between the theory an individual holds and some experience that the same individual has while holding it. This is what Quine seemed to have in mind when he used the expressions 'conflict with experience' (see Chapter 3) and 'recalcitrant experience' (see Chapter 4).

It is tempting to speculate that every experience brings with it some sort of report, which becomes lodged in the experiencer's theory whether the experiencer's epistemic norms approve of it or not. E.g. it is tempting to speculate that every English speaker who has a headache ineluctably acquires 'I have a headache', and that every English speaker who sees what looks to her like a hand ineluctably acquires 'Here is a hand'; thus Peirce:

> Even after the percept is formed there is an operation which seems to me to be quite uncontrollable. It is that of judging what it is that the person perceives.[8]

If this speculation were true, then perhaps each recalcitrant experience would bring a recalcitrant report; and if it did then we would be on familiar ground: the experiencer-cum-theorist could reason, either normatively or non-normatively, from the recalcitrant report to a revision of the rest of her theory.

Now the first thing I want to say about this speculation is that it holds a grain of truth, or at least it seems to me that it does, because usually (and perhaps always), when I have a sufficiently vivid experience (or perhaps any experience), I am compelled to accept some new sentence. But that is not to say that there is some particular new sentence that I am compelled to accept.

Occasionally there might be some particular new sentence that I am compelled to accept; e.g. when I have a headache, I might be compelled to accept 'I have a headache', but that is an unusual case. More often, there is leeway. E.g. when I see what looks like a hand in front of me, I might come to accept 'Here is a hand', and most times I do, but if I have the same experience while other strands of my theory say that I am watching a 3D movie, then I will not accept 'Here is a hand', and will accept 'Here is a stereoscopic projected image of a hand' instead; and if I cannot decide whether I am watching a 3D movie or not, then I will accept neither of those sentences, and venture to describe phenomena of shape and colour. Or when I am looking at a straight stick half submerged in water, I might be inclined to accept 'Here is a bent stick' but, because my theory includes some rudimentary optics, I accept 'Here is a straight stick' instead.

What, then, does it take for my current theory to conflict with my current experience?

Consider the stick. On one side, the side of theory, I deduce from historical information and mechanical laws that the stick is straight, then I apply laws of optics to deduce that, if the stick were in such-and-such a location and orientation and half submerged in water, the light arriving at my eyes would be the same as if the water was absent and the stick was bent. On the other side, the side of experience, I have an initial but inconclusive tendency to report 'Here is a bent stick' – inconclusive because it is subject to pushback from the side of theory. Yet there are limits to the legitimate pushing back. Theory may push me to replace a prima facie report (e.g. 'Here is a bent stick') with an amended report (e.g. 'Here is a straight stick'), but only if what I experience is compatible with what the theory, together with the amended report, leads me to expect to experience. If what I experience is incompatible with what the theory alone leads me to expect to experience, then no amended report can meet this condition. That is when conflict strikes: that is when I need to revise my theory.

A short time ago, we set out to examine the phrase 'conflict with experience', to make sure that it would not ensnare us in any way. In the comet example, we came up with a plan to eliminate the interesting terms 'conflict' and 'experience' from a fragment of our reasoning, so that, if their occurrence in that fragment led us into any kind of trouble, we would have a way out. Lately I have been trying to repeat the same modest accomplishment for cases of synchronous intrasubjective conflict, and the exercise has brought me around to depend on the terms 'incompatible' and 'experience'. The last part does not look like progress. For cases of synchronous intrasubjective conflict, therefore, we had better try something else.

♦

Perhaps Quine can offer us something. He had a great deal to say about the connection of theory to the theorist's input. It featured in many of his writings on scientific method, as well as on the learning and translation of language. He considered theories' connections to both distal and proximal inputs, and along the way he defined several salient categories of sentences – occasion sentences, observation sentences, observation categoricals and others – and treated some of those categories to different definitions in different publications. Through all the variations, though, there was one consistent message: a theory's connection to inputs goes via a subset of the theory's sentences. The following passage is typical:

> The sentences most directly connected with sensory stimulation ... are occasion sentences of a special sort, which I call *observation* sentences. By this I do not mean to suggest that they are about observation, or sense data, or stimulation. Examples are 'It's raining', 'It's milk', ... An observation sentence is an occasion sentence that the speaker will consistently assent to when his sensory receptors are stimulated in certain ways, and consistently dissent from when they are stimulated in certain other ways. If querying the sentence elicits assent from the given speaker on one occasion, it will elicit assent likewise on any other occasion when the same total set of receptors is triggered; and similarly for dissent. This and this only is what qualifies sentences as observation sentences for the speaker in question, and this is the sense in which they are the sentences most directly associated with sensory stimulation. ...
>
> The problem of relating theory to sensory stimulation may now be put less forbiddingly as that of relating theory formulations to observation sentences.[9]

To its credit, this view avoids the myth, entertained by some earlier empiricists, that every theory, or at any rate every a posteriori justified theory, includes descriptions of pure sensory phenomena. It is a myth that Quine elsewhere derided as 'the fancifully fanciless medium of unvarnished news',[10] and I applaud both the avoidance and the derision. I am less enthusiastic, however, about Quine's positive contribution, because it seems to me that he replaced the old myth with a myth of his own.

Quine's myth is typified by his claim that 'It's milk' meets his criterion of an observation sentence for an individual speaker, i.e. 'that the speaker will consistently assent to [it] when his sensory receptors are stimulated in certain ways, and consistently dissent from [it] when they are stimulated in certain other ways'. Of course that is not true. We have seen how assent to 'Here is a hand' or to 'Here is a bent stick' is influenced by the presence of other elements in one's theory, and the same can be said of 'It's milk'. A speaker who assents to 'It's milk' today will dissent from it tomorrow, under identical conditions of retinal stimulation, if her theory includes 'It came from a cow' today and includes 'It came from a paint factory' tomorrow.

If 'Here is a hand' and 'Here is a bent stick' and 'It's milk' do not count as observation sentences, then it is safe to say that observation sentences, if they exist at all, are rare. Certainly they are too rare for Quine's contention that 'the problem of relating theory to sensory stimulation may ... be put ... as that of relating theory formulations to observation sentences'.

To be fair, though, the passage above is immediately followed by acknowledgement of three difficulties (which I shall not go into) and an amendment of the view, as follows:

> We can withdraw to what I may call *observation categoricals* – sentences like 'Where there is smoke there is fire' or 'When it rains it pours' or 'When night falls the lamps are lit'. ...
>
> Here, then, is further progress in relating scientific theory to its sensory evidence. The relation consists in the implying of true observation categoricals by the theory formulation. And how do we know when an observation categorical is true? We never do, conclusively, by observation, because each is general. But observation can falsify an observation categorical. We may observe night falling and the lamps not being lit. We may observe smoke and find no fire.[11]

Now notice: observation categoricals have 'component observation sentences'. This entails that, if observation sentences are the rare birds that I take them to be, then observation categoricals are also rare. (E.g. 'When night falls the lamps are lit' is not an observation categorical, because 'Night falls' is not an observation sentence, because one can assent to it and dissent from it on different occasions, under identical conditions of retinal stimulus, depending on whether one's theory includes 'There is a total solar eclipse here'.[12]) Certainly, observation categoricals are too rare for Quine's contention that 'the relation [of scientific theory to its sensory evidence] consists in the implying of true observation categoricals by the theory formulation'.

We have been considering Quine's definition of 'observation sentence' for an individual speaker, but, in his earlier writings,[13] Quine defined 'observation sentence' differently. What counted there was not the constancy of one subject's assent/dissent responses to the sentence under the same stimulation across different occasions, but rather the constancy of assent/dissent responses to the sentence under the same stimulation across different speakers in a population.[14] He eventually abandoned that definition, due to problems defining sameness of stimulation across speakers, but, even if those problems could be solved and the definition applied, it would remain the case that observation sentences are rare. E.g. 'Night falls' would still not be an observation sentence, because speaker *A* will assent to it and speaker *B* will dissent from it, under a stimulation that is the same for both, if *B*'s theory includes 'There is a total solar eclipse here' and *A*'s theory does not; and 'Here is a straight stick' would still not be an observation sentence, because speaker *C* will assent to it and speaker *D* will dissent from it, under a stimulation that is the same for both, if *C*'s theory includes rudimentary optics and *D*'s theory does not; and so on.[15]

◆

The scarcity of observation sentences, under each of Quine's definitions, has drawn the attention of Peter Hylton:

> So almost no sentences in fact satisfy [the social criterion for being an observation sentence]. A similar argument shows that the individualistic criterion is not satisfied, even by most sentences which might appear to satisfy it.[16]

but it worries Hylton less than it worries me:

> Most of Quine's discussions of cognitive language, of how it functions and of how it might be learnt, proceed as if observation sentences were simply responses to stimulation. That view is untenable, as Quine came to see in the last years of his working life. How large a change in his general views does this fact require? Some change is certainly needed, but I think it is relatively modest.[17]

and he proceeds to offer a revised account of observation sentences, in which observationality is a matter of degree.[18] While apparently retaining Quine's idea that, for each speaker *S* and sentence *p* that is observational for *S*, *S* is disposed to assent to *p* under some stimulatory conditions and to dissent from *p* under others, Hylton departs from Quine by admitting that inference sometimes overrides those dispositions. To take one of his examples, there are conditions of retinal stimulation that dispose me to assent to 'There's a horse'. If those conditions are met, but my theory includes 'There are no horses in this region', then there are two possibilities: either (i) I follow my disposition to assent to 'There's a horse', and revise my theory accordingly, or (ii) I follow a deduction from 'There are no horses in this region', and it overrides my disposition, leading me to say, perhaps, 'It looks like a horse but is not really one'. Acknowledging this complexity is no major disruption to Quine's general view about language, since Quine's view is well equipped to describe both (i) and (ii).

I am persuaded that Hylton's account improves upon Quine's, in that Hylton's account stands a better chance of being true. My only complaint is that it does not solve the problem that is exercising us here. For recall our pending question: 'What does it take for my current theory to conflict with my current experience?' If my current theory includes 'There are no horses in this region' and I am receiving a retinal stimulus that disposes me to assent to 'There's a horse', then Hylton's account tells us that my theory might conflict with my experience, which is possibility (i), or it might not, which is possibility (ii). It is right to recognize both possibilities, but in doing so it leaves our pending question unanswered.

In the horse example, whether my current theory conflicts with my current experience depends on further details of the case. In most cases, my current, horse-denying theory will conflict with my equinoform visual experience, so I will need to revise the theory; but, in cases where the stimulus is as of a white horse and the theory includes 'There are plenty of albino zebras around here', there will be no conflict and the theory can stay as it is. Likewise there will be no conflict, and the theory can stay as it is, if it includes 'I am watching a 3D movie' or 'I am under the influence of a powerful hallucinogen'. Intuitively, it is easy to say what distinguishes the no-conflict cases – they are the ones in which what I experience is compatible with what my total theory leads me to expect to experience – but putting it that way only takes us in a circle. We had better try something else.

♦

I have bickered with Quine over his errors of fact, beginning with his claim that 'It's milk' fits his definition of 'observation sentence' for an individual speaker, but there is a more basic difference here, between Quine and me. Quine's errors of fact were symptoms of his tendency to speculate on questions of fact, and, though the errors were undoubtedly inadvertent, the speculation was not. It was a deliberate feature of his naturalized epistemology (as well as of his reflections on language learning and translation). I, on the other hand, aim to cut speculation to a minimum. Expansive speculation has its place, but its place is not here. As I see it, empiricism has attracted too much needless controversy by carrying too much inessential doctrine, so I want to lighten its load.

For the time being, let us remain focused on synchronous intrasubjective conflict. I propose to break it down as follows: a subject's theory generates an experiential expectation, and then the subject's sensory input, in the presence of that expectation, causes a reaction of surprise.

By *'sensory input'* I mean physical input to the subject's sense organs. It should probably be defined as some kind of proximal input, e.g. the pattern of firings of receptors at the subject's surface, but for present purposes I only require that it is some kind of input that we can study scientifically, so we do not need to speculate about it.

Experiential expectations are mental states, but I make no comment on the details, such as whether they are contentful states of some kind, e.g. propositional attitudes, or whether, if they are, their content refers somehow to external objects, or to sensory input, or to private phenomena, or to anything else. All I can tell you about an experiential expectation is that it disposes its subject to be surprised by some types of sensory input and not by others. So, when ontological precision is called for, we can identify an experiential expectation with a set of types of sensory input, viz. those that it disposes its subject to be surprised by.[19]

Nor shall I speculate on the process by which a theory *generates* an experiential expectation. Formal and informal deductions clearly play some part in it, as do the various items of germane and collateral information that I mentioned in the examples above, but I do not pretend to understand the mechanism. In particular, I take no position on whether it is ever channelled through a single sentence.

Finally, I do not speculate on whether sensory input brings about a 'realistic' report, such as 'Here is a hand'; a 'phenomenalistic' report, such as 'Red patch now'; or no report at all. It suffices that sensory input, when it confounds an experiential expectation, brings 'Uh-oh'.

'Uh-oh' is not a sentence, so it cannot serve as premise in any argument for a revision of theory. However, every conflict with experience (which is what 'Uh-oh' signifies) triggers an epistemic norm – either the norm of empirical correctness or the norm of sufficient logical explicitness – to demand that the theory not be retained in toto. So, if you have an 'Uh-oh' moment, please do revise your theory. It is a matter, not of drawing an inference, but of following a prescription.

Objection:

Some of us find synchronous intrasubjective conflict mysterious because it is an interaction between a theory and a non-linguistic thing, viz. experience. I was hoping that your analysis would show how that gap is bridged. Much to my disappointment, however, it relies on *generation* (as in 'a theory generates an experiential expectation'), which is an unanalysed interaction between a theory and another non-linguistic thing, viz. an experiential expectation. So that is no help at all, and I'm calling it out as *obscurum per obscurius*.

Reply: I agree that generation is unanalysed, and even mysterious, but bear in mind two points:

First, the subject doesn't need to understand generation, i.e. she doesn't need to know how her experiential expectations are made. All I ask her to do with her experiential expectations is to notice when her sensory input confounds them, and then respond by not retaining her incumbent theory whole.

Second, I reject the insinuation that generation is obscure. Mysterious, yes; obscure, no. That is to say, though we don't understand generation yet, there is no obstacle to theorizing about it from a third-person psychological standpoint. It is an interaction between a set of sentences that the subject accepts and a set of physical input types by which she is disposed to be surprised. Granted, neither acceptance of sentences nor disposition to surprise is *directly* observable (Is anything?), but, by psychological standards, both are pretty well observable.

◆

Earlier we examined a category of conflict with experience, typified by the comet example, in which one total theory both conflicts with experience and contains a verbal account of the experience with which it conflicts. There we were able to cut a key occurrence of the phrase 'conflict with experience' from the reasoning that leads to a revision of theory, and to replace it with steps of non-normative reasoning that we could in principle formalize. Then we turned to the category of synchronous intrasubjective conflict, in which one individual, at one time, both holds the theory that conflicts with experience and has the experience with which it conflicts. There, after some false starts, we saw how a theorist who follows our epistemic norms could decide to revise her theory using very little reasoning at all.

This two-category survey did not reveal any troubling presuppositions behind the phrase 'conflict with experience'; but was it exhaustive? In other words, do the two categories between them cover every conflict with experience that matters to our epistemology, or are there some conflicts that we still need to discuss?

Let us step through the possibilities. When our epistemology calls upon a theorist A to revise her, his or its theory T ('its' for the case where A is a community) in response to a conflict with experience E, there are two cases: either E is some other party's experience, or E is A's own experience. In case 1 (E is another party's experience), A could only have learnt of E by theorizing, so A's theory must include some verbal account of E, and we can treat this like the comet example. In case 2 (E is A's own experience), A must be an individual, and we must distinguish three subcases. Subcase 2.1: E is in A's present. This, by definition, is synchronous intrasubjective conflict. Subcase 2.2: E is in A's distant, poorly remembered past. Here A's best strategy is to find out about E by theorizing historically, treating herself as she would some other party, and then subcase 2.2 falls in with the comet example.[20] This leaves subcase 2.3: E is in A's recent, well-remembered past.

Subcase 2.3 typically arises shortly after a synchronous intrasubjective conflict. At time t, A had been surprised by an experience E, so she ceased to accept her incumbent theory T in toto and started casting about for a replacement. Now, at time t plus a moment, E has finished and A is assessing one or more candidate replacements for T. She must reject any candidate that conflicts with experience; in particular, she must reject any candidate that conflicts with E; and when she rejects some candidate T' on the grounds that it conflicts with E, that is subcase 2.3. Let us look into it.

At this time, t plus a moment, A is both rich and poor: rich because E is still fresh in her non-verbal memory, and poor because, having not yet incorporated E into any theory, she has no coherent verbal account of it. The lack of a coherent verbal account prevents her from theorizing psychologically about E, so her only option is to use her non-verbal memory.

The conflict between T' and E is not synchronous intrasubjective conflict, because it is not synchronous; and anyhow our analysis of synchronous intrasubjective conflict does not fit it, because T' is too late on the scene to generate an expectation in whose presence E can cause surprise. We must, therefore, recognize 2.3 as a distinct category of conflict with experience. It resembles synchronous intrasubjective conflict, insofar as A cannot use a verbal account of E; but, since there is no real expectation and no surprise, A can only *model* the expectation that T' would have generated, and notice that the recalled experience falls outside the modelled expectation.

I did not speculate on how generation works, and I shall not speculate on how modelling and non-verbal recall work; but all those processes have to work somehow, in order for conflict with experience to be possible in the full range of cases in which our epistemology's prescriptions hinge upon it. To that extent, and only to that extent, I concede that our norms have speculative psychological presuppositions.

17

Epistemology as the theory of knowledge

A typical university handbook defines 'epistemology' as 'the theory of knowledge'. All going well, it attracts students who have a passion for knowledge. They soon learn that knowledge has been analysed as justified true belief, which gives them a reason to care about justification (as well as about truth and belief); and even when Gettier cases disrupt the 'justified true belief' analysis, justification retains its cachet as a necessary condition for knowledge – but only until Timothy Williamson turns up with his 'knowledge first' approach and turns the order of analysis upside down.

Needless to say, this book has not followed that script. Here, the concept of knowledge has been neither analysed nor used to analyse anything else. In fact, knowledge has scarcely been mentioned. Justification has held the spotlight, with no position taken on its relation to knowledge. This is because I have a more direct, and also more urgent, reason to care about justification.

I think of the physicists who disagree about the origin of the universe, or about the best way to understand quantum mechanics, though they have no quarrel with each other's calculations or experimental results. Accusations of metaphysics fly, with no consensus on how to resolve them, and similar scenes play out across the frontiers of other fields, including cognitive science, semantics and ontology. In conflicts of this type, it seems to me that the theoretical differences, about the origin of the universe or whatever the issue might be, are symptoms of underlying differences about justification. If only the parties could agree upon a set of epistemic norms – i.e. criteria of justification – and bring the agreed norms to bear on the already agreed observational data, then they would be better placed to agree on what they *should* say about the world; and from there it is a short step to agreeing what *to* say about it.

The short, final step is from asserting 'We are justified in asserting p' to asserting p. I hesitate to call it an inference. Perhaps it is, but I will avoid calling it one because that would invite the unhelpful question 'Is it a good inference?' – as though the justification for asserting the so-called conclusion (i.e. p) depended on both (i) the truth of the so-called premise (i.e. 'We are justified in asserting p') and (ii) some logical or probabilistic connection from the so-called premise to the so-called conclusion. Of course there is no such dependency: the speakers' justification for asserting p is assured by (i) alone.

Notice that this step only works in the first person: there is no equivalent step from asserting 'They are justified in asserting p' to asserting p. But, in case a critic tries to burden me with any dubious notions about privacy or internality of reasoning, please observe that I do not require the first-person singular. My paradigm is '*We* are justified in asserting p'.

Most importantly, notice that the step from asserting 'We are justified in asserting p' to asserting p does not mention knowledge. Therefore, if there is a need to mention knowledge anywhere en route to agreement on p, it must be en route to 'We are justified in asserting p'. But is there a need to mention knowledge there?

Williamson has proposed a 'knowledge first' analysis of justification,[1] which employs the concept of knowledge in the following way: a proposition is justified if and only if there is sufficient evidence for it, where evidence consists of propositions, and a necessary condition for one proposition being evidence for another is that the former proposition is known. In support of this view, he argues that any other account of 'evidence for' as a proposition-to-proposition relation mishandles various non-deductive inferences. Rather than working through the detail of those arguments, though, let us simply grant *arguendo* that they succeed, proving that every account but Williamson's of 'evidence for' as a proposition-to-proposition relation is wrong. Surely this has no bearing on the merits of our Quinean epistemology, which (i) eschews propositions in favour of sentences, and (ii) eschews the evidential relation between sentences in favour of the evidential relation between the totality of experience and the totality of theory.

◆

My thesis, so far, is that epistemology can accomplish one major purpose without ever mentioning knowledge. But what about other purposes? English speakers are always asking who knew what and when, so they must have powerful motives to ask those questions, mustn't they? And epistemology ought to help them decide the answers, oughtn't it?

I am about to make the case for 'no' and 'no'. It starts with a bang.

A loaded gun has been fired, causing the death of a person. Police have identified and apprehended the shooter. These facts are not in dispute. There is considerable dispute, however, about the shooter's state of mind. It has become the talk of the town. Some say that she intended to kill the victim, so she is highly culpable and deserves a severe sentence, while others say that she was attempting a foolish, reckless, but not murderous practical joke, so she is somewhat less culpable and deserves a lesser sentence. There are myriad details, but it always seems to come down to one question: *Did she know that the gun was loaded?*

If we look a bit more closely, albeit still at a folk-psychological level, we can distinguish four possible states of the shooter's mind:

1. She knew that the gun was loaded.
2. She believed truly, but without justification, that the gun was loaded.
3. She believed truly, and with justification, that the gun was loaded, but she did not know that the gun was loaded; i.e. it was a Gettier case.
4. She did not believe that the gun was loaded (though it was).

In cases 1–3, the shooter's culpability is high, and equally high in all three cases, whereas in case 4 her culpability is somewhat lower. Ergo the degree of her culpability depends on whether she believed that the gun was loaded, not on whether she knew.[2]

I am making an exceptionally shallow point. It is merely that the townsfolk misspoke when they asked 'Did she know that the gun was loaded?' No doubt they will now correct themselves with a shrug and carry on, and no doubt we should be directing our attention to other examples, where questions of knowledge are raised without any mistake. Very well, then; let us look for some.

Second example. If you need the name of the capital of Honduras, and you prefer not to waste your time, you might decide that whether you take the trouble to ask any potential informant S will depend on *whether S knows a lot of geography*. But now you consider asking Siri™, your digital assistant. A pedant objects that Siri does not meet your stated requirement, because Siri does not have knowledge, because knowledge requires belief, and Siri cannot have beliefs because her mental life is not rich enough, or because she lacks a body, or because she is made of semiconductors, or for some other reason in that vein. That is all very engaging, but it is never going to stop you from asking Siri. What you will say to the pedant is, 'For present purposes, none of that stuff matters. I'm sorry I ever mentioned knowledge. When I said that my decision to ask S would depend on S's knowledge of geography, I simply misspoke. I meant to say that my decision would depend on S's ability to provide true answers to geography questions.'

Third example. Someone has asked you the name of the capital of Honduras, and you are weighing up whether to answer 'I don't know' or to respond in some other way. If you take the word 'know' at face value, then you will take your task to be to decide *whether you know the name of the capital of Honduras*; and then, even if you are pretty sure that it's 'Tegucigalpa', you will need to evaluate your basis for that claim and also somehow work out whether you are under the influence of a Gettier condition. But surely your actual task is not that hard. Either you have some fairly firm belief that you can express in the form 'The capital of Honduras is N', and you spit out the name N, or you don't, and you say 'I don't know'. As Quine and Ullian put it:

> Are there an even number of Paul Smiths in Boston? Will it rain in Pontiac next Labor Day? English being what it is, we answer 'I don't know', because it would be misleading to say 'I don't believe so'. But our state is simple nonbelief.[3]

Fourth example. It is often said that the purpose of teaching is to impart knowledge. So, if you need to evaluate the performance of teacher T, you might suppose that it depends on *whether S knows that* p, for various S and p such that T has tried to teach S that p. That cannot be the right test, though, because it is uniform where the goals of teaching are various. E.g. someone teaching the next generation of London cab drivers needs to impart a great many true beliefs, while a philosophy teacher's excellence can be measured, more nearly, by the skills that she imparts; and there are many other variations. So, in order to assess teaching, you must (i) decide what attributes the particular teaching is supposed to impart, and (ii) measure the degree to which it imparts them. And then you can stop. You have completed the teaching assessment, and you did it without either (iii) deciding whether the attributes you identified are necessary and/or sufficient conditions for knowledge or (iv) deciding whether S knows that p, for any values of S and p.

Fifth example. Under easily imagined circumstances, we say that how a cat will behave depends on *whether it knows that the ball is behind the sofa*. In point of fact, however, a cat who believes falsely, or irrationally, or Gettierly, that the ball is behind the sofa will, for as long as the belief lasts, behave identically to a cat who knows. So the behaviour depends on whether the cat believes that the ball is behind the sofa. When we said that it depends on whether the cat knows, we simply misspoke.[4]

And so on. I invite the reader to extend the series. Spend some days observing situations where it is asked 'Does/did/will S know that p?', and in each case investigate whether the questioner's actual purpose requires an answer to that question, or whether it requires an answer to some other question instead. If your experience runs like mine, then you will only find more cases of casual misspeaking. Each case is humdrum and easily corrected, but it chips away at the motive for elucidating an elusive literal use of 'S knows that p'. The cumulative effect for me, and perhaps for you too, is that the traditional problem of clarifying the concept of knowledge, i.e. clarifying the conditions under which S knows that p, comes to be seen as one of the least important problems in epistemology.

That is not to say that I find 'Does S know that p?' uninteresting. On the contrary, if I am right that it is almost always (if not always) asked by mistake, and if the mistakes are readily acknowledged and corrected on a case-by-case basis by the speakers who make them, and yet the rifeness of the mistakes has escaped general notice, then, as a social phenomenon, 'Does S know that p?' is very interesting indeed.

◆

The worst case is that 'Does S know that p?' is always asked by mistake, and that complete sentences of the forms 'S knows that p' and 'S doesn't know that p' are never asserted for any purpose other than to answer a misbegotten question. But, even in that worst case, it does not follow that every instance of 'know' is dispensable, for the word occurs in other contexts.

In particular, there is 'S wants to know …'. Sentences of this form contribute to the folk-psychological reasoning that explains certain observable behaviours, such as reconnaissance and experimentation, so we should not discard them lightly; and if we do not discard them then we should regiment them; but the devil is in the detail.

One dimension of that detail is the variety of expressions that can replace the ellipsis, e.g. 'where the ball is', 'who is at the door', 'what's in the box', 'when the mail arrives', 'how to ride a bicycle', 'the price of eggs', 'the way to San Jose'. That, however, is not the dimension I wish to investigate today, so let me narrow the discussion to sentences of the form 'S wants to know whether p'.

On the face of it, a sentence of the form 'S wants to know whether p' ascribes a desire about knowledge, so we could try to regiment it as a desire ascription where the content of the desire is about knowledge. The first step would be to replace it with 'S desires that (S knows that p or S knows that not-p)'; and from there we could proceed to regiment 'S desires that …' and 'S knows that …' in whichever style we usually use for propositional attitude ascriptions, be it sententialist (Part Three), Lewisian (Chapter 15) or other.

If we take this line then, just as Chapter 9 introduced the predicates 'believes' and 'desires' as formal counterparts of the vernacular 'believes that' and 'desires that', we will need to introduce a predicate 'knows' as a formal counterpart of the vernacular 'knows that'. Currently our only use case for this predicate puts it inside the content sentence of 'desires', which might seem strange, but surely it is no stranger than having a formal counterpart of the name 'Santa Claus', when its only use cases put it inside attitudinal contents (Chapter 12).

So let me come to the thing that really is strange. Bears sniff the air. Meerkats stand on their hind legs. A hawk circles a field. These are reconnaissance behaviours, whose folk psychological explanations may include 'S wants to know whether p', where the subject S is a bear, a meerkat or a hawk. So, if we regiment 'S wants to know whether p' in the manner we are now considering, we will be ascribing a second-order propositional attitude to an animal. This is strange because we are usually quite reluctant to ascribe second-order propositional attitudes to animals. E.g. most of us would baulk at saying that a meerkat believes that it believes that p, or that it believes that it desires that p, or even that it desires that it believe that p. Second-order ascriptions seem to imply that the subject has self-awareness, which some elite species apparently do demonstrate,[5] but reconnaissance behaviour seems too low a bar.

Now strangeness does not make the second-order treatment wrong, so we could try to stick with it. On the other hand, though, we are not stuck with it. Here is another option: we could try treating wanting to know as a first-order propositional attitude. That is to say, we could introduce a formal predicate 'wantstoknow', syntactically on par with our formal predicates 'believes' and 'desires', and we could regiment 'S wants to know whether p' in the same way as we regiment 'S believes that p' or 'S desires that p', only with 'wantstoknow' in place of the formal 'believes' or 'desires'. This approach seems artificial, and it is, but (i) that doesn't make it wrong, and (ii) the artificiality is to some extent down to chance, since, if the vernacular 'S is curious whether p' had caught our eye before 'S wants to know whether p', then the first-order treatment would have been the natural one.

And of course there is the null option: we could discard 'S wants to know whether p' without regimentation, whenever S is an animal that we judge to be non-self-aware. Our formal theory would then have to get by without counterparts of some ordinary-language explanations of accipitral field-circling etc., but its cupboard need not be completely bare: there could still be a regimentation of 'The hawk circles the field because hawks have an instinct to circle fields', and even of 'The hawk circles the field because it wants food, and it believes, to some degree, that if it circles the field then it will get food.'

So we have at least three options: we can extend our formal language with second-order attitude ascriptions to non-self-aware animals, we can extend it with a new class of first-order attitude ascriptions, or we can not extend it. The merits of any extension depend, as always, on its ability to simplify theory by converting unstructured data into deducible consequences (Chapter 3, Chapter 8), the unstructured data being, in this case, reports of observed reconnaissance behaviour by animals.

Thus we cannot judge either proposed extension by its ascriptions alone. We need to see, for each extension, the web of formal inferences that connect its ascriptions to the behavioural reports. So someone, philosopher or scientist, needs to design that web; but I hope you'll agree that 'philosopher or scientist' is a distinction without a difference.

Notes

Part One

1 Albert Einstein, 'Remarks Concerning the Essays Brought Together in This Co-operative Volume', in *Albert Einstein: Philosopher-Scientist*, ed. P. A. Schilpp (Evanston, IL: Library of Living Philosophers, 1949), 683–4. © The Hebrew University of Jerusalem, with permission of the Albert Einstein Archives.

1 Wanted: A normative epistemology in working order

1 Karl Popper, *Conjectures and Refutations*, 1963, 4th ed. (London: Routledge and Kegan Paul, 1972), 34.
2 Cf. the first two sentences of René Descartes's *Meditations*:

> Some years ago I was struck by how many false things I had believed, and by how doubtful was the structure of beliefs that I had based upon them. I realized that if I wanted to establish anything in the sciences that was stable and likely to last, I needed – just once in my life – to demolish everything completely and start from the foundations. (Descartes, *Meditations on First Philosophy*, 12)

Sentence one is similar to the early Popper, but the similarity ends in sentence two, where, rather than itemizing the 'many false things' and asking how they differ from other things, Descartes's mind turns to 'anything' and 'everything' – and to 'foundations'.

2 Epistemological dissociative disorder

1 The phrase 'leading to' worries me a little: if it means that the discoveries *should* lead the hero, *insofar as the hero is rational*, to the revised history, then it presupposes some set of epistemic norms, which in the present context would be question-begging. However, for the sake of the argument, I won't press that point.
2 Albert Einstein, *The Collected Papers of Albert Einstein*, edited by John Stachel, David C. Cassidy and Robert Schulmann (Princeton, NJ: Princeton University Press, 1994), 325.

3 Huw Price, 'Metaphysics after Carnap: The Ghost Who Walks?', 2007, in *Metametaphysics: New Essays on the Foundations of Ontology*, ed. D. Chalmers, D. Manley and R. Wasserman (Oxford: Clarendon Press, 2009), 321.
4 David Lewis, *On the Plurality of Worlds* (Oxford: Blackwell, 1986), 133.
5 W. V. Quine, 'Has Philosophy Lost Contact with People?', 1979, in *Theories and Things* (Cambridge, MA: Harvard University Press, 1981), 193.

3 Empiricism without (even mentioning) the dogmas

1 W. V. Quine, 'Two Dogmas of Empiricism', in *From a Logical Point of View: Nine Logico-Philosophical Essays*, 20–46 (Cambridge, MA: Harvard University Press, 1953), 42–3.
2 Ibid., 44.
3 Ibid., 45.
4 Some commentators have read Quine as offering general criteria for the confirmation of a part of one's total theory, and found that Quine, so interpreted, gets a great deal wrong. E.g. Elliott Sober writes:

> Quine's holism has a consequence that is even more radical. If I believe relativity theory, and this theory is confirmed by some observation that I make, then *everything* I believe is also confirmed. … [I]f I believe X and Y, anything that confirms X also confirms Y, even when X and Y are thoroughly unrelated. (Sober and Hylton, 'Quine,' 266)

Moral: do not read Quine as giving general criteria for the confirmation of relativity theory, or of any other X or Y that is less than one's total theory.
5 This conspicuous fact has not deterred some philosophers from questioning whether the norm should, or even could, guide us. Chapter 16 addresses this (to me rather surprising) controversy.
6 David Hume, *A Treatise of Human Nature* (Oxford: Clarendon Press, 1949), 196.
7 In *The Web of Belief*, Quine and Ullian went so far as to list *generality* as a virtue on par with simplicity. They, however, were discussing the virtues of individual hypotheses. When we are evaluating total theories, we can see the generality of a hypothesis as an aspect of simplicity, rather than as a separate norm, because, the more general the hypotheses, the more sentences it obviates from the compact presentation.
8 Is this the much-discussed 'indispensability argument'? I hesitate to say that it is, because the latter is sometimes characterized as something apart from the pursuit of simplicity. See, e.g. Gary Ebbs, 'Carnap and Quine on Truth by Convention',

in *Carnap, Quine, and Putnam on Methods of Inquiry* (Cambridge: Cambridge University Press), 60.
9 Here is the same point in the words of the later Quine:

> There is also another consideration, equally familiar, that incontestably gives truth a transcendent status in any likely sense of that redoubtable term. Namely, usage dictates that when in the course of scientific progress some former tenet comes to be superseded and denied, we do not say that it used to be true but became false. The usage is rather that we thought it was true but it never was. Truth is not the product of science, but its goal. It is an ideal of pure reason, in Kant's apt phrase. (Quine, 'Where Do We Disagree?', 164)

4 Conservatism is not a third norm

1 Carl Sagan, 'The Burden of Skepticism', *Skeptical Inquirer* 12 (Fall 1987). https://skepticalinquirer.org/1987/10/the-burden-of-skepticism/.
2 David Christensen, 'Conservatism in Epistemology', *Noûs* 28, no. 1 (March 1994): 69.
3 Quine, 'Two Dogmas of Empiricism', 43–6.
4 W. V. Quine, *The Roots of Reference* (La Salle: Open Court, 1974), 137–8; W. V. Quine and J. S. Ullian, *The Web of Belief* (New York: Random House, 1978), ch. 4.
5 W. V. Quine, 'On What There Is', in *From a Logical Point of View: Nine Logico-Philosophical Essays* (Cambridge, MA: Harvard University Press, 1953), 17.
6 As far as I know, the closest Quine ever came to acting on conservatism was in *The Roots of Reference*, where he was airing an objection to a somewhat technical aspect of his theory:

> I have called short leaps conservative. It is more illuminating to call them empiricistic. They are governed by this maxim of *relative empiricism*: Don't venture farther from sensory evidence than you need to. …
>
> The maxim would have us try to preserve the substitutional interpretation of quantification over abstract objects, if I have been right in supposing that this was genetically the prior interpretation. Considerations of overall simplicity of theory could outweigh this consideration and sustain the objectual interpretation, but at any rate there should be a deliberate weighing of considerations. (Quine, *The Roots of Reference*, 138)

It is not clear to me that the maxim 'Don't venture farther from sensory evidence than you need to' is any kind of conservatism, but, be that as it may, Quine did not let the maxim win. For all the confected suspense about 'deliberate weighing of

considerations', the 'considerations of overall simplicity' prevailed, and Quine sided with the objectual interpretation of quantification.
7 W. V. Quine, 'Things and Their Place in Theories', in *Theories and Things* (Cambridge, MA: Harvard University Press, 1981), 10.
8 Christensen, 'Conservatism in Epistemology', 74.
9 Ibid.
10 Ibid.
11 Quine and Ullian, *The Web of Belief*, 55–6.
12 Scott Soames, *Philosophical Analysis in the Twentieth Century, vol. 1: The Dawn of Analysis* (Princeton, NJ: Princeton University Press, 2005), 299.
13 Gideon Rosen provides two more examples: scepticism about induction and scepticism about abstract objects:

> the skeptical doubt which traditional discussions of induction purport to address, viz., the doubt of the agent who declines to believe that the sun will rise tomorrow *simply because he cannot prove that the future will resemble the past.* This timid Humean freak is a paradigm of unreason … because his standards for good reasoning are absurdly high. The nominalistically minded skeptic about science is likewise unreasonable. It may well be that our basic assumptions about abstract objects do not admit of independent justification 'from below'. Still, to take this as grounds for opting out of modern science altogether would be an egregious overreaction—a paradigm case of unreasonable epistemic caution. (Rosen, 'Nominalism, Naturalism, Epistemic Relativism', 73)

14 Lewis, *On the Plurality of Worlds*, 134.

5 Sufficient logical explicitness is norm zero

1 Quine, 'Two Dogmas of Empiricism', 42.
2 For reasons that emerge in Chapter 16, I am taking care to avoid saying that (3) itself conflicts with experience.
3 I.e.: they are formed in a way that leaves no doubt as to when they fit the role of premises in the logical laws, and, whenever they are used in that role, they give rise to conclusions that are also so formed.

Part Two

1 W. V. Quine, *Word and Object* (Cambridge, MA: MIT Press, 1960), 161. © 1960 Massachusetts Institute of Technology, by permission of the MIT Press.

7 The armchair

1. W. V. Quine, 'Mr Strawson on Logical Theory', in *The Ways of Paradox and Other Essays* (Cambridge, MA: Harvard University Press, 1976), 151.
2. James Andrew Smith Jr puts it well:

   > Quine denies that methods of paraphrase provide analyses of the meaning of the sentences we use; even if they did, he does not think it matters: '[s]ynonymy ... is not a notion we can readily make adequate sense of ...; and even if it were, it would be out of place in [cases of paraphrase].' [Quine, *Word and Object*, 159]. ... [O]n Quine's view, the philosopher does not aim to simplify and clarify science in the sense of aiming for a simpler and clearer formulation of the content of current scientific theories. Rather, she aims to *make* science simpler and clearer by devising simpler and clearer scientific theories. (Smith, 'Quine on Naturalism, Nominalism, and Philosophy's Place Within Science', 1558)

3. Quine, 'Mr Strawson on Logical Theory', 151.
4. Quine, *Word and Object*, 159.
5. Price, 'Metaphysics after Carnap', 321. Hylton, likewise, detects the ironic twist:

   > There is considerable historical irony here. Quine would certainly have less sympathy with ... non-scientific metaphysics than he has with the views of Carnap. His arguments against Carnap, and against Logical Positivism more generally, however, undermined the idea that there was a basis on which attempts at metaphysics could definitely be ruled out as meaningless. By doing that, Quine's work may well have had the effect of encouraging a revival of just the sort of metaphysics which he would strongly oppose. (Hylton, *Quine*, 367)

6. The obstacle, for me, is Price's use of the word 'pragmatism'. Apparently, if you hold a theory for pragmatic reasons, you are taking a 'deflationary' stance that you are not taking when you hold a theory for 'more-than-pragmatic' reasons. My epistemology has no counterpart of these terms. There is a norm of simplicity, which bears some resemblance to pragmatism (and, as I hint in Chapter 13, Quine might have come to it by merging two forms of pragmatism); but I see nothing 'deflationary' about simplicity. I see it as a normal and wholesome reason for accepting theories in any field.
7. Quine, 'On What There Is', 13.
8. Ibid., 1.
9. Quine, *The Roots of Reference*, 136.
10. Quine, 'Facts of the Matter', in *Essays on the Philosophy of W. V. Quine*, edited by R. W. Shahan and C. Swoyer (Norman, OK: Harvester, 1978), 168.
11. Quine, 'Things and Their Place in Theories', 9.

Adam Sennet and Tyrus Fisher heed this message to some extent when they write 'On Quine's view, it isn't the case that paraphrase reveals what an unparaphrased sentence "really" means' (Sennet and Fisher, 'Quine on Paraphrase and Regimentation', 92); but they seem not to have absorbed the message entirely, for they also write 'Quine … propose[s] that we regiment in order to assess our commitments' (ibid., 92). The tension leads to a hybrid account: 'Regimentation is partly a matter of displaying ontological commitment, but also partly a matter of selecting the commitments you are willing to take on' (ibid., 106). My countersuggestion, based on the extracts from *The Roots of Reference*, 'Facts of the Matter' and 'Things and Their Place in Theories', is that the second part of the hybrid alone represents Quine's mature view.

Regimentation, on this view, is a matter of selecting the commitments we are willing to take on; but what are *commitments*? To regiment is to replace informal sentences with formal ones, and typically the latter commit us, via formal logic, to accepting further formal sentences. Sometimes they commit us to accepting existential quantifications, e.g. '$\exists x$ (x is a number)', and then I may describe the situation by saying, 'I have chosen to quantify over numbers'; but still my commitment is to accepting *sentences*. It is part and parcel of developing my theory of the world, which I do as best I can by following my three Quinean norms.

Sennet and Fisher, by contrast, ask 'What *objects* am I committed to?', and in answering they feel a need for interpretation and/or translation (ibid., §4). That soon embrangles them in Quine's doctrines of the inscrutability of reference and the indeterminacy of translation, culminating in this wall of worry:

> Acquiescing in the home language, however, fails to alleviate the main problem with indeterminacy. As van Fraassen points out, if the semantics of the home language were known and determinate, then acquiescing in it would enable its users to 'know what they are talking about' [van Fraassen, 'Review of *Pursuit of Truth*', 853]. But this doesn't seem to help if the meanings of a language's sentences are determinate only relative to a translation manual and there are multiple, inequivalent, and equally good translation manuals [van Fraassen, 'Review of *Pursuit of Truth*', 853]. One may acquiesce in the home language, but it seems that such acquiescence amounts to merely settling for one manual amongst many, and simply ignoring the relativity. It is, thus, at best an open question what acquiescing in the home language actually achieves. (Ibid., 104)

This breed of brooding may well be the lot of specialists, whose topic is semantics, but it need not afflict the rest of us, as we develop our theories in accordance with our epistemic norms; for we can carry on without even one translation manual. Indeed, we can carry on without even broaching the topic of translation.

(Here I concur with Gary Kemp that 'the finished claims of ontology are as non-semantical as those of physics or tennis commentary and are as absolute as anything in Quine's scheme' (Kemp, 'In Favor of the Classical Quine on Ontology', 236). However, I suspect that Kemp's reasoning differs from mine. Certainly his argument is longer than mine, and it mobilizes many aspects of Quine's philosophy, with naturalism at the centre. All I rely on is my usual shtick of isolating Quine's epistemic norms from any semantic doctrines.)

12 David Lewis, 'Counterpart Theory and Quantified Modal Logic', in *Philosophical Papers, vol. I* (Oxford: Oxford University Press, 1983), 26.
13 Lewis, *On the Plurality of Worlds*, 2.
14 David Hume, *An Enquiry Concerning Human Understanding* (Chicago: Open Court, 1924), 166:

> When we run over libraries, persuaded of these principles, what havoc must we make? If we take in our hand any volume of divinity or school metaphysics, for instance, let us ask, Does it contain any abstract reasoning concerning quantity or number? No. Does it contain any experimental reasoning concerning matter of fact and existence? No. Commit it then to the flames, for it can contain nothing but sophistry and illusion.

8 Adapting to predicate logic

1 Quine, 'Two Dogmas of Empiricism', 43.
2 Quine, *Word and Object*, 170.
3 Quine, 'Things and Their Place in Theories', 9.
4 Quine, 'On What There Is', 4.
5 W. V. Quine, *From Stimulus to Science* (Cambridge, MA: Harvard University Press, 1995), 57.
6 Lewis, *On the Plurality of Worlds*, 4.
7 Ibid., 135.
8 Ibid., 134. These lines immediately precede the passage quoted in Chapter 4.
9 Quine, 'Predicate Logic', in *Quiddities: An Intermittently Philosophical* Dictionary (Cambridge, MA: Harvard University Press, 1987), 158.

Part Three

1 Quine, 'Intensions Revisited', 121.

9 Destination and horizon

1. Or we might not. If it turns out that our regimented propositional attitude psychology applies alike to humans, octopodes and robots, while the alternative is a collection of wildly diverse deductions from different branches of physiology and mechatronics, then the relative uniformity of the psychological deductions might be reason enough to retain them. Cf. Chapter 3's second 'white swans' example.
2. David Lewis (in Lewis, *Convention*) offers a promising approach to the study of meaning, but it takes as a starting point that subjects have beliefs and preferences (i.e. desires), including beliefs and preferences about the beliefs and preferences of others. And, even with such an advanced starting point, Lewis needs many more steps to work up to a theory of meaning for the sort of languages we are used to.
3. The uncharitable idea that we depend on imagined verbal behaviour was conjectured in Quine, *Word and Object*, 219:

   > All of [the propositional attitudes] can be thought of as involving something like quotation of one's own imagined verbal response to an imagined situation.
   > ... [W]e find ourselves attributing beliefs, wishes and strivings even to creatures lacking the power of speech, such is our dramatic virtuosity. We project ourselves into what from his behaviour we imagine a mouse's state of mind to have been, and dramatize it a belief, wish, or striving, verbalized as seems relevant and natural to us in the state thus feigned.

4. Donald Davidson, 'Belief and the Basis of Meaning', in *Inquiries into Truth and Interpretation* (Oxford: Clarendon Press, 1984), 144:

   > There is a principled, and not merely a practical, obstacle to verifying the existence of detailed, general, and abstract beliefs and intentions, while being unable to tell what a speaker's words mean. We sense well enough the absurdity in trying to tell without asking him whether someone believes there is a largest prime .... The absurdity lies ... in the fact that we have no good idea how to set about authenticating the existence of such attitudes when communication is not possible.

5. Quine, 'Facts of the Matter', 168:

   > When we attribute a belief about ancient history to someone, ... we are dependent on what he says – even though we are loath to equate belief with lip service. If the believer is a foreigner, our attribution may be subject also to the vagaries of translation of his testimony into our language.

6. Tarski, 'The Concept of Truth in Formalized Languages', §1. See also W. V. Quine, 'Three Grades of Modal Involvement', in *The Ways of Paradox and Other Essays*

(Cambridge, MA: Harvard University Press, 1976), 161; W. V. Quine, 'The Scope and Language of Science', in *The Ways of Paradox and Other Essays* (Cambridge, MA: Harvard University Press, 1976), 240; Quine, *Word and Object*, 143–4; W. V. Quine, *Pursuit of Truth* (Cambridge, MA: Harvard University Press, 1992), 69; W. V. Quine, 'Promoting Extensionality', in *Confessions of a Confirmed Extensionalist and Other Essays*, ed. Dagfinn Føllesdal and Douglas B. Quine (Cambridge, MA: Harvard University Press, 2008), 147; Quine, *From Stimulus to Science*, 95; and Donald Davidson, 'On Saying That', in *Inquiries into Truth and Interpretation* (Oxford: Clarendon Press, 1984), 97.

7 Were it not for Curtailments #5 and #6, we would probably add a third place, for the degree to which the belief or desire is held, and a fourth place, for the time at which it is held.
8 Quine, 'Confessions of a Confirmed Extensionalist', 498.
9 Ibid., 499.
10 This is one of the respects in which my motivation aligns with McDermott's:

> To those with thoroughly modern tastes in philosophy of psychology, the project will look like a 'Quinean fantasy'. They think that common-sense psychology, stated in common-sense terms, is presumptively a good theory, and does not need to be re-stated in any artificial notation. But common-sense complacency will not answer the charge that the common-sense theory has a hidden reliance on a notion of linguistic meaning. (McDermott, 'Empiricism and Common Sense', 165–6n.4)

11 Quine, *Pursuit of Truth*, 68.
12 If your ears do not accept this, then you might conclude that 'Fidus believed that Cicero was dangerous' is not *de re* after all. However, another option is to say that it is *de re*, and that 'Fidus believed that the author of *In Catilinam I–IV* was dangerous' is *de dicto*, and to change the definition of '*de re* ascription' so that substitutivity of identity is only demanded when the substitution produces a *de re* ascription. Something would then need to be done about the apparent circularity.
13 McDermott and Hylton spell out two species of this specious view:

> The view I criticise here is supported by a popular account of the truth conditions of *de re* ascriptions. It is held that the *de dicto* reading of ['Oedipus wants to marry Jocasta'] is 'psychologically stronger' than the *de re* one – it 'tells us more about the character of the mental causes of behaviour'. On a *de dicto* construal, ['Oedipus wants to marry Jocasta'] tells us how Oedipus 'represents to himself' the object of his desire. Whereas on the *de re* construal ['Oedipus wants to marry Jocasta'] tells us merely that Jocasta is the object of his desire 'under *some* description' – we are not told which one. (McDermott, 'A Russellian Account of Belief Sentences', 150–1)

One way to think of the problem is this: we attribute beliefs by considering what we would be inclined to say if we were in (what we take to be) the subject's place. ... But this is, in the first place, evidence for *de dicto* belief attributions. The semantics of such attributions has its problems, ... but the subject's sincere, earnest assertions generally give us a good guide here. For *de re* ascriptions they do not ... . So we need some idea of when it is correct to infer a *de re* attribution from *de dicto* attributions. (Hylton, *Quine*, 347)

10 Sententialism

1 Those terms will nonetheless occur in the content sentences, because the content sentences do not have them between quotation marks. (But how can they not occur in the fully regimented ascriptions, if they occur in the content sentences? It's because the content sentences do not occur in the fully regimented ascriptions either. Tarski's transformation replaces each entire quoted content sentence with an expression formed of letter names and the concatenation operator.)

2 W. V. Quine, 'Quantifiers and Propositional Attitudes', in *The Ways of Paradox and Other Essays* (Cambridge, MA: Harvard University Press, 1976), 194. The point about ocean currents and clocks deserves renewed notice nowadays, because it answers an objection from Jerry Fodor (Jerry Fodor, 'Propositional Attitudes', in *RePresentations: Philosophical Essays on the Foundations of Cognitive Science* (Cambridge, MA: MIT Press, 1981), 192, point 4). Fodorian question: How can a mouse's attitude to a sentence be causally efficacious, when a sentence is powerless with respect to mice? Quinean answer: The same way that an ocean's clockwise current can be causally efficacious, when a clock is powerless with respect to oceans. In each case we identify a state by reference to something powerless, but that is not to say that the state we have identified is powerless.

3 I find them important, but some philosophers have held that a regimented psychology can do without some of these steps, viz. the ones that track a subject's deductions. See Chapter 15.

4 Paul M. Churchland, *Scientific Realism and the Plasticity of Mind* (New York: Cambridge University Press, 1979), 104. I have taken some liberty in adapting Churchland's notation. Although he is willing to be taken as quantifying over sentences (ibid., 103), he prefers the sentential variables to be seen, not as arguments of the psychological predicates, but somehow as parts of the predicates. I find this confusing because I do not know what a predicate is, except as defined by the absence of variables and the *substituenda* of variables.

5 I must also say that I find the computer analogy unhelpful as a way of understanding how we might ever discover the mentalese language. That is because I have never heard of a case in which a computer scientist discovered a machine language. Real machine languages are *designed*, either before or together with the computers that implement them. Moreover, if a computer scientist ever did claim to have discovered a machine language (e.g. for some computer that she found in an attic, without any manuals), then I would not know how to evaluate the so-called discovery – e.g. to decide between it and incompatible rival 'discoveries' concerning the same computer – unless I am to understand it as a conjecture about what was designed.
6 Adapted from an example in Michael McDermott, 'The Narrow Semantics of Names', *Mind* 97, no. 386 (April 1988): 234.
7 Adapted from an example in Michael McDermott, 'A Russellian Account of Belief Sentences', *Philosophical Quarterly* 38, no. 151 (April 1988): 148.
8 Clitheroe and Lisarow are actual towns.
9 The weasel words are to allow for two kinds of variation in the missing clauses: (i) those clauses will use variables that the context supplies, i.e. not always '*s*', '*g*' and '*k*', or '*s*', '*n*' and '*o*'; and (ii) there may be not one but two kinds of missing clause: one for laws that quantify over general terms and kinds and one for laws that quantify over names and objects.
10 See Fred Dretske, *Knowledge and the Flow of Information* (Cambridge, MA: MIT Press, 1981).
11 Why the proviso, 'if exists'? It is because I am assuming that singular terms, including names, will be regimented in a way that ensures that any atomic sentence that uses a vacuous singular term is false. Thus 'The North Pole accommodates Santa Claus' is false because 'Santa Claus' is vacuous, and ' 'Santa Claus' designates Santa Claus' is false for the same reason. (At least I *assume* that 'Santa Claus' is vacuous. You might disagree, if you either subscribe to an ontology of unactualized possibles or are very young. In either case I must ask you to choose your own example of a genuinely vacuous name.)
12 See Hartry Field, 'Tarski's Theory of Truth', *Journal of Philosophy* 69, no. 13 (July 1972): especially §IV.
13 Modulo further regimentation of the terms that we use ourselves. Although Curtailment #6 is in force now, a complete regimentation will have us speaking the language of predicate logic, and then the general terms we use ourselves will no longer have the dichotomy of adjectives and common nouns, let alone the erraticism of the plural '*s*'. When our own lexicon changes in those ways, disquotation will push the same changes into the content language. I count that as a point in disquotation's favour.

11 From sententialism to Russellianism

1. Quine, *Word and Object*, 142:

   > Here we have a criterion for what may be called *purely referential position*: the position must be subject to the *substitutivity of identity*.

   See also W. V. Quine, 'Reference and Modality', in *From a Logical Point of View: Nine Logico-Philosophical Essays* (Cambridge, MA: Harvard University Press, 1953), 140.

2. Quine, *Word and Object*, 146:

   > It would be wrong to suppose that an occurrence of a term within an opaque construction is barred from referential position in every broader context. Examples to the contrary are provided by the occurrences of the personal name in [' "Tully was a Roman" is true' and ' "Tully" refers to a Roman']

   See also Quine, 'Reference and Modality', 141:

   > Our criterion of referential occurrence makes the occurrence of the name 'Giorgione' in ['Giorgione played chess'] referential, and must make the occurrences of 'Giorgione' in [' 'Giorgione played chess' is true'] and [' 'Giorgione' named a chess player'] referential by the same token, despite the presence of single quotes … . The point about quotation is not that it must destroy referential occurrence, but that it can (and ordinarily does) destroy referential occurrence.

3. Leibniz wrote '*Eadem sunt, quae sibi mutuo substitui possunt, salva veritate*' (Those things are identical that can be mutually substituted while preserving truth), which Frege quoted with approval (Frege, 'On Sense and Reference', 64). Even in Quine's phrase 'purely referential occurrence', it is easy to hear the intimation that a term *refers* normally, despite Quine's criterion being substitutivity of identity. E.g. it would seem that McDermott understood that phrase as being about reference when he wrote:

   > Russell's paradigm was:
   > (1) Othello believes that Desdemona loves Cassio.
   > He saw this as a relation between four things – three people and loving. Not only do the names 'Desdemona' and 'Cassio' have purely referential occurrence in the content-sentence, so also does the predicate 'loves'; it refers to loving. (McDermott, 'A Russellian Account of Belief Sentences', 141)

4. Or perhaps 'believes(Fidus, '__ is __', Cicero, dangerous-kind)'.
5. See W. V. Quine, 'Intensions Revisited', in *Theories and Things* (Cambridge, MA: Harvard University Press, 1981), 118–20.

6 Suggested but not pursued in McDermott, 'A Russellian Account of Belief Sentences', 143.
7 Or '... and Fidus believes '__ is dangerous' of x'; or '... and Fidus believes <'__ is dangerous', x>'.
8 Or '... then s comes to believe 'There's a __' of k'; or '... then s comes to believe <'There's a __', k>'.
9 Or '... then s believes '__ is dangerous' of o'; or '... then s believes <'__ is dangerous', o>'.
10 Or 'Galen believes '__ is __' of Cicero and cordate-kind'; or 'Galen believes <'__ is __', Cicero, cordate-kind>'.
11 Quine, 'Intensions Revisited', 114.
12 Much of what follows is due to Kaplan (Kaplan, 'Opacity'), but the clarifying idea that the objects under discussion are *sequences* was Quine's suggestion (Quine, 'Reply to David Kaplan', 292).
13 Kaplan ('Opacity', 273) saw the problem and proposed a solution; however Kaplan's discussion was not explicitly about sequences, and it is not clear how his solution applies when the concatenation operator is understood as *sequence* concatenation. Quine, who suggested the use of sequences, offered a solution of his own, but, frankly, I do not know what to make of it:

> [Kaplan] revives Russell's idea, which has seemed so bizarre, of letting all manner of objects figure as components of propositions – thus 'Mont Blanc (with all its snowfields), ... the object "Quine" (with all its vowels)', the object Quine (with all its bowels). His resulting propositions are what he calls valuated sentences, or $entences. They are amalgams of expressions and other things. Such an amalgam presents no ontological problem. I think of it as a sequence, in the mathematical sense, whose elements are atomic signs or other things. In an appendix Kaplan incorporates some pointy brackets (*spitze Klammern*) into his $entences at certain points to avert, I gather, a subtle confusion of use and mention. Where they bracket a non-expression, such as Mont Blanc, perhaps the pointy brackets can be seen as quotation marks to form a name of the object – as if we were to plant a open-quote in France and a close-quote in Italy in such a way as to bracket Mont Blanc and all its snowfields. The interpretation of $entences as sequences can take the pointy brackets in its stride. (Quine, 'Reply to David Kaplan', 292)

14 We could, e.g. reserve a special character set for symbols that occur in content hybrids in the *usual* way. Then the 'and' in Andrew's content hybrid could not be confused with the 'ȧŋd' that occurs whenever someone has a conjunctive belief. This is, of course, no more than a hint toward a solution.

15 See the discussion of Oedipus in McDermott, 'A Russellian Account of Belief Sentences', 151.

12 Sententialism with non-designating names

1 Adapted from an example in McDermott, 'A Russellian Account of Belief Sentences', 146.
2 E.g. McDermott considers 'Bernard J. Ortcutt' (ibid.).
3 This assumption could fail if we brought designating names into the content language in other ways, e.g. by casting designating names into the role of arbitrary names, as in: 'Sandra believes 'Cicero will come'; Sandra believes 'If Cicero will come, then I will get a present if I do stocking-hanging'; (44); (45); ∴ (46)'. But we have no reason to do this. Whatever it might achieve can be achieved just as well with a made-up name (e.g. 'Schmanta Schlaus'), which, because it is non-designating, will not upset the uniform substitutivity of co-designating names.

Part Four

1 Voltaire, 'To the Countess of Fontaine-Martel', in *Miscellaneous Poems by Mr de Voltaire, vol. XXXII* , trans. T. Smollet, T. Francklin et al. (Salisbury: J. Newbery, R. Baldwin, W. Johnston, S. Crowder, T. Davies, J. Coote, G. Kearsley and B. Collins, 1764), 47.

13 The 'Two Dogmas' argument

1 Quine, 'Two Dogmas of Empiricism', 20.
2 Another adjective that would fit here is 'tragic'. I shudder to think how many students have failed to grasp the positive message in Quine's §6 because they were put off by the dusty reading prerequisites of the negative sections.
3 George Berkeley, *A Treatise Concerning the Principles of Human Knowledge*, ed. J. Dancy (Oxford: Oxford University Press 1998), §1.
4 E.g. Quine, 'Epistemology Naturalized', 71, mentions Hume, whose 'explanation of body in sensory terms was bold and simple: he identified bodies outright with sense impressions', and also A. B. Johnson, who 'nearly a century after Hume's *Treatise*, [espoused] the same view. "The word iron names an associated sight and feel", Johnson wrote.'

5 Bertrand Russell, 'The Relation of Sense-Data to Physics', in *Mysticism and Logic* (London: Allen and Unwin 1963), 115.
6 Scholars of Carnap are divided over whether he saw himself as advancing Berkeley's phenomenalistic project. For my purposes, however, what counts is that this is what Quine saw Carnap as attempting. For evidence that Quine saw Carnap that way, and for references to the dissenting scholarship, see Sander Verhaegh, *Working from Within* (Oxford: Oxford University Press, 2018), 21n.11.
7 Carnap, 'Empiricism, Semantics, and Ontology', in *Semantics and the Philosophy of Language*, ed. Leonard Linsky (Urbana: University of Illinois Press, 1952), 219.
8 In the category of external questions, Carnap includes some that present an appearance – a misleading appearance, in his view – of being about something else. Carnap calls these *pseudo-object*, or *quasi-syntactical* questions. That is to say, although the question is about which linguistic framework ought to be adopted, it appears to be about objects. (See ibid., 211: 'Those who raise the question of the reality of the thing world itself have perhaps in mind not a theoretical question as their formulation seems to suggest, but rather a … question … concerning the structure of our language.') This applies especially to questions of very general scope, which concern all the objects of some *category*. Quine has dubbed these 'category questions' (Quine, 'On Carnap's Views on Ontology', 207). However, as Quine recognized, category questions are for Carnap also sometimes taken literally as (trivial) internal questions of existence.
9 'Everyone is at liberty to build up his own logic, i.e. his own form of language, as he wishes. All that is required of him is that, if he wishes to discuss it, he must state his methods clearly and give syntactical rules' (Carnap, *Logische Syntax der Sprache*, 52). This occurs under the heading, 'The Principle of Tolerance in Syntax'. In a revealing passage of his intellectual autobiography, Carnap suggests 'it might perhaps be called more exactly the "principle of conventionality of language forms"' (Carnap, 'Intellectual Autobiography', 55).
10 Rudolf Carnap, *Der Logische Aufbau der Welt*, trans. R. George as *The Logical Structure of the World* (London: Routledge and Kegan Paul, 1967), §§126–7.
11 See also W. V. Quine, *From Stimulus to Science* (Cambridge, MA: Harvard University Press, 1995), 13:

> A law of least action gets built into our very standard of what to count as real. This was a deep insight of Carnap's. It is a stick-figure caricature of what the scientist actually does, early and late, in devising theories. It is the scientist's quest of the simplest solution.

12 Perhaps along the lines of Lewis, *Convention*, §V.3 and §V.5, summarized on p. 207:

> So I claim to have filled Quine's order: I have given an account of the proper kind of analyticity – analyticity relative to a population of language users.

> See also McDermott, 'Empiricism and Common Sense', 184:
>
>> But if we can make use of the concepts of belief and desire without fear of circularity, the prospects for an analysis of the concept of linguistic meaning seem to be greatly enhanced. That is enough to defeat Quine's argument against meaning. I do not have an analysis to offer. I have no opinion, for example, on whether meaning is a matter of *rules* or *conventions*. But either way, we may assume, it would be constituted by a pattern of beliefs and desires concerning the use of language. The point is that a non-circular analysis no longer seems impossible, if we can make use of the concepts of belief and desire.

13 On this admittedly rather inconsequential point I disagree with some of the mainstream commentary on Quine, e.g.:

> The failure and untenability of reductionism … rules out [a] way in which the concept of analyticity might have been explained. (Kemp, *Quine: A Guide for the Perplexed*, 25)

> Quine's emphasis on the link between meaning and evidence in fact leads him to deny that we can, in general, make clear sense of the idea of the meaning of a sentence. The crucial point here is holism. (Hylton, *Quine*, 57)

14 'Carnapian' rather than 'Carnap's' because this position has the norm of internal pragmatism where Carnap had the principle of least action.

15 'Close' rather than 'identical' because the conclusion has the norm of total logical explicitness where I have the norm of sufficient logical explicitness.

16 Quine, 'Two Dogmas of Empiricism', 36.

17 Ibid., 36–7.

18 Paul A. Gregory goes some way to defending Quine's claim that the truth of a sentence depends partly on language. In Gregory, *Quine's Naturalism*, ch. 3, he considers what it takes for a speaker to be plausibly seen as speaking the language of the surrounding community, and he arrives at a necessary condition, to the effect that the speaker counts as true a significant mass of sentences that the community counts as true, including a significant mass of sentences that would not traditionally be classed as analytic.

I do not dispute Gregory's analysis, nor do I cavil at his tendency to use 'S is speaking meaningfully' as though it were always at least materially equivalent to 'S is plausibly seen as speaking the language of the surrounding community', since that may well be how it looks from an external point of view. However, as my present concern is with epistemology rather than semantics, I need to question the relevance of all this to the speaker-cum-theorist. Thus suppose you face a choice between theories T and U, and suppose that to accept T would be to speak meaningfully in Gregory's sense and to accept U would be to speak non-meaningfully in Gregory's sense. Why should this circumstance affect your decision? If U is the simplest sufficiently logically explicit total theory available to you that is empirically correct *vis-à-vis* the totality of experience available to you, then why not choose U and forgo meaningfulness in the Gregory sense?

Granted, this choice will lead to some awkward conversations with the neighbours, but you can take heart in the fact that Quine put himself in this predicament so often that his workaround – semantic ascent – became standard operating procedure for him. Here is a typical use case:

> 'Of course there are miles. Wherever you have 1760 yards you have a mile.' 'But there are no yards either. Only bodies of various lengths.' 'Are the earth and the moon separated by bodies of various lengths?' The continuation is lost in a jumble of invective and question-begging. When on the other hand we ascend to 'mile' and ask which of its contexts are useful and for what purposes, we can get on; we are no longer caught in the toils of our opposed uses. (Quine, *Word and Object*, 272)

(For more on Quine's non-conservatism, see Chapters 4 and 7. For a critique of Quine's categories of observation sentence and observation categorical, which are prominent in Gregory's discussion, see Chapter 16.)

19 Quine, *Methods of Logic* (London: Routledge and Kegan Paul, 1974), xiii.
20 W. V. Quine, 'Posits and Reality', in *The Ways of Paradox and Other Essays* (Cambridge, MA: Harvard University Press, 1976), 257.
21 Quine, *Word and Object*, 3.
22 Quine, 'Carnap and Logical Truth', in *The Ways of Paradox and Other Essays* (Cambridge, MA: Harvard University Press, 1976), 152.

14 Naturalized epistemology

1 On this point we resemble Penelope Maddy's 'second philosopher':

> Philosophers, speaking of her in the third person, will say that such an inquirer operates 'within science', that she uses 'the methods of science', but she herself has no need of such talk. When asked about why she believes that water is H_2O, she cites information about its behavior under electrolysis and so on; she doesn't say 'because science says so and I believe what science says'. (Maddy, *Second Philosophy*, 15)

But there is also this difference: while we have our three epistemic norms, and they counsel us to say many of the same things as the second philosopher would say about water, etc., the second philosopher does not profess those norms, and appears to shun codified epistemic norms tout court. Thus there is, as far as I can tell, no such thesis as second philosophy. This lacuna is bound to inconvenience the second philosopher in debates with non-second-philosophers, for, though she can and does critique their epistemologies, she cannot formulate an invitation to them to take up hers.

In depicting the second philosopher, Maddy is fond of the phrase 'natural-born naturalist' (ibid., 118n.5). To be naturally born a naturalist may well be good fortune, but it is not a characteristic that one can invite others to share. (Also, if truth be told, the birth metaphor *understates* the unshareable privilege with which the second philosopher entered the world. She is a character drawn by an epistemologist, so, for her, *l'essence précède l'existence*.)

2 The false dichotomy, stated literally, is 'Epistemology either abstains from natural science or is just more natural science'. It can also take the form of an invalid argument: 'Epistemology does not abstain from natural science; therefore, epistemology is just more natural science.' I sense that this, or something very much like it, has begun to take root in the literature on Quine's naturalism, e.g.:

> When Quine is ... concerned with 'the theory-building process' he is nonetheless taking for granted 'the theory that is being built', with its fully realistic attitude towards light rays, nerve endings, human beings, sensory nerves, and what have you. This is the way in which Quine's naturalism is revolutionary: he denies that there is a distinctively philosophical standpoint from which we can reflect on knowledge. (Hylton, *Quine*, 22)

> The epistemologist is not ... pursuing a task fundamentally different from the scientist. This is in complete accord with the ... point about beginning from within ongoing theory. There is no special standpoint other than ongoing theory, no cosmic exile, from which the philosopher proceeds. (Gregory, *Quine's Naturalism*, 63)

> Consider [this version] of Quine's naturalism: ... Science contains epistemology in the sense that engaging in epistemology presupposes an accepted scientific framework as background. (Harman and Lepore, 'Introduction: Life and Work', 5)

3 W. V. Quine, 'Naturalism; Or, Living within One's Means', in *Confessions of a Confirmed Extensionalist and Other Essays*, ed. Dagfinn Føllesdal and Douglas B. Quine (Cambridge, MA: Harvard University Press, 2008), 462.
4 W. V. Quine, 'Five Milestones of Empiricism', in *Theories and Things* (Cambridge, MA: Harvard University Press, 1981), 72.
5 Ibid.
6 Quine, 'Epistemology Naturalized', 82.
7 Ibid., 75.

8 Verhaegh, *Working from Within*, 68.
9 I doubt that Verhaegh's interpretation is right, because (i) Quine's presentations of naturalized epistemology in 'Epistemology Naturalized' and 'Five Milestones of Empiricism' did not claim to be normative; (ii) as we are about to see, Quine's presentations of naturalized epistemology that did claim to be normative found their normativity in one or another brand of instrumentalism; and (iii) as we are about to see, none of those instrumentalisms are deflationary in Verhaegh's sense, i.e. none of them equate good practice with actual practice.

Verhaegh (ibid., 68n.28) cites Bredo Johnsen, who appears to share Verhaegh's interpretation of Quine:

> So far is [Quine in 'Epistemology Naturalized'] from proposing to abandon the normative that he is proposing instead to *discover* the norms that govern theorizing by discovering the norms that we conform to in our theorizing. … [P]sychology will identify the norms we adhere to, and philosophy will tell us that, *by virtue of* their being the ones we adhere to, they are the ones we *are to* adhere to. (Johnsen, 'How to Read "Epistemology Naturalized"', 88, italics in the original)

However, this is not Johnsen's final position. When he goes on (as we soon shall) to consider Quine's view of epistemology as engineering, Johnsen allows that normative epistemology may 'perhaps modify the most general norms that guide our scientific theorizing' (ibid., 90–1).

10 Quine, *The Roots of Reference*, 136–7.
11 Quine, 'Reply to Morton White', in *The Philosophy of W. V. Quine*, ed. L. E. Hahn and P. A. Schilpp (La Salle: Open Court, 1986), 664–5.
12 Quine, *Pursuit of Truth*, 19.
13 Since this is a completely general standard for evaluating theories, it may be contrasted with the kind of epistemological modesty that Ebbs attributes to Quine in 'Quine Gets the Last Word', §5, e.g.:

> This aspect of Quine's philosophy – the uncompromising core of his scientific naturalism – can seem puzzling. For if there is no legitimate standpoint on justification that is independent of any particular scientific theories we accept, then there are no substantive general principles for evaluating or justifying our acceptance of particular scientific statements or the theories of which they are a part. (Ibid., 123)

> Quine [invites] us to subtract the assumption that there are substantive general principles for evaluating and justifying assertions from the practical and theoretical grasp of what it is to justify, defend, and revise assertions in a given scientific discipline that we achieve by study and practice of that discipline. (Ibid., 125)

14 Quine, *Pursuit of Truth*, 20. Contrast Paul A. Gregory, *Quine's Naturalism: Language, Theory, and the Knowing Subject* (London: Continuum, 2008), §5.4, which attempts to answer the question 'Why should we, or science, aim at predictive success?' ('Gregory, *Quine's Naturalism: Language, Theory, and the Knowing Subject*', 109).
15 Quine, 'Reply to Morton White', 665.
16 Quine, 'Comment on Haack', in *Perspectives on Quine*, ed. Robert B. Barrett and Roger F. Gibson (Oxford: Blackwell, 1990), 128. Contrast Gregory, *Quine's Naturalism*, 107: 'At present … there is no better candidate for the terminal parameter than sensory prediction. This is largely because there is no other plausible candidate.'
17 Quine, 'Ontological Reduction and the World of Numbers', in *The Ways of Paradox and Other Essays* (Cambridge, MA: Harvard University Press, 1976), 212–13.
18 And parts of mathematics, for as Quine remarks, 'the set theorist [ventures] ever upward and outward on his lofty ontological limb. The farther he ventures, the less it matters even to science, let alone common sense' (Quine, *The Roots of Reference*, 131.)
19 Quine, *Pursuit of Truth*, 20.
20 See also Quine, *Pursuit of Truth*, 15:

> But the ultimate objective is so to choose the revision as to maximize future success in prediction … . There is no recipe for this, but maximization of simplicity and minimization of mutilation are maxims by which science strives for vindication in future predictions.

21 Quine, 'Naturalism; Or, Living within One's Means', 462. See also W. V. Quine, 'Comment on Haack' in *Perspectives on Quine*, ed. Robert B. Barrett and Roger F. Gibson (Oxford: Blackwell, 1990), 49 and Quine, *From Stimulus to Science*, 49.
22 W. V. Quine, 'On the Nature of Moral Values', in *Theories and Things* (Cambridge, MA: Harvard University Press, 1981), 55.
23 Quine, 'Five Milestones of Empiricism', 72.

15 Attitudes to sets of *possibilia*

1 Lewis, 'Attitudes *De Dicto* and *De Se*', in *Philosophical Papers,* vol. I (Oxford: Oxford University Press, 1983) and Lewis, *On the Plurality of Worlds*, 28–30.
2 Lewis, *On the Plurality of Worlds*, 28–9.
3 Lewis, *On the Plurality of Worlds*, ch. IV.
4 Ibid., 32–4.
5 Ibid., 36.
6 Ibid., 37.

7 For Lewis, the causes of belief are to be specified by a version of the principle of charity that states that beliefs are the results of normal perceptual and inductive processes (Lewis, 'Radical Interpretation', 112–13; Lewis, 'New Work for a Theory of Universals', *Australasian Journal of Philosophy* 61, no. 4 (December 1983), 375). This view survives in *On the Plurality of Worlds*, but there it is embedded in a complex discussion of 'contingency plan' cases (Lewis, *On the Plurality of Worlds*, 37–8).

8 Lewis espoused a classical theory of practical reason, or decision theory. In Lewis, 'Radical Interpretation', 113–14, it is called 'the Rationalization Principle', and in Lewis, *On the Plurality of Worlds*, 36 it is called 'the principle of instrumental rationality'.

9 Lewis, *On the Plurality of Worlds*, §1.8.

10 Lewis, *On the Plurality of Worlds*, 33: the examples of Pierre, Fred and Peter.

11 Lewis Carroll, *Symbolic Logic, Part I: Elementary*, reprinted with additions in *Symbolic Logic and the Game of Logic* (New York: Dover, 1958), 119, 133.

12 Lewis, *On the Plurality of Worlds*, 34.

13 Ibid., 34–5.

16 The mythical given

1 W. Sellars, 'Empiricism and the Philosophy of Mind', in *Minnesota Studies in the Philosophy of Science, Volume I: The Foundations of Science and the Concepts of Psychology and Psychoanalysis*, ed. H. Feigl and M. Scriven (Minneapolis: University of Minnesota Press, 1956), 267.

2 Donald Davidson, 'A Coherence Theory of Truth and Knowledge', in *Truth and Interpretation: Perspectives on the Philosophy of Donald Davidson*, ed. Ernest Lepore (Oxford: Blackwell, 1986), 310.

3 Stich, *From Folk Psychology to Cognitive Science* (Cambridge, MA: MIT Press, 1983), 242.

4 The position at which we arrived comes close to fitting Susan Haack's initial characterization of foundherentism:

> Foundherentism may be approximately characterized thus:
> (FH1) A subject's experience is relevant to the justification of his empirical beliefs, but there need be no privileged class of empirical beliefs justified exclusively by the support of experience, independently of the support of other beliefs; and:
> (FH2) Justification is not exclusively one-directional, but involves pervasive relations of mutual support. (Haack, *Evidence and Inquiry*, 19)

All it would take to secure my agreement is to substitute 'sentences' for 'beliefs' and for 'empirical beliefs', and to substitute 'holistic support' for 'relations of mutual support'. Nevertheless, I do not join Haack in drawing the following inference (with 'sentences' substituted for 'beliefs'):

> But from even this very sketchy characterization it will be apparent that …, since beliefs will be seen to be justified partially by experience and partially by other beliefs, the account will be gradational rather than categorical. (ibid., 20)

The claim that justification is a matter of degree deserves serious consideration, even if I have not pursued it in these pages; but it is not apparent to me that this claim follows from the fact that justification depends on two things. (Compare Haack's argument with the following parallel but patently invalid argument: In a two-premise syllogism, the conclusion is justified partly by premise one and partly by premise two; therefore, its justification is gradational rather than categorical.)

5 One epistemologist who apparently shared this view was C. S. Peirce:

> It appears, then, that *Logica utens* consisting in self-control, the distinction of logical goodness and badness must begin where control of the processes of cognition begins; and any object that antecedes the distinction, if it has to be named either good or bad, must be named *good*. (Peirce, *Collected Papers vol. 5* (Cambridge, MA: Harvard University Press, 1934), paragraph 114)

6 It has always struck me that normative ethicists have a better grip on Niebuhrian serenity than most normative epistemologists do. Normative ethicists have Kant's formula 'ought implies can', which brings a swift and permissive conclusion to any ethical deliberation about an action that is beyond the agent's control: if you cannot do it, then you are under no obligation to do it; but if you are compelled to do it, i.e. you cannot refrain, then you are permitted to do it, i.e. you are under no obligation to refrain. I would very much like to see belief-oriented epistemologists borrow Kant's formula and repurpose it with an epistemic 'ought', like so:

> If I ought to refrain from believing that I have a headache, then I can refrain from believing that I have a headache. [Ought implies can.]
> It is not the case that I can refrain from believing that I have a headache. [Assumed]
>
> ∴ It is not the case that I ought to refrain from believing that I have a headache. [Modus tollens]

7 Subtlety alert: The conflict arises via informal logic and not otherwise, so the violation is of the norm of sufficient logical explicitness, not the norm of empirical correctness. However, when we revise the theory to repair the violation, we do not necessarily have to make it *more* logically explicit than it already is. Changing the supposed trajectory of the comet might be enough to cut the informal path to

conflict with experience, thus rendering the theory *sufficiently* logically explicit (as well as empirically correct).
8 Peirce, *Collected Papers*, vol. 5, paragraph 115.
9 W. V. Quine, 'Empirical Content', in *The Ways of Paradox and Other Essays* (Cambridge, MA: Harvard University Press, 1976), 25.
10 Quine, *Word and Object*, 2.
11 Quine, 'Empirical Content', 27–8.
12 Corollary: observation alone cannot falsify 'When night falls, the lamps are lit'. Right now, as I face the street outside and see darkness all around, I dissent from that sentence, but I did not dissent from it on occasions when my theory included 'There is a total solar eclipse here', even if the retinal stimulus was identical.
13 E.g. Quine, *Word and Object*, 37–43.
14 Ibid., 42–3.
15 McDermott comes to a similar conclusion by considering a different kind of example:

> In real languages like English, there are *no* observation sentences. Even such a favourable case as 'This is red' is only approximately observational. (Feeling a familiar object in the dark, I agree that it is red; but the same stimulus would not prompt assent in *all* competent speakers.) (McDermott, 'Empiricism and Common Sense', 128)

16 Hylton, *Quine*, 136.
17 Ibid., 137.
18 Ibid., §5.IV.
19 Cf. McDermott:

> If we want to explain theory content in terms of the prompting of assent and dissent, the simplest solution would be: the content of a theory, for a speaker at a time, is the stimulations that would prompt him to *abandon* it (i.e. that would prompt dissent from at least one of its component sentences). This is, indeed, what you would expect Quine to arrive at, combining the basic idea that content is determined by confirmation conditions with (i) a holistic focus on theories rather than statements, (ii) a Popperian emphasis on disconfirmation rather than confirmation, and (iii) a behaviouristic replacement of disconfirming experiences by stimuli prompting dissent. (McDermott, 'Empiricism and Common Sense', 128, italics in the original)

Clearly, this has much in common with my view, but there is this difference: McDermott is defining a notion of *theory content*. This leads him to draw conclusions that I would not draw.
20 See the discussion in Chapter 4 of Christensen's example involving the populations of India and the United States.

17 Epistemology as the theory of knowledge

1 Timothy Williamson, *Knowledge and Its Limits* (Oxford: Oxford University Press, 2009), ch. 9.
2 To put it another way (which amounts to the same thing in this case, since it's true that the gun was loaded), the shooter's culpability depends on whether she knew *in the criminal law sense* that the gun was loaded, where this sense is as described by Alexander F. Sarch:

> Note that knowledge that proposition, p, is true, in the criminal law, is typically taken to mean a subjective belief amounting to practical certainty in p plus the truth of p—not justified true belief plus an anti-Gettier condition, as in the philosophical literature. (Sarch, 'Condoning the Crime', 141n.40)

3 Quine and Ullian, *The Web of Belief*, 13.
4 Williamson (*Knowledge and Its Limits*, 62–4) offers a more elaborate example to show that non-verbal behaviour can depend on knowledge. Here the behaviour (a burglar ransacking a house all night) depends, not only on what the subject believes, and not only on what the subject believes truly, but also on other aspects of his state; and Williamson would have us explain it by ascribing knowledge (knowledge that there is a diamond in the house). Now the same behaviour could be explained by citing a detailed feature of the subject that is not necessary and sufficient for knowledge (e.g. true belief without reliance on false lemmas), and Williamson concedes this; but he retorts that, no matter what detailed feature D one chooses, if D is not necessary and sufficient for knowledge, there will be a variant of the example in which knowledge explains the subject's behaviour and D does not.

I agree with Williamson's retort, which is to say, I agree that it is true; but what does it show? It refutes an ambitious opponent, who claims that there is some detailed feature D, not equivalent to knowledge, such that, for any context C in which knowledge explains behaviour, D can replace knowledge in C. And this seems to be the opponent Williamson has in mind, when he writes of 'the search for a substitute for knowing in causally explanatory contexts' (ibid., 63). But his retort does not refute a more modest opponent, who claims that, for any context C in which knowledge explains behaviour, there is some detailed feature D, not equivalent to knowledge, such that D can replace knowledge in C. If the modest opponent is right, then knowledge is dispensable in each and every causally explanatory context. Therefore, if Williamson wants to show that knowledge has an indispensable psychological role, he needs to answer the modest opponent.
5 See Amanda Pachniewska, 'List of Animals That Have Passed the Mirror Test', Animal Cognition website. Accessed 1 February 2022. http://www.animalcognition.org/2015/04/15/list-of-animals-that-have-passed-the-mirror-test/.

Bibliography

Ayer, A. J. *Language, Truth and Logic*. 2nd ed. 1946. Reprint. Hammondsworth: Penguin, 1982.
Berkeley, George. *A Treatise Concerning the Principles of Human Knowledge*. 1710. Edited by J. Dancy. Oxford: Oxford University Press 1998.
Carnap, Rudolf. 'Empiricism, Semantics, and Ontology'. 1950. In *Semantics and the Philosophy of Language*, edited by Leonard Linsky, 208–28. Urbana: University of Illinois Press, 1952.
Carnap, Rudolf. 'Intellectual Autobiography'. In *The Philosophy of Rudolf Carnap*, edited by P. A. Schilpp, 1–42. La Salle: Open Court, 1963.
Carnap, Rudolf. *Der Logische Aufbau der Welt*. 1928. 2nd ed. Translated by R. George as *The Logical Structure of the World*. London: Routledge and Kegan Paul, 1967.
Carnap, Rudolf. *Logische Syntax der Sprache*. 1934. Translated by Amethe Smeaton as *The Logical Syntax of Language*. Chicago: Open Court, 2002.
Carroll, Lewis. *Symbolic Logic, Part I: Elementary*. 1897. Reprinted with additions in *Symbolic Logic and the Game of Logic*. New York: Dover, 1958.
Christensen, David. 'Conservatism in Epistemology'. *Noûs* 28, no. 1 (March 1994): 69–89.
Churchland, Paul M. *Scientific Realism and the Plasticity of Mind*. New York: Cambridge University Press, 1979.
Davidson, Donald. 'Belief and the Basis of Meaning'. 1974. In *Inquiries into Truth and Interpretation*, 141–54. Oxford: Clarendon Press, 1984.
Davidson, Donald. 'A Coherence Theory of Truth and Knowledge'. 1983. In *Truth and Interpretation: Perspectives on the Philosophy of Donald Davidson*, edited by Ernest Lepore, 307–19. Oxford: Blackwell, 1986.
Davidson, Donald. 'On Saying That'. 1968. In *Inquiries into Truth and Interpretation*, 93–108. Oxford: Clarendon Press, 1984.
Descartes, René. *Meditations on First Philosophy*. 1641. Translated by John Cottingham, Robert Stoothoff and Dugald Murdoch in *The Philosophical Writings of Descartes*, vol. 2, 3–62. Cambridge: Cambridge University Press, 1984.
Dretske, Fred. *Knowledge and the Flow of Information*. Cambridge, MA: MIT Press, 1981.
Ebbs, Gary. 'Carnap and Quine on Truth by Convention'. 2011. In *Carnap, Quine, and Putnam on Methods of Inquiry*, 57–94. Cambridge: Cambridge University Press, 2017.

Ebbs, Gary. 'Quine Gets the Last Word'. 2011. In *Carnap, Quine, and Putnam on Methods of Inquiry*, 113–27. Cambridge: Cambridge University Press, 2017.

Einstein, Albert. *The Collected Papers of Albert Einstein*. Edited by John Stachel, David C. Cassidy and Robert Schulmann. Princeton, NJ: Princeton University Press, 1994.

Einstein, Albert. 'Remarks Concerning the Essays Brought Together in This Co-operative Volume'. 1949. In *Albert Einstein: Philosopher-Scientist* (The Library of Living Philosophers: Volume 7), edited by P. A. Schilpp, 665–88. Evanston, IL: Northwestern University, 1949.

Euclid, *The Elements*. C. 300 BCE. Translated by Thomas L. Heath in *The Thirteen Books of Euclid's Elements*. New York: Dover, 1956.

Field, Hartry. 'Tarski's Theory of Truth'. *Journal of Philosophy* 69, no. 13 (July 1972): 347–76.

Fodor, Jerry. 'Propositional Attitudes'. 1978. In *RePresentations: Philosophical Essays on the Foundations of Cognitive Science*, 177–203. Cambridge, MA: MIT Press, 1981.

Frege, Gottlob. 'On Sense and Reference'. 1892. Translated by Max Black. In *Translations from the Philosophical Writings of Gottlob Frege*. 2nd edn, edited by Peter Geach and Max Black, 56–78. Oxford: Blackwell, 1960.

Gregory, Paul A. *Quine's Naturalism: Language, Theory, and the Knowing Subject*. London: Continuum, 2008.

Haack, Susan. *Evidence and Inquiry: Towards Reconstruction in Epistemology*. Oxford: Blackwell, 1993.

Harman, Gilbert, and Lepore, Ernie. 'Introduction: Life and Work'. In *A Companion to W. V. O. Quine*, edited by Gilbert Harman and Ernie Lepore, 1–13. Chichester, England: Wiley-Blackwell, 2014.

Hume, David. *An Enquiry Concerning Human Understanding*. 1748. Chicago: Open Court, 1924.

Hume, David. *A Treatise of Human Nature*. 1739. Reprinted in one volume. Oxford: Clarendon Press, 1949.

Hylton, Peter. *Quine*. New York: Routledge, 2007.

Johnsen, Bredo. 'How to Read "Epistemology Naturalized"'. *Journal of Philosophy* 102, no. 2 (February 2005): 78–93.

Kaplan, David. 'Opacity'. In *The Philosophy of W. V. Quine*, edited by L. E. Hahn and P. A. Schilpp, 229–89. La Salle: Open Court, 1986.

Kemp, Gary. 'In Favor of the Classical Quine on Ontology'. *Canadian Journal of Philosophy* 50, no. 2 (2020): 223–37.

Kemp, Gary. *Quine: A Guide for the Perplexed*. London: Continuum, 2006.

Lewis, David. 'Attitudes *De Dicto* and *De Se*'. 1979. In *Philosophical Papers* vol. 1, 133–56. Oxford: Oxford University Press, 1983.

Lewis, David. *Convention: A Philosophical Study*. Oxford: Blackwell, 1969.

Lewis, David. 'Counterpart Theory and Quantified Modal Logic'. 1968. In *Philosophical Papers*, vol. 1, 26–39. Oxford: Oxford University Press, 1983.

Lewis, David. 'New Work for a Theory of Universals'. *Australasian Journal of Philosophy* 61, no. 4 (December 1983): 343–77.
Lewis, David. *On the Plurality of Worlds*. Oxford: Blackwell, 1986.
Lewis, David. 'Radical Interpretation'. 1974. In *Philosophical Papers*, vol. 1, 108–18. Oxford: Oxford University Press, 1983.
Maddy, Penelope. *Second Philosophy: A Naturalistic Method*. Oxford: Oxford University Press, 2007.
McDermott, Michael. 'Empiricism and Common Sense'. Unpublished manuscript, 2015. PDF file.
McDermott, Michael. 'The Narrow Semantics of Names'. *Mind* 97, no. 386 (April 1988): 224–37.
McDermott, Michael. 'A Russellian Account of Belief Sentences'. *Philosophical Quarterly* 38, no. 151 (April 1988): 141–57.
Pachniewska, Amanda. 'List of Animals That Have Passed the Mirror Test'. Animal Cognition website. Accessed 1 February 2022. http://www.animalcognition.org/2015/04/15/list-of-animals-that-have-passed-the-mirror-test/.
Peirce, C. S. *Collected Papers*, vol. 5. Cambridge, MA: Harvard University Press, 1934.
Popper, Karl. *Conjectures and Refutations*. 1963. 4th ed. London: Routledge and Kegan Paul, 1972.
Price, Huw. 'Metaphysics after Carnap: The Ghost Who Walks?'. 2007. In *Metametaphysics: New Essays on the Foundations of Ontology*, edited by D. Chalmers, D. Manley and R. Wasserman, 320–46. Oxford: Clarendon Press, 2009.
Quine, W. V. 'Carnap and Logical Truth'. 1954. In *The Ways of Paradox and Other Essays*. Rev. ed., 107–32. Cambridge, MA: Harvard University Press, 1976.
Quine, W. V. 'Comment on Haack'. 1990. In *Perspectives on Quine*, edited by Robert B. Barrett and Roger F. Gibson, 128. Oxford: Blackwell, 1990.
Quine, W. V. 'Confessions of a Confirmed Extensionalist'. 2001. In *Confessions of a Confirmed Extensionalist and Other Essays*, edited by Dagfinn Føllesdal and Douglas B. Quine, 498–506. Cambridge, MA: Harvard University Press, 2008.
Quine, W. V. 'Empirical Content'. In *The Ways of Paradox and Other Essays*. Rev. ed., 24–30. Cambridge, MA: Harvard University Press, 1976.
Quine, W. V. 'Epistemology Naturalized'. 1968. In *Ontological Relativity and Other Essays*, 69–90. New York: Columbia University Press, 1969.
Quine, W. V. 'Facts of the Matter'. 1977. In *Essays on the Philosophy of W. V. Quine*, edited by R. W. Shahan and C. Swoyer, 155–69. Norman, OK: Harvester, 1978.
Quine, W. V. 'Five Milestones of Empiricism'. 1975. In *Theories and Things*, 67–72. Cambridge, MA: Harvard University Press, 1981.
Quine, W. V. *From Stimulus to Science*. Cambridge, MA: Harvard University Press, 1995.
Quine, W. V. 'Has Philosophy Lost Contact with People?' 1979. In *Theories and Things*, 190–3. Cambridge, MA: Harvard University Press, 1981.
Quine, W. V. 'Intensions Revisited'. 1977. In *Theories and Things*, 113–23. Cambridge, MA: Harvard University Press, 1981.

Quine, W. V. *Methods of Logic*. 1952. 3rd ed. London: Routledge and Kegan Paul, 1974.
Quine, W. V. 'Mr Strawson on Logical Theory'. 1953. In *The Ways of Paradox and Other Essays*. Rev. ed., 137–57. Cambridge, MA: Harvard University Press, 1976.
Quine, W. V. 'Naturalism; Or, Living within One's Means'. 1995. In *Confessions of a Confirmed Extensionalist and Other Essays*, edited by Dagfinn Føllesdal and Douglas B. Quine, 461–72. Cambridge, MA: Harvard University Press, 2008.
Quine, W. V. 'On Carnap's Views on Ontology'. 1951. In *The Ways of Paradox and Other Essays*. Rev. ed., 203–11. Cambridge, MA: Harvard University Press, 1976.
Quine, W. V. 'On the Nature of Moral Values'. 1978. In *Theories and Things*, 67–72. Cambridge, MA: Harvard University Press, 1981.
Quine, W. V. 'On What There Is'. 1948. In *From a Logical Point of View: Nine Logico-Philosophical Essays*, 1–19. Cambridge, MA: Harvard University Press, 1953.
Quine, W. V. 'Ontological Reduction and the World of Numbers'. 1964. In *The Ways of Paradox and Other Essays*. Rev. ed., 212–20. Cambridge, MA: Harvard University Press, 1976.
Quine, W. V. 'Posits and Reality'. 1955. In *The Ways of Paradox and Other Essays*. Rev. ed., 246–54. Cambridge, MA: Harvard University Press, 1976.
Quine, W. V. 'Predicate Logic'. 1987. In *Quiddities: An Intermittently Philosophical Dictionary*, 156–9. Cambridge, MA: Harvard University Press, 1987.
Quine, W. V. 'Promoting Extensionality'. 1994. In *Confessions of a Confirmed Extensionalist and Other Essays*, edited by Dagfinn Føllesdal and Douglas B. Quine, 143–51. Cambridge, MA: Harvard University Press, 2008.
Quine, W. V. *Pursuit of Truth*. 1990. Rev. ed. Cambridge, MA: Harvard University Press, 1992.
Quine, W. V. 'Quantifiers and Propositional Attitudes'. 1955. In *The Ways of Paradox and Other Essays*. Rev. ed., 185–96. Cambridge, MA: Harvard University Press, 1976.
Quine, W. V. 'Reference and Modality'. 1953. In *From a Logical Point of View: Nine Logico-Philosophical Essays*, 139–59. Cambridge, MA: Harvard University Press, 1953.
Quine, W. V. 'Reply to David Kaplan'. In *The Philosophy of W. V. Quine*, edited by L. E. Hahn and P. A. Schilpp, 290–4. La Salle: Open Court, 1986.
Quine, W. V. 'Reply to Morton White'. In *The Philosophy of W. V. Quine*, edited by L. E. Hahn and P. A. Schilpp, 663–5. La Salle: Open Court, 1986.
Quine, W. V. *The Roots of Reference*. La Salle: Open Court, 1974.
Quine, W. V. 'The Scope and Language of Science'. 1954. In *The Ways of Paradox and Other Essays*. Rev. ed., 228–45. Cambridge, MA: Harvard University Press, 1976.
Quine, W. V. 'Things and Their Place in Theories'. 1981. In *Theories and Things*, 1–23. Cambridge, MA: Harvard University Press, 1981.
Quine, W. V. 'Three Grades of Modal Involvement'. 1953. In *The Ways of Paradox and Other Essays*. Rev. ed., 158–76. Cambridge, MA: Harvard University Press, 1976.
Quine, W. V. 'Two Dogmas of Empiricism'. 1950. In *From a Logical Point of View: Nine Logico-Philosophical Essays*, 20–46. Cambridge, MA: Harvard University Press, 1953.

Quine, W. V. 'Where Do We Disagree?' 1999. In *Quine in Dialogue*, edited by Dagfinn Føllesdal and Douglas B. Quine, 159–65. Cambridge, MA: Harvard University Press, 2008.
Quine, W. V. *Word and Object*. Cambridge, MA: MIT Press, 1960.
Quine, W. V., and J. S. Ullian. *The Web of Belief*. 1970. 2nd ed. New York: Random House, 1978.
Rosen, Gideon, 'Nominalism, Naturalism, Epistemic Relativism'. *Noûs* 35, no. 15 (2001): 69–91.
Russell, Bertrand. 'The Relation of Sense-Data to Physics'. 1910. In *Mysticism and Logic*, 108–31. London: Allen and Unwin 1963.
Sagan, Carl. 'The Burden of Skepticism'. *Skeptical Inquirer* 12 (Fall 1987). https://skepticalinquirer.org/1987/10/the-burden-of-skepticism/.
Sarch, Alexander F. 'Condoning the Crime: The Elusive Mens Rea for Complicity'. *Loyola University Chicago Law Journal* 47, no. 131 (2015): 131–77.
Sellars, W. 'Empiricism and the Philosophy of Mind'. In *Minnesota Studies in the Philosophy of Science, Volume I: The Foundations of Science and the Concepts of Psychology and Psychoanalysis*, edited by H. Feigl and M. Scriven, 253–329. Minneapolis: University of Minnesota Press, 1956.
Sennet, Adam, and Fisher, Tyrus. 'Quine on Paraphrase and Regimentation'. In *A Companion to W. V. O. Quine*, edited by Gilbert Harman and Ernie Lepore, 89–113. Chichester, England: Wiley-Blackwell, 2014.
Smith, James Andrew, Jr. 'Quine on Naturalism, Nominalism, and Philosophy's Place Within Science'. *Synthese* 198 (2021): 1549–67.
Soames, Scott. *Philosophical Analysis in the Twentieth Century, Volume 1: The Dawn of Analysis*. 2003. Princeton, NJ: Princeton University Press, 2005.
Sober, Elliott, and Hylton, Peter, 'Quine'. *Proceedings of the Aristotelian Society, Supplementary Volumes* 74 (2000): 237–99.
Stich, *From Folk Psychology to Cognitive Science*. Cambridge, MA: MIT Press, 1983.
Tarski, Alfred. 'The Concept of Truth in Formalized Languages'. 1931. In *Logic, Semantics, Metamathematics*, translated by J. H. Woodger, 152–278. Oxford: Clarendon Press, 1956.
van Fraassen, Bas. 'Review of *Pursuit of Truth*'. *Times Literary Supplement* 4558 (1990): 853.
Verhaegh, Sander. *Working from Within*. Oxford: Oxford University Press, 2018.
Voltaire. 'To the Countess of Fontaine-Martel', 1732. In *Miscellaneous Poems by Mr de Voltaire, vol. XXXII*, translated by T. Smollet, T. Francklin et al., 46–8. Salisbury: J. Newbery, R. Baldwin, W. Johnston, S. Crowder, T. Davies, J. Coote, G. Kearsley, and B. Collins, 1764.
Williamson, Timothy. *Knowledge and Its Limits*. 2000. Oxford: Oxford University Press, 2009.

Index

a priori 45, 113
abductive inference 18–19, 21, 27, 43, 94
analyticity. *See* analytic–synthetic distinction
analytic–synthetic distinction 15, 65, 105, 108–10
arbitrariness 81, 94
architecture, theoretical. *See* theoretical architecture
atoms 7–9
attitude–attitude interaction 78–9, 85, 89–91
Ayer, A. J. 5

backsliding 39–40, 47–8, 51–4
behaviour 70–1, 125–6, 150; *see also* verbal behaviour; *see also* nonverbal behaviour
belief 36, 108, 133–5, 147, 149–50; *see also* propositional attitudes
Berkeley, George 106–7
bivalence 61
Bradley, F. H. 11–12
bridging laws 81–2, 85, 89–91, 94, 99–100, 127–8, 136
bridging steps 79–80, 82, 84–5, 92, 127–8, 131–2

Carnap, Rudolf 5–6, 51, 77, 107–11
Carroll, Lewis 128
category questions 169n. 8
causal theories of reference 82
causation 63–5
character sequences 72, 77, 88, 90
checkpoint. *See under* prediction
Christensen, David 26, 28–30
Churchland, Paul 79
circularity 4
classical mechanics 30, 119–20
co-designating names 74–5, 86–7, 92, 96–102, 126
coextensive general terms 74, 87, 92, 126

commitment. *See* implicit theory, ontological commitment
common sense 5, 46–50, 60–1; *see also* conservatism, informal logic
compact presentation 17–19, 35, 62, 81, 94, 98, 156n. 7
compartmentalized thinking 124, 130–2
compulsion 17, 135, 137
computer analogy 80
concatenation operator 73, 90
conditionals 72; *see also* counterfactual conditionals
conflict with experience 15, 34, 135–45; *see also* empirical correctness, sufficient logical explicitness
conservatism 25–32, 43, 48–9, 63–4, 78, 119–21
content language 79–80, 84, 93
content predicate 88–90
content sentence 77, 89
contextual definition 106
convention. *See* linguistic convention
counterfactual conditionals 63–5
counterpart relation 125, 127
curiosity. *See* wanting to know
curtailments 71–3

Davidson, Donald 72, 134, 162n. 4, 163n. 6
de dicto 75, 87, 127
deferential epistemology 113, 115
deflation 115, 159n. 6
degree of belief/desire 72, 124, 163n. 7
de re 75, 127
Descartes, René 4, 155n. 2 (Chapter 1)
descriptive epistemology 114–15
de se. *See* egocentric attitudes
desire. *See* propositional attitudes
disquotation. *See* disquotational theory of reference
disquotational theory of reference 83–5, 89

disquotational-sententialist psychologies. *See* DS psychologies
distal input and output 92, 99–100
doxastic alternatives. *See* doxastic and orectic alternatives
doxastic and orectic alternatives 123–32
Dretske, Fred 165n. 10
DS psychologies 85–7, 93, 96
DS+ psychologies 87–8, 91, 93

Ebbs, Gary 156n. 8, 173n. 13
egocentric attitudes 125
Einstein, Albert 1, 10; *see also* relativity, theories of
empirical correctness 16–17, 25, 34–7, 109, 143, 176n. 7
engineering, epistemology as. *See* instrumental epistemology
entailment 35
epistemological dissociative disorder 7–13
ethics 3, 113, 116, 122
existence. *See* ontology
existential quantification. *See* quantification
experience 32, 45, 49, 58; *see also* conflict with experience, falsifiability, foundational empiricism
experiential expectation 142–4
experimentation 16, 23, 38–9, 121–2
explanation 70; *see also* abductive inference
explicit theory 33–5
extensionality 70, 74, 77, 91, 126–7
external pragmatism 107, 109
external questions 107, 109

falsifiability 4, 7–12, 43
fictional characters 60
Field, Hartry 165n. 12
first philosophy 4, 113
Fodor, Jerry 164n. 2; *see also* Language of Thought hypothesis
folk psychology. *See* experience, propositional attitudes
formal logic. *See* logic
foundational empiricism 106, 133–5
foundationalism 3, 5, 155n. 2 (Chapter 1); *see also* foundational empiricism
foundherentism 175–176n. 4
four-dimensional view. *See* tense

Frege cases 92, 98–102
Frege, Gottlob 166n. 3; *see also* Frege cases
future-proofing 23, 38–9, 95–7, 101

Galileo Galilei 49
general substitutivity 87, 98
generality 81–2, 119, 156n. 7
generation of experiential expectation 142–4
Gettier cases 147, 149
Gödel, Kurt 62
Gregory, Paul A. 170–1n. 18, 172n. 2, 174n. 14

Haack, Susan. *See* foundherentism
Harman, Gilbert. *See* lost evidence, argument from
Harman, Gilbert and Ernie Lepore 172n. 2
Hawking, Stephen 45
Heidegger, Martin 11
heliocentrism 18–19, 49
Hempel, Carl. *See* raven paradox
heuristics 27, 119–21
holism 9–10, 16, 21, 57, 108, 134, 148, 156n. 4 (Chapter 3)
Hume, David 4, 18–19, 54, 168n. 4
hybrids 90–1
Hylton, Peter 141–2, 159n. 5, 163–4n. 13, 170n. 13, 172n. 2
hypocrisy 3, 31, 36, 38, 40

if-then. *See* conditionals
illusion 91–2, 100–1
implicit theory 33–5
inclusion thesis 114–22
incomplete belief systems 124, 130–1
inconsistent belief systems 124, 130
incorrigibility. *See* compulsion
incredulous stare 12
indeterminacy of translation 160n. 11
indispensability argument 156n. 8
inductive inference 18–21, 27, 43
inference to the best explanation. *See* abductive inference
informal logic 34–9, 43, 60–1, 102, 135
informational theories of reference 83
inscrutability of reference 160n. 11
instrumental epistemology 115–21
intensional isomorphism 77

intention 71
internal pragmatism 108–9
internal questions 107–9

James, William 18
Johnsen, Bredo 173n. 9
Johnson, A. B. 168n. 4
justified true belief 147

Kant, Immanuel. *See* ought implies can
Kaplan, David 90
Kemp, Gary 161n. 11, 170n. 13
knowledge 147–52

Language of Thought hypothesis 80
least action, principle of 107
Leibniz, Gottfried Wilhelm von 166n. 3
Lewis, David 32, 54, 63; *see also* doxastic and orectic alternatives, incredulous stare, modal realism
  Convention, 36, 162n. 2, 169n. 12
limit (mathematics) 62
linguistic convention 36, 107–11
linguistic rule. *See* linguistic convention
logic 27, 57, 106; *see also* logical laws, predicate logic
logical explicitness 33–40, 43, 46, 57, 102, 118; *see also* sufficient logical explicitness, total logical explicitness
logical laws 16–18, 33–5, 47, 83; *see also* logical explicitness
logical positivism 12; *see also* Ayer, A. J., Carnap, Rudolf
lost evidence, argument from 28–30

Maddy, Penelope. *See* second philosophy
mathematics 9, 21–2, 27, 43, 58, 62, 174n. 18
McDermott, Michael 69, 163n. 10, 163n. 13, 165n. 6, 165n. 7, 166n. 3, 167n. 6, 168n. 15, 168n. 1 (Chapter 12), 168n. 2 (Chapter 12), 170n. 12, 177n. 15, 177n. 19
meaning 72, 77–8, 106–7, 110–11
mental representation 82
metaphor 40
metaphysics 5, 11–12, 22, 43–5, 51–5, 62, 113
misadventure 100
modal realism 12, 54, 63, 127–8

modality 54, 63–5
modelling of experiential expectation 145
modesty 119
Moore, G. E. 31
moral values. *See* ethics

narrow psychology 100
naturalism. *See* naturalized epistemology
naturalized epistemology 113–22, 142
Newton, Isaac. *See* classical mechanics
Niebuhr, Reinhold. *See* serenity
non-designating names 93–101, 128; *see also* vacuous names
nonverbal behaviour 72, 78, 129, 150–3
nonverbal memory 145
null general terms 86
numbers 52–3, 61–2, 118

objects. *See* ontology
objects of propositional attitudes 74, 77, 123
observation categorical 140
observation sentence 138–41
ontological commitment 52–3
ontology 5, 52–4, 59–63, 118
oppression 12
ordinary language. *See* backsliding, common sense
orectic alternatives. *See* doxastic and orectic alternatives
ought implies can 176n. 6

Pachniewska, Amanda 178n. 5
passive behaviour 70
Peirce, C. S. 137, 176n. 5
perception 71
philosophy of psychology 71
physics 27, 45–6, 147
plenitude, principles of 126
Popper, Karl. *See* falsifiability, What is the difference?
possibilia. *See* possible objects
possible objects 54, 63, 126; *see also* doxastic and orectic alternatives
possible worlds. *See* possible objects
pragmatism 109, 159n.6; *see also* external pragmatism, internal pragmatism
predicate logic 57–8, 165n. 13
prediction 16, 22–3, 39, 118
  as checkpoint, 116–17, 119–21

Price, Huw 11, 51
probability. *See* probability and statistics
probability and statistics 73, 120–1
propositional attitudes 63, 69–102, 123–32, 151–3
propositions 35–6, 123, 148
proximal input and output 91–2, 100, 101, 142
pseudo-object questions 169n. 8
purely referential position 88

quantification 51–4, 60–3, 118, 126, 157–8n. 6
quasi-syntactical questions. *See* pseudo-object questions
quotation 72, 77

raven paradox 20–1
reconnaisance behaviour 151–3
reductionism 15, 105, 108
refutability 119
regimentation 46–53, 57, 63–102, 123, 125, 151–3
relativity, theories of 30, 156n. 4 (Chapter 3)
Rosen, Gideon 158n. 13
Russell, Bertrand, 106–7: *see also* Russellianism
Russellianism 88–93, 98
Rutherford, Ernest 19

Sagan, Carl 25
Sarch, Alexander F. 178n. 2
scepticism 3, 5, 17, 28, 31, 106, 110–11, 155n. 2
scientism 47
second philosophy 171–2n. 1
second-order propositional attitudes 151–2
self-awareness 152–3
Sellars, Wilfrid 134
semantic analysis 48, 63, 113
semantic ascent 171n. 18
semantics. *See* meaning, semantic analysis
Sennet, Adam and Tyrus Fisher 160n. 11
sentences within sentences 73
sensory input 133, 136, 138–44; *see also* distal input and output, proximal input and output
sententialism 77–102
serenity 135

simplicity 17–22, 25, 27–8, 35–7, 43, 57, 62–3, 81, 107–9, 119–21, 159n. 6
Smith, James Andrew Jr. 159n. 2
Soames, Scott 31
Sober, Elliot 156n. 4 (Chapter 3)
speculation 134, 137, 142, 145
Stalnaker, Robert 130–1
statistics. *See* probability and statistics
Stich, Stephen 134
stimulation. *See* sensory input
sufficient logical explicitness 37–9, 44, 143, 176–7n. 7
surprise. *See* experiential expectation
synchronous intrasubjective conflict 137–8, 142–4
synonymy. *See* meaning
syntheticity. *See* analytic–synthetic distinction

Tarski, Alfred 72, 90
teaching 150
tense 58–9
term-introducing laws 81–2, 85, 89, 94–5, 97
term-introducing steps 79–82, 84–5, 94, 127–8
testimony 29–30, 45, 49
theoretical architecture 50–1, 57, 153
theoretical conservatism. *See* conservatism
time: *See* tense
total linguistic explicitness 107, 109
total logical conformance 107, 109
total logical explicitness 36, 109
truth 22

uh-oh. *See* experiential expectation
uniform substitutivity 86–7, 96–8, 101–2

vacuous names 86, 92–4, 96, 125, 165n. 11
van Fraassen, Bas 160n. 11
variables 70, 73, 89, 164n. 4; *see also* quantification
verbal behaviour 71–2, 74–5, 77–8, 94, 125
Verhaegh, Sander 115, 169n. 6
Voltaire 103

wanting to know 151–3
What is the difference? 4–5, 26, 28–9, 31
Williamson, Timothy 147–8, 178n. 4
Wittgenstein, Ludwig 12

www.ingramcontent.com/pod-product-compliance
Lightning Source LLC
Chambersburg PA
CBHW052120300426
44116CB00010B/1736